PC POWER PROTECTION

PC POWER PROTECTION

Mark Waller

Power Management Associates
P.O. Box 875
Montrose, CA 91020-0875

HOWARD W. SAMS & COMPANY
A Division of Macmillan, Inc.
4300 West 62nd Street
Indianapolis, Indiana 46268 USA

To J. Fredrick Kalbach, who grew young as he helped an industry mature.

FIRST EDITION
FIRST PRINTING—1988

International Standard Book Number: 0-672-22637-5
Library of Congress Catalog Card Number: 88-63207

Acquisitions Editor: *James S. Hill*
Development Editor: *James Rounds*
Manuscript Editor: *Frank N. Speights*
Illustrator: *T. R. Emrick*
Technical Reviewer: *Ben Crosby, ONEAC Corp.*
Cover Illustrator: *Visual Graphic Services, Indianapolis*
Indexer: *Ted Laux*
Compositor: *Cromer Graphics, Indianapolis*

Printed in the United States of America

Contents

Preface

When I tell people that I write books and give workshops about computer electrical power, they get a sort of far-off look in their eyes and either say, "Oh, that's nice," or they ask, "How did you learn so much about power supplies?" I patiently explain that computer power products are external devices that "clean up" the normal utility power so the computer can use it, not power supplies which are internal to the CPU, and then they say, "Oh, that's nice."

Every now and then, however, I run into an ardent PC user who wants to know exactly what I am talking about. These are people who have been burnt and don't want it to happen again. Once users learn to depend on their computer, especially if it helps them make a living, they are literally lost without it. A power disturbance can render that personal system you have grown so fond of useless in a few milliseconds.

There is also another kind of person who is worried about being burnt by bad power—the corporate DP manager who is in charge of hundreds of PCs scattered throughout a major facility. Each department looks to this professional to protect their investment in equipment and keep them up, no matter how "dirty" the power is. There are a vast number of people caught up in the growing culture of databases, spreadsheets, interfacing, networking, and publishing who will simply not tolerate power problems. And they want answers.

Anyone who has had any repairs done by qualified field-service personnel knows what it can cost. The kind of high energy capable of being carried by that simple innocuous electrical wire in the wall can cause enough damage to make equipment replacement far more economical than equipment repair. Imagine dumping what might seem to be a perfectly good CPU into the trash and buying a new one instead of opting to repair it. A few years ago that would have been unheard of. But today, the cost of a new modem or printer might well be under, or equal to, the cost of repairing a nonfunctioning unit. Of course, we all know that these babies contain modular components, and we can no longer replace just the offending transistor or capacitor. Now we must buy an entire subassembly. Add the cost of labor to the price of a damaged module and the decision to buy or repair is often made on the spot.

Depending on the circumstance, we might be able to rationalize losing a little data or replacing some damaged equipment. Even a few days of twiddling our thumbs while our PC is in the shop isn't the end of the world. None of us really believe this, but let's pretend that we can actually do without our precious little darling for a moment. So, what's the big deal? So, we repair the thing. So what? Networking and desktop publishing, that's what.

Suddenly we can "connect" to everything. PCs can be linked to mainframes, minis, other PCs, and FAX machines via branch offices, LANs, satellites, and electronic mail. On the other hand, company after company is investing in desktop publishing. Every department or small business wants to save time and money on forms, newsletters, and the like. Every ambitious executive knows that the ability to produce pretty reports is several times more important than producing accurate reports.

We've all seen the TV ad where two managers are taking a "red eye" somewhere. One shows the other this amazing report that is full of clever graphs and crisp-looking print. No mention is made that the underlying data might be utter nonsense. It is automatically assumed that anything that looks that good must be accurate. What a management tool! For this reason as much as any other, such as saving on printing costs, desktop publishing is touching every area of corporate America.

The point is that what once was an isolated power problem has now attained the capability of creating a disaster of biblical proportions. More people will be affected by a single computer power problem than ever before, and "Uptime" means productivity for greater numbers of people. Professionals in the large-systems arena have struggled with the problem for many years. This struggle gave birth to the computer power industry. But even today, the same people buy huge backup power systems with little understanding of what it is all about.

This power situation was the inspiration for my first book, *Computer Electrical Power Requirements*. When I wrote the book, I was worried that no one would understand what the book was all about, but once the book was in print, eager readers made it a huge success. It seemed that DP managers, field engineers, and facilities managers had long been waiting for some kind of orientation to the whole subject of computer power. Even though *Computer Electrical Power Requirements* was an overview (it did include a chapter on PC power), I soon discovered there was much, much more to tell.

Meanwhile, a plethora of PC power products appeared on the market purporting to do amazing things for us. Some actually worked. Some did not. Some were dangerous, having serious safety problems. Many didn't even have a UL label on them. But sales of devices have been brisk despite the fact there has been almost no reliable source of information to warn the buyer. And, I'm sure that as many sales have been made based on bright colors, sophisticated packaging, and slick marketing as have occurred because of informed buying.

What is all the noise about surges and spikes? Do we need protectors, conditioners, or backups? What works? What doesn't?

PC Power Protection attempts to take that which seems like so much smoke and mirrors and tries to explain it in plain terms. What the book will not do is compare one product against another. But, it will compare one technology against another. We will take each approach to computer-power problem solving, analyze it, explain how it works, and then take a look at its relative strengths and weaknesses.

In other words, when you have finished this book, you will know the difference between various types of surge protectors, know when their use is appropriate, and when it is not. And, the same thing will be done with all of the various protective devices on the market. We will look at power and learn why we need to do something about its use and application. We will discuss networks and other special applications, and will see what technologies might best apply in each case.

A word of caution is appropriate at this point. The word is MONEY. It costs money to do things right. Quality always has a price. We will touch on price issues as we go along, but please bear in mind that solving a power problem and saving money are two mutually exclusive things. It is possible to find a good value. But, without the proper priorities, it is more likely that you will be apt to save pennies at the expense of dollars.

Put a little more simply, it is one thing to find the cheapest surge suppressor on the market. It is quite another thing to discover that a surge suppressor was entirely the wrong product for your application. You may have saved a few bucks on the purchase only to find that all the money spent was wasted.

PC Power is an exciting field. There are over one hundred companies in the market vying for a share of the consumer's mind and pocketbook. *PC Power Protection* will be your guide through the sideshow of hype, barter, and glitter. When our tour is over, you will know what to ask and how to determine if the answer applies to your needs. Armed with the facts, you will be the *master* of PC electrical power.

MARK WALLER

Acknowledgements

I would like to acknowledge my editor, Jim Hill, whose belief in me and the subject made this second book a reality, and the patience and help of Sams' editors Jim Rounds and Frank Speights, who assisted me in rounding out the rough edges and shaping the finished product.

A special word of thanks goes to Ben Crosby, who enthusiastically reviewed every word of the book for technical accuracy and overall consistency.

I would like to thank Tex Morphis of the Cañada Camera Shop for his superb work in developing the photographs for this book.

The computer power industry is young and, as such, has no settled body of work from which to draw. As a result, the concepts and ideas expressed here are the culmination of many hours of telephone conversations and cups of hot coffee with experts and friends who took the time to enhance my understanding. Therefore I must acknowledge Don Tollefson, Robert McLoughlin, Milton Hanson, William Carpenter, Peter Nystrom, Fred Schlines, and Doug Caldwell.

Fred Kalbach and Warren Lewis deserve note here. Their writing, work, and friendship helped me build the foundation that launched this project.

Of course, this would not be complete without thanking my wife, Jan, for her support and love. And thanks go to Petra and Abigail, who have finally discovered what Daddy does nights and weekends.

1 Introduction

It must have been quite a shock to those pioneering data-processing people who installed the first large mainframes when they realized what it was going to take. The computer of yesteryear filled a room. Then, the room had to have a raised floor. Temperature and humidity had to be just right. Special fire equipment had to be installed. The electrical power had to be brought in just so. And, the list goes on.

Today, the situation for mainframe computers is much the same. Planning for a proper environment for the computer can cost as much as 10% to 20% of the total cost of the computer. Planning a major data center is not a trivial matter. It is not uncommon for a company to employ an architect, an electrical engineer, a mechanical engineer, a variety of contractors, and a special consultant to interface between the players—the user and the various vendors involved in the project.

By contrast, a small-business person might purchase a local area network, take it to the office, plug it in, and start using it. That is a big contrast! Today, few minicomputers require an engineered environment. Some of the most powerful machines on the market are purported to operate in a typical office from regular utility power, with no special exotic installation considerations.

Large and Small Computers

Can there be that much difference between a mainframe and a PC, so that one setup requires a special room with all the extras and another does not? Are the large computers so much more sensitive? Are the little computers tougher, more rugged? Are there any significant technological differences? Let's analyze this, one step at a time. What does a mainframe computer have that a PC does not?

Both have a CPU. Also, both have disk drives, printers, tape storage, modems, and multiplexers. True, there are differences in designs from one type to another, but the basic mechanical and electronic structure of the products is very much the same. There are few technologies found in mainframes that have not been duplicated to one degree or another in microcomputers.

Peripheral Speeds

One difference that existed for a few years was *clock speed.* But, a new generation of processors is now blurring the performance differences of one machine over another. The speed, architecture, and bit size of the basic microcomputer chip is changing rapidly.

Printers are also not too different. Again, speed is the main difference. A large computer center can afford a superfast printer, but printer speed is not a significant reason to build a computer room.

Data Storage

What about *data storage*? Are little disk drives less susceptible to dust and dirt corruption than big disk drives? We must admit there are some differences between a simple floppy disk and the disk drive of a mainframe, but do differences in size, speed, and capacity call for an engineered environment?

This whole discussion might make great grist for an argument between PC and mainframe design engineers, but at the same time, it might be leaving you a little cold. Well, let me warm things up a bit. The simple fact is that from a *technological standpoint*, there is just as much reason to have an engineered environment for a PC as there is for a mainframe computer. We don't want our PC to overheat, and we don't want the humidity to get so low that we zap it with static electricity. Also, we don't want fire sprinklers to hose it down when the power is on. We don't want our storage media to get dirty, causing data to be lost or destroyed. And we don't want power problems to interfere with continuous data processing. Looked at this way, our concerns are very similar to the concerns facing the manager of a major data center.

Main Differences

So what is the difference? It is a difference of degree. Obviously, when you crowd a lot of electronic equipment in a room, heat will be generated. Thus, cooling the air so equipment overheating does not occur is important. On the other hand, one PC in an office does not contribute enough heat to the environment to justify the installation of additional air conditioning. Even if the room air conditioning failed and the PC cooked, the financial loss would be far less than the cost of adding additional air conditioning. In contrast, the overheating of a mainframe computer might cost $100,000 to repair. That is the other big difference. A proper environment for a mainframe computer is designed to protect the huge investment in capital that has been made.

However, there is another cost that must be factored into our discussion—*downtime*. Imagine the plight of a major airline. When their computer system goes down, their nationwide reservation system is out. Customers can't make reservations, so they take their business elsewhere. Every minute that the airline's computer is down, a finite dollar amount can be assigned to the cost of lost business. It might be as much as several hundred thousand dollars per minute. Thus, few minutes of downtime can pay for a large investment in proper computer installation.

For us, however, downtime takes on somewhat smaller proportions. But everything is a matter of perspective. A few years ago, when the microcomputer was first being introduced in kit form, downtime was expected. In fact, it was part of the challenge of the hobby. No self-respecting, soldering-iron wielding, PC pioneer would have been satisfied without the challenge of keeping the thing running. Today, we are far more dependent on our PCs and their operation (uptime). While the price of hardware may have fallen dramatically, no one can doubt that the dollar value of the tasks being performed has increased astronomically. Environmental considerations are becoming more of an issue for both the home and business user.

Quality of Power

This brings us to the subject of this book. The single biggest area of concern for a PC's environment is the quality of the AC utility power that is provided for it. Power problems can cause a variety of processing errors, interruptions, and even equipment damage. Solving those problems is economically and technologically within the reach of every user. A myriad of devices are available that plug in to the wall socket.

So why write a book on the subject? Everyone knows you just go out and buy a "black box" that fixes the power. Right? There's the rub. There are dozens of "boxes" that are advertised to do certain things. The problem is that few perform as advertised, and many of the devices themselves are misapplied or misused by the user.

Let me state my point a little more forcefully. As a professional who spends his business day in and around computer installations large and small, as a problem solver who deals with the full range of computer power problems, as a writer who's job is to research the industry, I can say without hesitation that most of the money spent on PC power products is wasted. That's right, wasted!

How? Either by buying products that don't work properly, or by trying to apply one technology to solve a problem when another technology is the only appropriate option. At a recent workshop, I cited some examples of the very thing that we will cover later in this book. The DP professionals in the room grew more and more agitated as the day wore on. Finally, I interrupted my presentation to ask them what was wrong, and was told that they wanted to get to the computers and start looking behind the walls and under the floors to see how much trouble they were really in. Like so many others, these folks had developed a false sense of security, thinking that they had protected themselves from disaster when actually they had made matters considerably worse.

Obviously, to solve a power problem we must know what *power* is. This is where we will start. A few fundamentals about electricity will pave the way for most of what follows in later chapters. This may be old hat to some, but to many it will be the first time they have seen what electrical power actually looks like. Don't feel lonely if this describes you. I recently addressed a group of sales people from a large electrical wholesaler, who make their living from sales to electrical contractors. Throughout my presentation, I made reference to the "AC sine wave." I learned later that only one person in the room knew what I was talking about. We will cover that ground right away.

Power Devices

It is difficult to solve a power problem that you don't understand, so we will clearly define what power problems are, and what terms should be attached to each. We will learn, for example, that a "surge suppressor" will do nothing to an actual surge, and it doesn't suppress anything. This is not just semantics. The darn things are dangerous if not used properly. Another surprise will come when we learn that *uninterruptible power supplies (UPS)* are usually not uninterruptible. But all that will come later, after we clearly define power and power problems, and cover a few more topics like lightning, noise, static, and grounding. Then, we will discuss the product technologies and how they work, and when and how to use them. We will even talk about laser printers and LANs as they might relate to our subject matter.

Along the way, we will be using some very sophisticated tools to show in graph, as well as photographic form, what things really look like. At first, oscilloscope tracings and displays might appear a little daunting. One might be tempted to skip over something that looks too technical. Don't! You will miss the reward of this book. You are going to get a real-time view of what electrical power is. It may seem strange at first, but a picture of what your PC actually sees when you plug it into the electrical wall outlet is fascinating. A picture of what it sees when you use a power product is also a learning experience.

We will explain exactly what is happening as we go along. Remember, we are not testing products. We are showing various technologies at work.

Now, it's time to move on to the good stuff. But let's put on safety glasses and a hard hat. Yes, there will be danger and high voltage. But more importantly, we will be blasting away at myths, trying to discover reality. In a way, we will come to know the power of truth as we explore the truth about power.

2 Basic Electricity

Let's not kid ourselves. We are not going to cover all of basic electricity in just one chapter. What we are going to attempt to do is to touch on those elementary principles on which the rest of this book is based. Every computer power problem or problem-solving product uses the tools of basic electricity.

Most of us remember some of the experiments done in science class many years ago. We attached a lantern battery to a switch and constructed a circuit using either a light bulb or a small motor. When we closed the switch, the motor started or the light lit. Possibly we felt the wire carrying the electricity get warm as current flowed through it. Or, we may have put some kind of resistor in the circuit to cause the light to dim. Also, most of us wound insulated wire around a tenpenny nail and created an electromagnet. We might have sprinkled iron filings on a piece of paper so we could observe the arrangement of magnetic lines of force. It may come as a shock to some to learn that this is not the same electricity as that which is flowing through the wires of your home or office.

The electricity flowing from a source like a battery is called *direct current* or *DC*. The electricity that comes from our local utility company is called *alternating current* or *AC*. The two kinds of current flow have dramatically differing properties.

AC Power

Direct current was used extensively many years ago for commercial use. When it became necessary to transmit power over vast distances, however, AC power was found to be a better alternative. In order to understand AC power, we must start where the utility company starts—at the generator.

A magnetic field is a bundle of invisible lines of force called *flux*. Long ago, it was discovered by the early electrical pioneers that a wire conductor would produce a current flow when it was moved through a magnetic field. This led to the application of the basic principles of electric generation. Let's look at an example of a simple generator (Fig. 2-1). The two blocks represent electromagnets. The space between the two blocks is filled with flux. The more flux lines the conductor cuts through, the greater the current flow in the conductor.

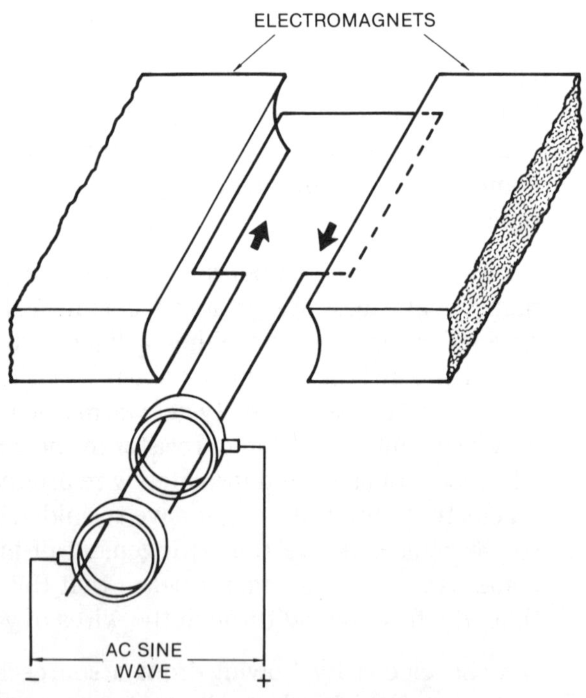

Fig. 2-1. A conductor cuts through a magnetic field and induces a voltage in a rotating conductor.

As the conductor rotates, it reaches a position which is perpendicular to the lines of force or flux. This means that no flux is being cut by the conductor (Fig. 2-2). At this point, current flow drops to zero. A quarter turn

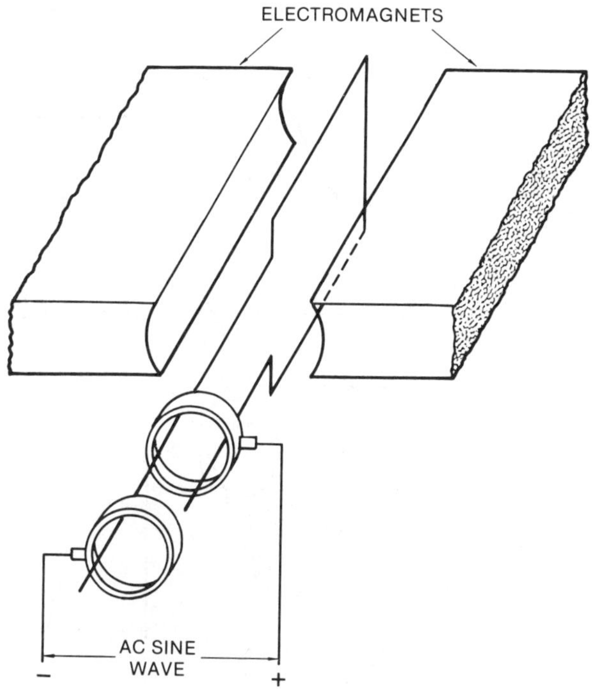

Fig. 2-2. When the conductor passes between lines of flux, no lines are cut by the conductor and no current flows.

later, the conductor has rotated so that maximum flux lines are again being cut, but the direction of current flow in the conductor has reversed because the position of the conductor has rotated 180° (Fig. 2-3).

This is exactly how a real generator creates power. Mechanical energy is converted to electrical energy by the use of the rotational mass of a spinning generator. Turbines driven either by steam or water are used to provide the spinning force. Therefore, the generator spins in a 360-degree revolution. Using the principle we have discussed and graphing the voltage we would measure at the terminals of our crude generator, we would get the sine wave shown in Fig. 2-4. This waveform is called a *sine wave* because it replicates the graph generated by the sine function in trigonometry.

Clearly we have left a lot out of this simplified example, but it does show how the alternating characteristic of AC power is produced. In actual practice, the large generators used at dams or steam plants have three sets of windings inside of them. This produces three sine waves, each displaced 120° from the next (Fig. 2-5). This results in the production of *three-phase*

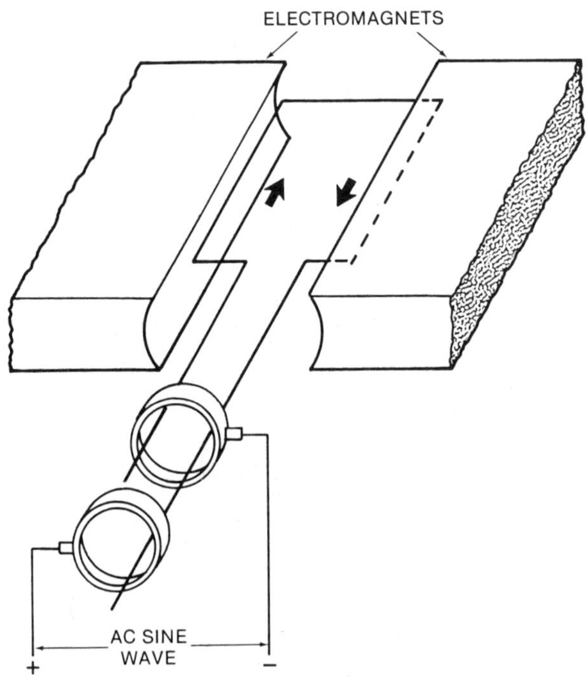

Fig. 2-3. Current flows in the opposite direction since the conductor is 180° from where it started.

power, the kind of power that feeds most commercial buildings. Three-phase power is then split into its three phases, to power everyday equipment like PCs.

Well, all this theory is fine, you say, but seeing is believing. If we plug an oscilloscope into an electrical outlet, we can get an actual picture of what electricity looks like. Fig. 2-6 is a photo that shows us what the sine wave looks like at the receptacle. This picture actually changes sixty times a second. Remember the spinning generator with its conductor cutting through lines of force? There are sixty such 360° revolutions happening every second. That's why we say the frequency of utility power is 60 hertz, or 60 cycles per second. You may notice that many of the pictures of sine waves in this book look distorted. We will find out why this is true as we go along. The photo was taken in a severe environment (my office). This is not unlike the sine wave that might appear in older buildings, where nearby heavy loading may cause the building service transformer to drive into saturation, thus causing flattopping of the waveshape and other distortions.

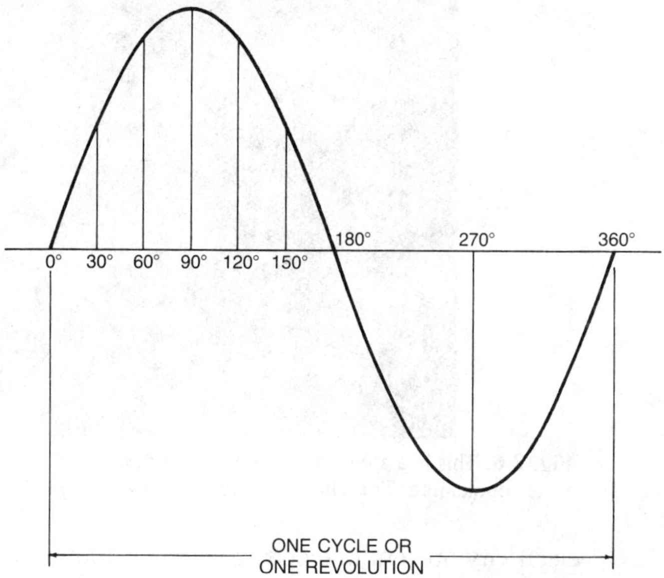

Fig. 2-4. As the conductor turns through 360°, the flow of current and the magnitude of the voltage, when plotted, traces a sine wave.

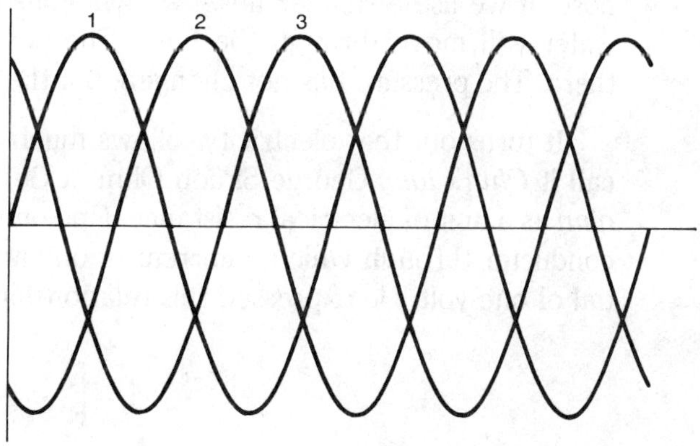

Fig. 2-5. Three-phase generation produces three sine waves whose peaks are 120° from one another.

Ohm's Law

The flow of electricity is like the flow of water. Well, not really, but let's see if the analogy can help us understand the three fundamental components of

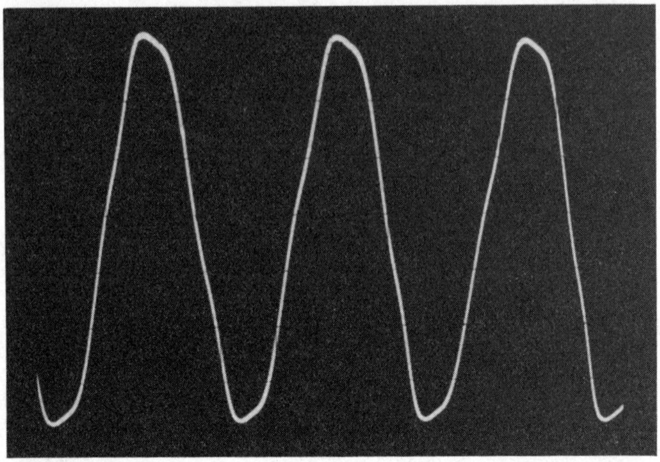

Fig. 2-6. This is a snapshot of the screen of an oscilloscope, showing what utility power looks like. This shows a sine wave that is repeated sixty times per second.

electricity present in electrical circuits. Imagine that we have a water faucet with a hose attached to it. The faucet has the potential of providing a certain water pressure through the hose. The flow of water is determined by two things—the size of the hose and the pressure forcing water through the hose. If we use a smaller hose, we will constrict the flow of water and less water will move through the hose. The potential for a larger flow is still there. The pressure has not changed, but the actual flow is less.

It turns out that electricity follows much the same set of principles. We call it *Ohm's law*. George Simon Ohm, a German physicist, established the *ohm* as a unit of electrical resistance. One ohm is equal to the resistance of a conductor through which a current of one ampere is produced by a potential of one volt. He expressed this relationship in the equation:

$$I = \frac{E}{R} \qquad \text{(Eq. 2-1)}$$

We can deduce that this relationship can be expressed using two other equations:

$$E = IR \qquad \text{(Eq. 2-2)}$$

and

$$R = \frac{E}{I} \qquad \text{(Eq. 2-3)}$$

where,

R is the electrical resistance in ohms,
I is the electrical current in amperes,
E is the electromotive force or electrical potential in volts.

If we have a circuit with a pressure of 120 volts and a resistance of 10 ohms, we can determine that 12 amperes of electricity will flow (Equation 1-1). And, like our garden hose in the analogy, if the resistance is changed to 100 ohms, then the current will be only 1.2 amperes.

Ohm's law is the foundation for much of the discussion in this book. The relationship of current, voltage, and resistance is at the heart of every power problem and every technology used to solve those problems. Take some time with a calculator if you are not familiar with Ohm's law. Try and get comfortable with these three equations. Then your understanding of the discussions in this book—and a lot of the hype in the marketplace—will be greatly enhanced.

Power

The real benefit of electricity is that it allows us to get work done. As luck would have it, we have another mathematical expression which describes work that is done by electricity. The unit of work is called a *watt* after an early pioneer in electricity, James Watt. One watt is the work done in one second by the action of one volt of electricity moving one ampere of current through a resistance of one ohm. This leads to the mathematical expression:

$$P = EI \qquad \text{(Eq. 2-4)}$$

where,

P is the power in watts,
E is the voltage in volts,
I is the current in amperes.

So if we have a computer that draws 2 amperes at 120 volts, it does 240 watts worth of work. If we look back at Ohm's law (Equation 2-2), we see that we can substitute one equation for another, or

$$P = (IR)I \qquad \text{(Eq. 2-5)}$$

Equation 2-5 can also be written:

$$P = I^2R \qquad \text{(Eq. 2-6)}$$

We can now solve our earlier example for R. If P = 240 watts and I = 2 amperes, then R must equal 60 ohms. These are extremely important equations. Every power product is sized for the amount of power it must handle. The power used by any computer or peripheral device is clearly marked on a plate or sticker attached to the back of the unit. This identification plate (Fig. 2-7) is usually fastened near where the power cord enters the chassis of the device.

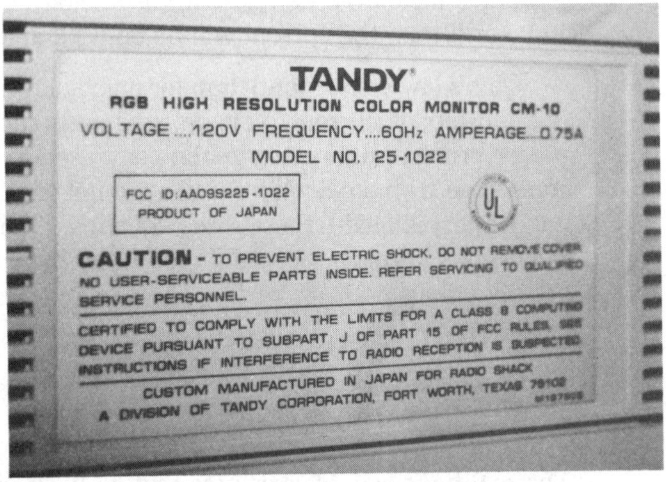

Fig. 2-7. The plate or sticker containing the power information specs is usually located near where the power cord enters the device chassis.

Normally, the pertinent information will be given in watts. Often, however, it is given in amperes. Given amperes, it is easy, using Equation 2-4, to determine the power in watts. We do this by multiplying the current (in amperes) times 120 volts. Do not use any value (number) other than 120 volts; for example, like 110 or 115 volts. The standard voltage supplied by the utility company is 120 volts.

Impedance

It is time to wade into water that becomes deeper and just a little murky. Earlier we said that there were important differences between AC and DC power. These differences will show mainly as changes in the way we think of resistance (R) in our equations. These changes in resistance (R) will affect current and voltage in AC circuits; we will get to that shortly.

In electronics, there are three basic components that get little attention. We are always hearing about vacuum tubes, integrated circuits, transistors, and a whole array of other exotic components. But, from the standpoint of electricity, there are really only three kinds of components that we need discuss—resistors, capacitors, and inductors. The schematic symbols used for these circuit elements are given in Fig. 2-8.

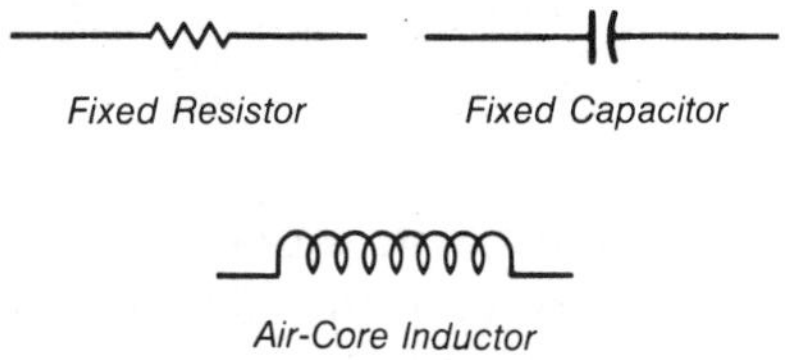

Fig. 2-8. Electronic schematic symbols.

Resistors

A resistor is a resistor is a resistor. It has a constant ohmic value and acts the same no matter what kind of current is flowing through it. This is true for direct current (DC), alternating current (AC), or radio-frequency AC (RF). When we see a resistor in a circuit, we needn't take any special notice of anything except its value when doing any calculating.

Capacitors

As the symbol indicates, a capacitor is a gap in a circuit, which usually appears between two plates called *electrodes*. The space between the plates may be air or some other insulating dielectric, like glass, or mica, or paper.

It should come as no surprise that to DC, a capacitor is an open circuit. True, a charge will build up on the faces of the capacitor electrodes, and that charge can be dissipated by a load across the capacitor's terminals. But, a capacitor presents no path for current flow after its initial charging. In an AC circuit, however, a capacitor takes an active role. A capacitor displays a differing reactance depending on the frequency of the current being presented across its terminals. The capacitor's *capacitance*, a characteristic of the physical construction of the capacitor, is expressed in *farads*. To a 60-Hz electrical signal, the reactance of a given capacitor will be totally different than that for a radio signal of 10 MHz. For example, a 60-Hz signal might see a capacitor of a certain value as an open circuit. Therefore, no current would flow across this path. A 10-MHz radio signal might see the same capacitor as a short circuit and thus the capacitor would become part of this signal's circuit. We will see this characteristic used in some of the product technologies we will discuss in later chapters.

More detail on how a capacitor reacts in various circuits is really beyond the scope of this book. What is important to us is that at different frequencies, the reactance of the capacitor causes an impedance to current flow, expressed in ohms. The formula for calculating this reactance is:

$$X_C = \frac{1}{2\pi fC} \qquad \text{(Eq. 2-7)}$$

where,

X_C is the capacitive reactance in ohms,
π is the constant Pi (3.1416),
f is the frequency in hertz,
C is the capacitance in farads.

Inductors

At first glance, our symbol for an inductor (Fig. 2-8) looks like a coil of wire. In most cases, it is. To direct current, an inductor is important only as a source of pure resistance (of the wire). To alternating current, an inductor has more curious properties since current flowing through the coil of wire forms a constantly changing magnetic field. This property of an inductor, expressed in *henrys*, means that its reactance (expressed in ohms) changes as the frequency of the signal passing through it changes.

This changing reactance offers a changing opposition to current flow. A certain inductor might offer a low impedance to a 60-Hz power signal while offering a high impedance to a radio signal. This effect has given some inductors the additional term of "choke," because they literally choke off the flow of signals at certain frequencies. Inductive reactance also presents an ohmic value of impedance to current flow in the circuit, but this impedance is different from the impedance presented by capacitive reactance. Inductive reactance is the opposite of capacitive reactance. The formula used to derive inductive reactance is:

$$X_L = 2\pi fL \qquad \text{(Eq. 2-8)}$$

where,

X_L is the inductive reactance in ohms,
π is the constant Pi (3.1416),
f is the frequency in hertz,
L is the inductance in henrys.

Impedance is a term that will be used over and over again in this book. Impedance is expressed in ohms and is used along with the term "load" to

Bookmark

HOWARD W. SAMS & COMPANY

DEAR VALUED CUSTOMER:

Howard W. Sams & Company is dedicated to bringing you timely and authoritative books for your personal and professional library. Our goal is to provide you with excellent technical books written by the most qualified authors. You can assist us in this endeavor by checking the box next to your particular areas of interest.

We appreciate your comments and will use the information to provide you with a more comprehensive selection of titles.

Thank you,

Vice President, Book Publishing
Howard W. Sams & Company

COMPUTER TITLES:

Hardware
- ☐ Apple 140 ☐ Macintosh 101
- ☐ Commodore 110
- ☐ IBM & Compatibles 114

Business Applications
- ☐ Word Processing J01
- ☐ Data Base J04
- ☐ Spreadsheets J02

Operating Systems
- ☐ MS-DOS K05 ☐ OS/2 K10
- ☐ CP/M K01 ☐ UNIX K03

Programming Languages
- ☐ C L03 ☐ Pascal L05
- ☐ Prolog L12 ☐ Assembly L01
- ☐ BASIC L02 ☐ HyperTalk L14

Troubleshooting & Repair
- ☐ Computers S05
- ☐ Peripherals S10

Other
- ☐ Communications/Networking M03
- ☐ AI/Expert Systems T18

ELECTRONICS TITLES:
- ☐ Amateur Radio T01
- ☐ Audio T03
- ☐ Basic Electronics T20
- ☐ Basic Electricity T21
- ☐ Electronics Design T12
- ☐ Electronics Projects T04
- ☐ Satellites T09
- ☐ Instrumentation T05
- ☐ Digital Electronics T11

Troubleshooting & Repair
- ☐ Audio S11 ☐ Television S04
- ☐ VCR S01 ☐ Compact Disc S02
- ☐ Automotive S06
- ☐ Microwave Oven S03

Other interests or comments: ______________________________

____

____

Name ______________________________
Title ______________________________
Company ______________________________
Address ______________________________
City ______________________________
State/Zip ______________________________
Daytime Telephone No. ______________________________

A Division of Macmillan, Inc.
4300 West 62nd Street Indianapolis, Indiana 46268

22637

indicate the resistance through which current must flow. Let's look at the circuit diagram given in Fig. 2-9. Here we see that the load in this circuit is consuming 240 watts of power. (The electrical load in a circuit is that device which consumes power.) In this circuit, the load is a 60-ohm resistor.

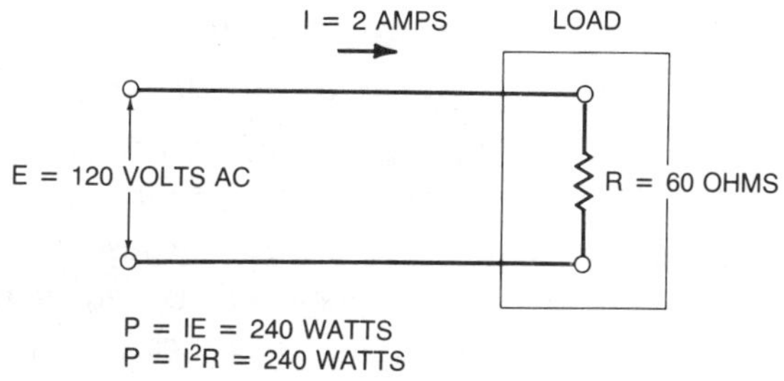

Fig. 2-9. A circuit containing a pure resistive load.

In Fig. 2-10, we see a load whose impedance (Z) of 60 ohms is partially made up of a resistor, which represents the pure resistive elements of the circuit (like the wire itself). Also, we see that there are capacitive and inductive elements in the load, which contribute to the impedance in the circuit. Impedance, then, is a function of the overall opposition to current flow in a circuit.

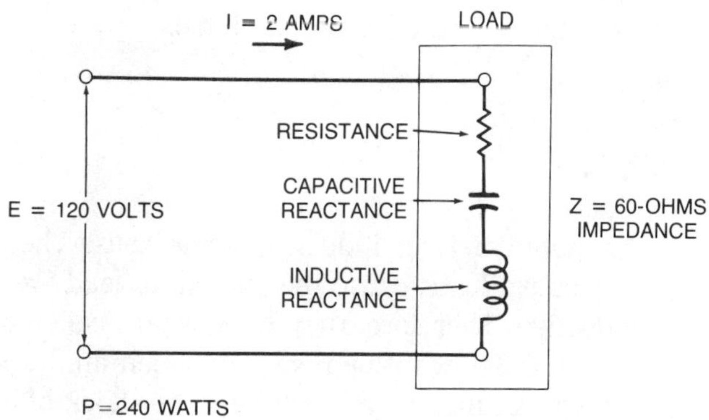

Fig. 2-10. This circuit has an impedance that is a function of three different circuit elements.

I was almost tempted to say that the elements shown in Fig. 2-10 each add impedance, but, "add" would have been an unfortunate term in this context since capacitive and inductive reactance to current flow cannot be expressed by just adding two ohmic values. They must be added algebraically. The formula for this is:

$$Z = \sqrt{R^2 + (X_L - X_C)} \quad \text{(Eq. 2-9)}$$

where,

Z is the impedance in ohms,
X_L is the inductive reactance,
X_C is the capacitive reactance.

Earlier, we said that capacitors and inductors affect the flow of AC power in circuits. This doesn't just refer to their characteristic impedance. Capacitive elements in an AC circuit cause current to lead the voltage while inductive elements in a circuit cause current to lag the voltage. If the capacitive reactance were exactly equal to the inductive reactance, the effects of the two would exactly cancel and then the overall impedance of the load would be equal to the purely resistive elements in the circuit. Of course, this is never the case unless this feature is intentionally designed into a circuit. (A circuit where capacitive reactance is equal to inductive reactance is called a *resonant* circuit.)

What we are trying to say here is that the impedance of the circuit shown in Fig. 2-10 is not determined by just adding three ohmic values. It is a more complex mathematical process. Nevertheless, the load does ultimately present a characteristic impedance that is expressed in ohms. We will use the term impedance (Z) often in future chapters. In Ohm's law, impedance can be used by substituting Z for R, with Z being equal to the impedance in the circuit (in ohms).

Power Factor

As stated before, inductive loads cause the current to lag the voltage. Capacitive loads cause the current to lead the voltage. Computer loads are inductive. Therefore, they have what's called a *lagging power factor*. If we took the 240-watt load we have been analyzing and measured the power with a wattmeter, we would get the shock of our life. Let's assume that the load is a personal computer. Our wattmeter might show that only 204 watts are being used. But, wait a minute! We defined watts earlier as "real power."

Let's check the situation out by looking at the voltage and current. We take a voltmeter and we measure 120 volts. A clamp-on ammeter shows the current to be 2 amperes. According to Equation 2-4, that's equal to 240 watts. Persons concerned with measuring computer power call this measurement "volts time amps," or *voltamperes*. Voltamperes, abbreviated VA, is defined as "apparent power."

The difference between *apparent power* and *real power* is used in computing the "power factor," and mathematically can be expressed by the formula:

$$\frac{\text{Real power}}{\text{Apparent power}} = \frac{\text{Watts (W)}}{\text{Voltamperes (VA)}} = \text{Power Factor (PF)} \qquad \text{(Eq. 2-10)}$$

In this case, we substitute and have

$$PF = \frac{\text{Real power}}{\text{Apparent power}} = \frac{204}{240} = 0.85$$

Remember that we said that computers are inductive loads where current lags the voltage by a certain amount. Fig. 2-11A shows the phase relationship between voltage and current in a purely resistive circuit. Fig. 2-11B shows this relationship in a pure inductive circuit. What happens is that energy, which is not actually used, is circulated inside the load. The capacitive and inductive elements of the load allow current to flow, current which is not converted into work. At some point in each AC cycle, this unused power is actually returned to the power source. It is important that the equipment that provides power to a load be sized for apparent power. Often computer power equipment is rated in VA as well as watts.

This phenomenon can also occur in other kinds of equipment. Fig. 2-12 is a photo of the voltage and current waveforms present in the circuits of a water cooler. Notice that the inductance of the motor windings of the compressor motor have caused the current to lag the voltage. Now look at Fig. 2-13. Here, we have the voltage and current waveforms of a purely resistive load (a radiant space heater). Notice that for a purely resistive load, the current and voltage waveforms are synchronized.

Transformers

Without transformers, the distribution of modern utility power would be impossible. Transformers perform two important functions. First, they enable voltage to be transformed from one level to another. Secondly, a transformer can electrically isolate one part of a power system from another. We will save this topic for a later chapter.

When electricity is generated at a generating plant, voltages with potentials on the order of 4800 volts to 18,000 volts might be expected to appear at the terminals of a generator. This voltage is then stepped up by transformers to prepare it for the long trek cross-country to city power distribution plants. The high-voltage transmission level is often roughly

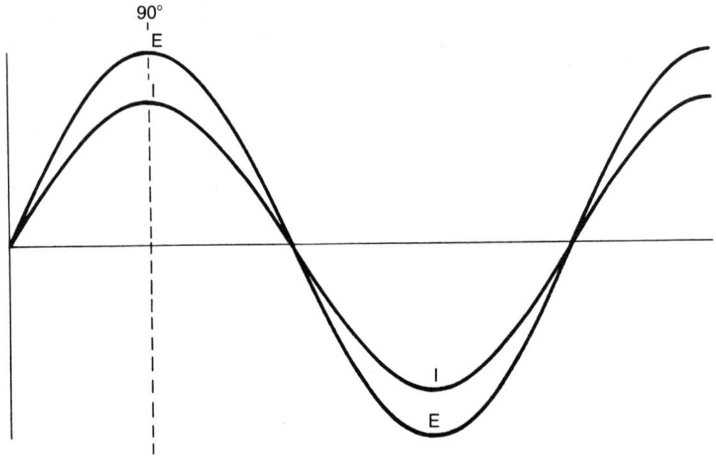

(A) In a purely resistive circuit, peaks occur at the same time.

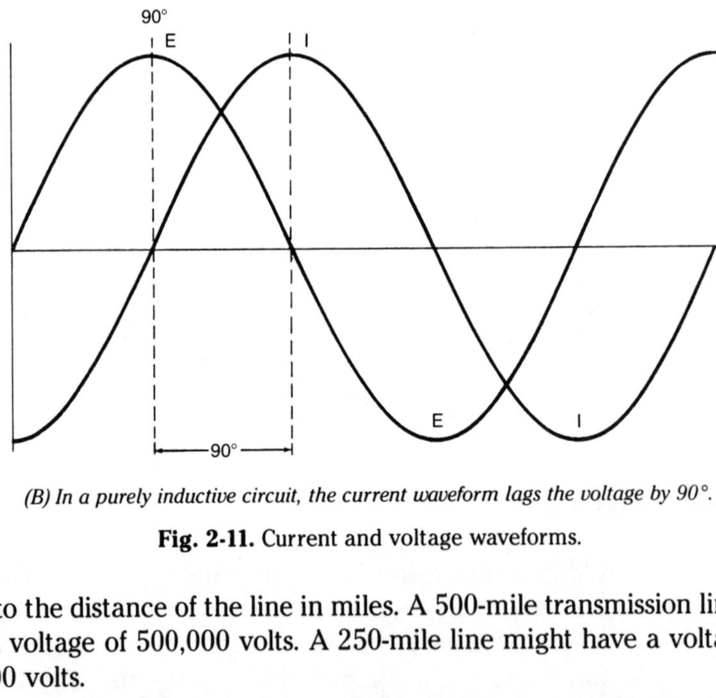

(B) In a purely inductive circuit, the current waveform lags the voltage by 90°.

Fig. 2-11. Current and voltage waveforms.

equal to the distance of the line in miles. A 500-mile transmission line might have a voltage of 500,000 volts. A 250-mile line might have a voltage near 250,000 volts.

Once the power reaches a city, it is stepped down to voltages like 34,500 volts and then routed to electrical substations, where it is stepped down again to about 4800 volts and sent out over the primary distribution lines to neighborhood homes and businesses.

How is all this stepping up and stepping down accomplished? A transformer makes this possible. Fig. 2-14 shows a typical transformer symbol. It

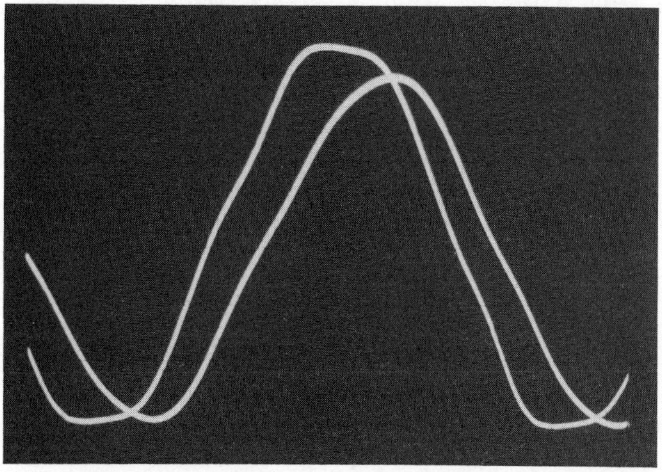

Fig. 2-12. The voltage and current waveforms measured in the circuits of an office water cooler. The current is lagging the voltage by a few degrees.

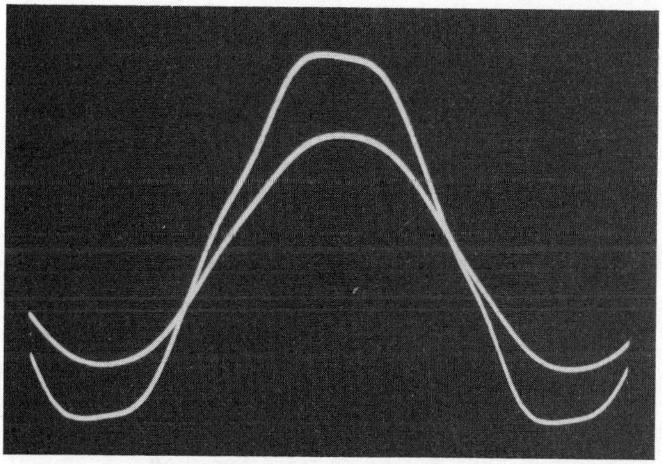

Fig. 2-13. The voltage and current waveforms of a purely resistive load (a radiant space heater). Note that the waveforms are in synchronization.

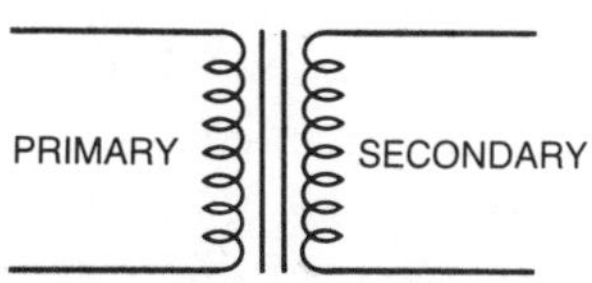

Fig. 2-14. A transformer has a primary winding, a secondary winding, and a laminated iron or steel core. This transformer has a transfer ratio of 1:1 since the number of windings in the primary equals the number of windings in the secondary.

has a primary winding and a secondary winding. These are wound around a common core of iron.

We stated earlier that alternating current (AC) flowing in an inductor produces a rapidly changing magnetic field. When this inductor is placed close to another inductor, the rapidly changing field produces a proportional current in the second inductor. This is the same effect that made generators work in our previous discussion. The expanding and contracting magnetic flux lines produced by a primary inductor will cut through the windings of a secondary inductor and will produce a current flow.

Many years ago, it was discovered that a coil wound around a laminated iron core would allow flux to penetrate 10,000 times better than it would in a coil with an air core. In more technical terms, air has a higher "reluctance" to the passage of flux lines and iron is far more "permeable." Sometimes electronic symbols can mislead. The physical construction of a transformer is such that the primary and secondary windings are wound close to one another in "jelly roll" style, around the iron or steel core.

An important thing to remember about properly designed transformers is "power in equals power out." Transformers are amazingly efficient. Losses in the transformation process are so small that we will ignore them. The second important thing to remember is the concept of the "transformation ratio."

Using the transformer symbol shown in Fig. 2-14, let's assume that there are 240 watts of power flowing in the primary winding. Theory tells us that there must also be 240 watts of power flowing in the secondary winding. If the primary voltage is 120 volts and there is 2 amperes of current flowing in the primary windings, then the same would be true of the voltage and current in the secondary windings.

Now look at the transformer diagram shown in Fig. 2-15. This transformer has twice as many turns of wire, or windings, in the secondary as it does in the primary. If we were to measure the current and voltage carefully, and the voltage and current levels were the same as in the previous transformer, we would find that we had 240 watts of power entering the primary and 240 watts of power available for a load in the secondary. However, measurements would show that our secondary voltage was two times that of the primary, or 240 volts, and that only 1 ampere of current was flowing. Remember the power formula, $P = E \times I$. This effect has some very practical benefits in the world of power transmission. The subject is discussed in more detail in my book, *Computer Electrical Power Requirements*, published by Howard W. Sams & Company.

In any event, these two properties of transformers, the *transformation ratio* and *power in equals power out*, explain the stepping up and down of voltage by the utility companies.

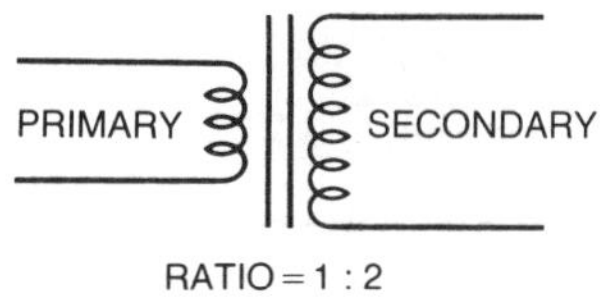

Fig. 2-15. The secondary winding has twice as many turns as the primary.

Voltages We Use

If we remove the faceplate of a common wall outlet, we will find three wires (don't try this at home) in the box behind the plate. One wire will be black, one will be white, and one will be green. Each wire is important and each has a distinct function.

The black wire is called the phase wire or hot wire. The white wire is called the neutral. The green wire is the ground. There are two ways that 120-volt power reaches us. One way is as part of a single-phase system (Fig. 2-16); the other is as part of a three-phase system (Fig. 2-17). Unless your computer is in or near a computer room, it is probably being fed from a single-phase portion of the building's distribution system.

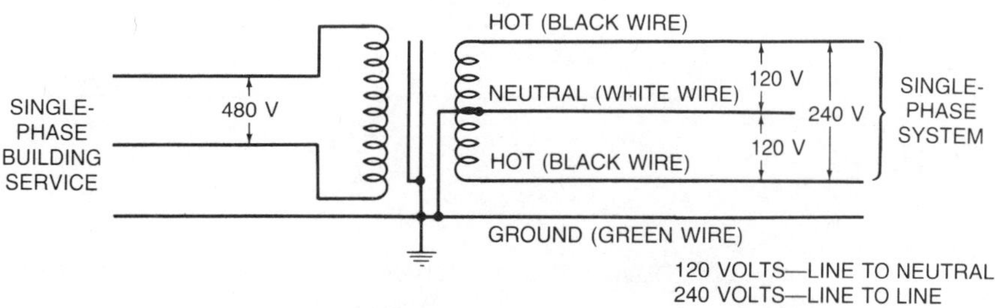

Fig. 2-16. A single-phase electrical distribution system.

One important point should be made here. It may not come up again, but it is a good thing to know. In Fig. 2-18, we have shown a three-phase transformer with a "Y-wound" secondary. This design creates a neutral connection where the current from all three legs or phases of the transformer return to complete a circuit. The current from each leg combines with the other two legs in the

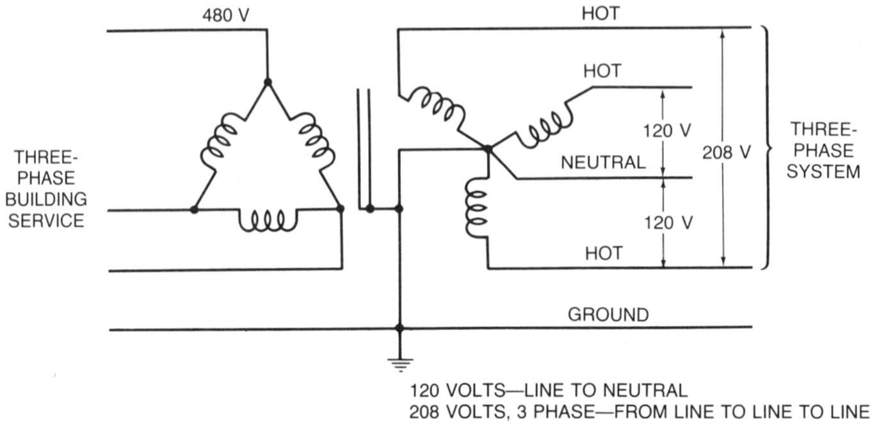

Fig. 2-17. A three-phase electrical distribution system.

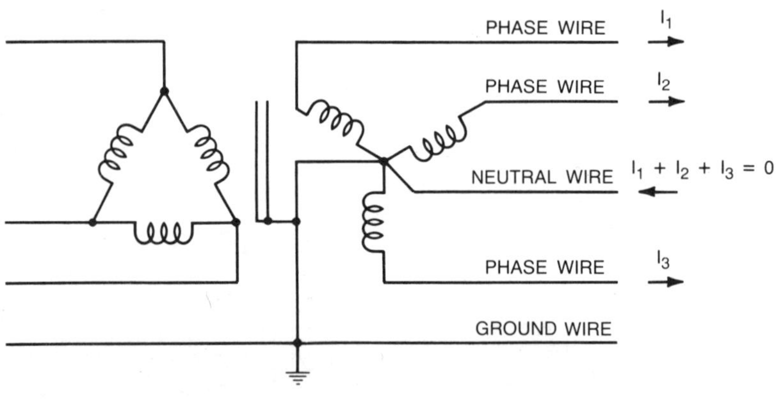

Fig. 2-18. Diagram for a transformer with a delta-wound primary and a Y-wound secondary, which creates a neutral point.

neutral line. Since the current in each leg is 120° out of phase with each of the other two, the current flow is theoretically cancelled in the neutral line. In other words, the algebraic sum of the three phases is zero, when added in the neutral line.

Later, we will see that the power supplies used in personal computers cause some interesting problems in this respect. Also, notice that the neutral and ground wires are bonded together at the transformer. This will come up again. For now, just keep these two concepts in the back of your mind.

Kirchhoff's Law

Fig. 2-19 shows a circuit with parallel paths through which the current can flow. It is difficult to know the actual amount of current that might be flowing in each branch of the circuit. To aid us in determining this, we have *Kirchhoff's law*. This law states that the current flowing toward a point in a circuit must be equal to the current flowing away from that point. This might seem fairly simple to understand while viewing Fig. 2-19, but this statement will come up again in the chapter on "Grounding." For now, just remember that electricity flows in circuits, and it is not possible to have a circuit where current flow just disappears. Kirchhoff's law helps us see that.

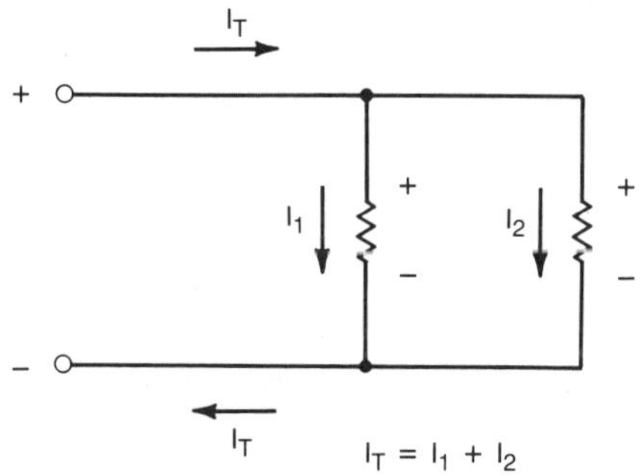

Fig. 2-19. Circuit illustrating Kirchhoff's law, which states that the current flowing to a point in a circuit is equal to the current flowing away from that point.

A Word of Caution

If it feels like we have covered a tremendous amount of turf here, we have. This was meant to be an overview, nothing more. What comes next is inextricably interwoven with the concepts we have presented here, and the book would not be complete without this chapter. If this has served as a light refresher, great. If we have covered ground that you might not have walked before, let me pass on some encouragement.

These basic principles of electricity undergird the remainder of this book and are at the heart of reliable computer operation. Many fine books have been written over the years on the subject. Time spent becoming comfortable with the topics given in this chapter will serve you well in the chapters to come, and in many other areas of the personal computer field.

Now that we have some understanding of what power is, let's look at the power we receive from the utility companies and see how it relates to the power the computer needs.

3 Recognizing Power Problems

In this chapter, we will define power problems for what they are and will explore their causes. At the outset, it is important that we recognize the truth about utility power. It is a product that has been around in the same basic form for years. The technology of generating, transmitting, and distributing power has remained frozen in time throughout the computer revolution. Is that bad? No. The alternative would be to have a utility bill each month that rivaled the cost of a PC.

Public utilities bring an amazingly clean product to our home and offices. It is economical and reliable. The plain and simple fact is that modern electronic equipment simply will not run on it. We will find out why in this and later chapters. The point here is to acknowledge the fact that we will never solve computer power problems by attacking the electrical utilities. In fact, many of the more enlightened companies in the field have launched programs to assist customers in solving their problems. These efforts range from mere public relations to actually selling computer power products.

The greatest exposure the power-distribution system has comes from birds, weather, errant motorists, and other factors that are mostly beyond the control of the utility companies. If the companies built redundancy into their system or adopted more defensive installation procedures, the net effect would be dramatic rate increases. Even if the utilities were willing to do it, computer users would still find themselves facing an alarming array of factions that are opposed to higher energy costs.

So for the foreseeable future, we will have to put up with some frequent (and some infrequent) perturbations on the power line. What are these strange occurrences? Where do they come from?

Definitions

Definitions are important. It is sometimes hard to understand this left brain penchant we all have of naming things—defining them in minute detail. Take olives, for example. To one person, Greek olives and Italian olives might be similar in many ways. They are both dark colored and salty tasting. But ignoring the fine distinctions might get the man at the Italian deli a little hot under the collar. The differences are like night and day to him.

Power problems have definitions but not every source defines every event in exactly the same terms. One of the biggest differences is in the matter of time. Some events are distinguished from another only by the fleeting nature of the event. Not all experts agree on these event durations. The definitions that we give here are an amalgamation from a number of sources. They are arranged in order of duration with the swiftest events listed first.

Impulses

An *impulse* is a disturbance of the voltage waveform for a duration of less than roughly 1 millisecond. An impulse may be additive or subtractive in nature (Fig. 3-1) and it may have a ringing or oscillatory characteristic. Some slang words that might be associated with this precise term are: spike, notch, transient, whisker, and glitch.

A *spike* is an imprecise term for an additive or positive-going impulse, while a *notch* is generally a subtractive impulse. A *transient* is an often misused word that merely describes the nonrepetitive nature of an impulse.

The slang term, *whisker*, refers to the thin line that an impulse of short duration traces on the screen of an oscilloscope. *Glitch* is a word used to describe almost anything.

Noise

Noise is a term used to describe repetitive, high-frequency impulses. We will see noise riding on a sine wave in a later chapter. Suffice it to say that noise

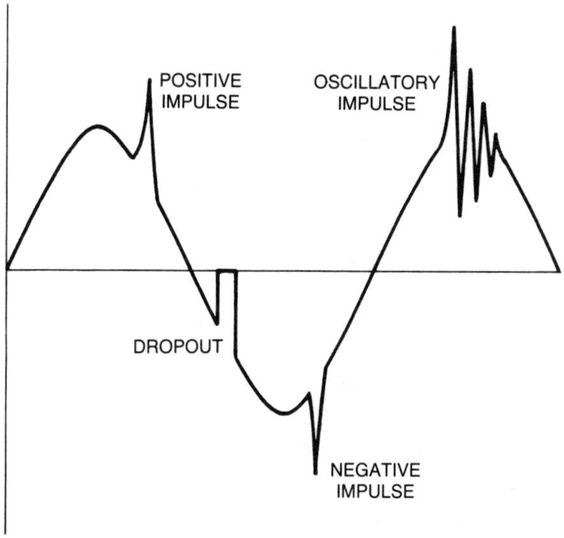

Fig. 3-1. Impulses on a sine wave.

occurs as impulses, and, in that way, is really a slightly different category or class of impulses. Noise, even though it is not a precise term, is an important concept which we will deal with in detail later.

Dropouts

A *dropout* is a total loss of power for a short period, from about 1 millisecond to 1 second (Fig. 3-1). Utility switching is the normal cause of dropouts.

Surges

This is as good a time as any to run our razor-sharp rapier through a commonly held misconception. A *surge* is not an "impulse" or a "spike." A surge is a *transient* condition where a series of peak sine-wave voltages exceed the set standard voltages for a period of time—from about one half cycle to possibly several hundred cycles (Fig. 3-2). This might also be defined as from about 8 milliseconds to 2.5 seconds.

The controversial point to be made here is that a surge is not an impulse. And the computer product we normally hear mentioned, the *Surge Suppressor* or *Surge Protector*, may not suppress surges at all. These devices are designed to suppress impulses of a high magnitude. Perhaps this may seem like a fine point, but the truth is that there are electronic products that we will talk about which cure impulses and there are other products that

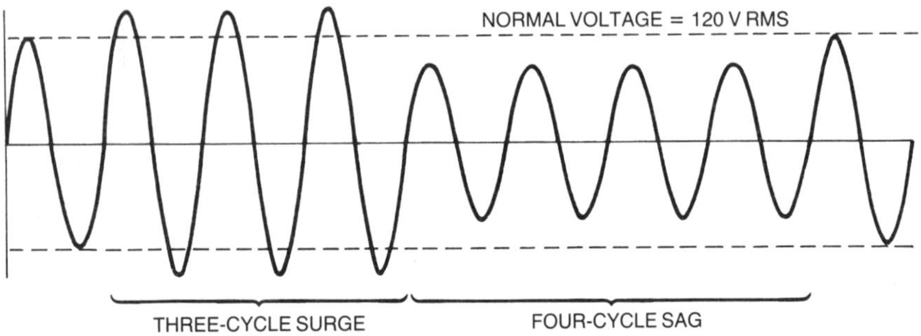

Fig. 3-2. Sags and surges are short-term increases or decreases in voltage.

cure surges or slow-moving over-voltage conditions. When it comes to shelling out hard-earned dollars, we don't want to buy the wrong product for the wrong reasons.

Sags

A *sag* is identical to a surge except that the peak sine-wave voltage has decreased from the set standards for a period of time, rather than increasing. A couple of slang terms which you might hear associated with sags are "flickers" and "dips."

A *flicker* refers to intensity variations in lights. Of course, incandescent electric lighting flickers 60 times a second, but our eyes can't see it. In order for the eye to perceive a flicker, an event of several hundred milliseconds has to occur. Of course, as we will see later, this is an eternity for a computer. Countless times I've heard a DP manager say, "Oh, the power didn't go out. The lights just 'flickered'." This may seem sort of ignorant in the context of a book about power problems, but I have seen tens of thousands of dollars wasted, based on this kind of silly misinterpretation of the facts.

The term *dip*, which is slang for sag, usually relates to an event inside the building—an event which is not utility related. Dips are caused by heavy step load changes that demand large starting currents. More on this shortly.

Overvoltage and Undervoltage

The terms *overvoltage* and *undervoltage* refer to conditions like sags and surges that last longer than a few seconds.

Brownouts

A long-term undervoltage condition that is actually planned by the utility, or is the result of excessive loading, is called a *brownout.* There are many locations throughout the United States that experience chronic brownout conditions. These may be caused by seasonal use of air conditioning or by heavy loading during certain times of the day.

Blackouts

A *blackout* is a widespread loss of utility power, either accidental or planned.

Outages

An *outage* is a localized loss of power that usually lasts from 1 to 5 minutes.

Computer Tolerances

The simple fact is that power is very dirty. In an earlier photo, we saw what appeared to be a relatively clean sine wave. Using a special filter, we can look at the noise that might typically appear riding on that sine wave (Fig. 3-3). Even if the magnitude of this noise is not particularly large, we should be shocked to see this much dirt on the line. What this means is that at any given time, a computer is seeing some unwanted signal as part of the power that appears on the power line. If this is true, there are evidently some power disturbances that won't affect a computer. After all, we have just shown that there are always some disturbances on the line; just because they are there doesn't mean we have a problem.

On the other hand, there are obvious limits to this optimistic view. There are two major considerations in determining when a power problem becomes a real problem. Those two considerations are *duration* and *magnitude.* The longer an unwanted excursion lasts, the greater the chance that it will affect computer operations. And, the larger the event, in terms of peak energy, the greater the chance that it will affect computer operations.

A computer's susceptibility also depends on what kind of power it was designed to expect. Most personal computers have power supplies designed to demand large amounts of current, but they are not too fussy about the level of voltage that appears at their terminals. Some older devices have altogether different power supplies that must see that voltage held to within

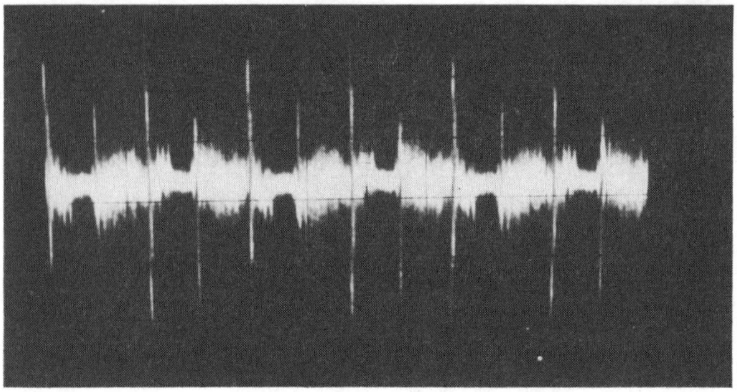

Fig. 3-3. High-frequency noise.

a certain rigid range or problems will develop. We will cover this later in our chapter on power supplies.

Fig. 3-4 makes this point graphically. We see an area (designated by the shading) where events can occur without causing problems for the computer. The area under the curve describes events that are so short in duration that their effect is not felt. As we trace the curve to the right along the "x" axis, we see that magnitude becomes a greater factor. The area under the curve (the cross-hatched area) is now bounded much more tightly than it was for shorter-duration events. What this means is that excursions above or below these longer-duration limits cannot be tolerated.

There are two points to be made about the graph in Fig. 3-4. This is an approximation of what one might expect to be design criteria for PC power tolerances. We can only approximate since there are so many manufacturers in the market that no firm standards are being followed. For larger systems, the criteria has been set by a group called the *Computer Business Electronics Manufacturers Association.* This group, CBEMA, has agreed on input power standards for larger systems. PCs are somewhat different from larger systems in that they are less critical about the power they receive.

The second point to be made about the graph is that the power supplies in today's PCs will pass certain kinds of noise directly into the computer. This is a change from earlier computer power-supply designs which were substantially immune to noise. But we will cover this in more detail later.

Survival Time

So what is the survival time of a PC? How long can it go without normal AC power before it crashes? For most PCs, the answer is about 20 to 40 milliseconds, or about $1^1/_2$ to $2^1/_2$ cycles. (Some lightly loaded PCs will ride

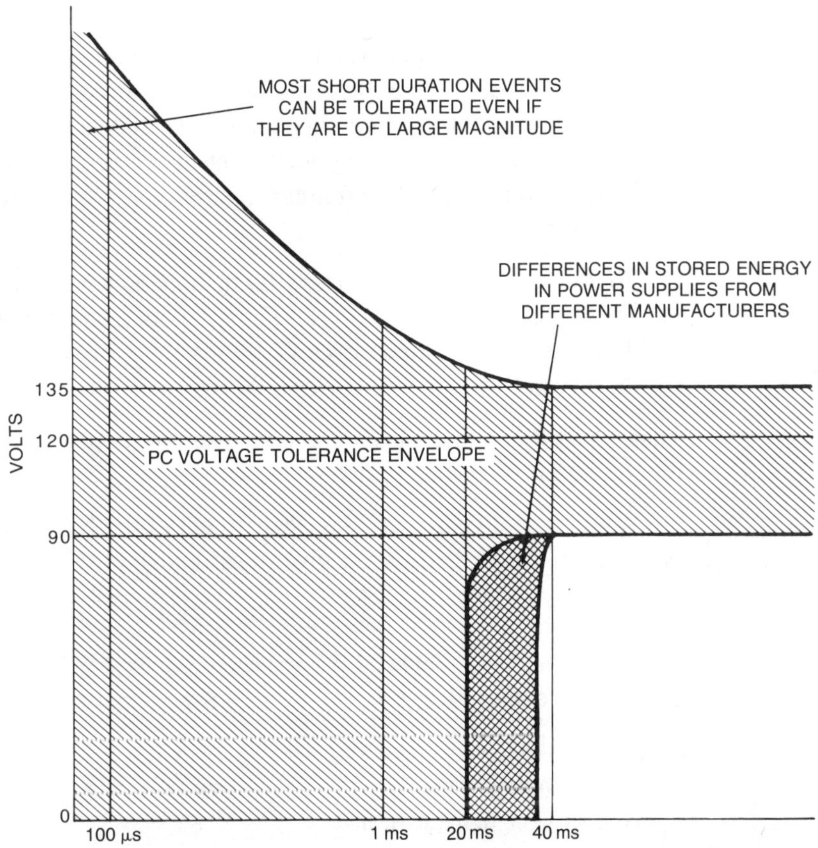

Fig. 3-4. A graph showing the estimated susceptibility profile for voltage variations and disturbances in PCs.

through 3 to 4 cycles without power.) This is a wide variance when you consider that a mainframe will die after about 10 milliseconds. The reason for this is that in the mad rush to build the cheapest PC, many manufacturers succeeded in building a cheap power supply. Cheaper designs use smaller components which have less electrical capacity and, therefore, provide less ride-through capability. Better-built power supplies have a greater tolerance for power interruptions due to the energy-storing capability of the components.

This tolerance is also an indication of the power supply's ability to provide for the instantaneous current demand of the computer during low line voltage conditions. In plainer language, we mean that the greater the energy-storage capacity of the power supply, mainly in the large filter capacitors, the greater will be its ability to provide large quantities of current, even when the line voltage may have dropped. We will explore this subject in detail later.

Power Quality

In 1984, Con Edison published a pamphlet entitled *Electric Power and the Computer.* The utility warned customers that transient voltage fluctuations are a recurring fact of life. Before we explore why this happens, let's see how often it happens. Con Edison is very forthright in predicting how often a sag might occur that would affect computer operations. On a 120-volt system, they estimate sags:

To 90 volts (25%) for 6 cycles (100 ms) once or twice a month.
To 90 volts (25%) for 30 cycles (500 ms) once or twice a year.
To 55 volts (54%) for 12 cycles (200 ms) once or twice a year.
To 0 volts (100%) for 12 cycles (200 ms) very rarely.

That adds up to some 14 to 28 events every year that may cause an interruption of data processing.

A number of years ago, the Department of the Navy did a survey of power problems at six sites. Table 3-1 gives a summary of what was found.

Table 3-1. Power-Related Computer Failures

Recorded Cause	Sags	Outages	Total Failures
Wind and Lightning	37%	14%	51%
Utility equipment failure	8%	0%	8%
Construction or Traffic accidents	8%	2%	10%
Animals	5%	1%	6%
Tree limbs	1%	1%	2%
Unknown causes	21%	2%	23%

The Bell System Survey

From May 1977 through September 1979, the Bell System conducted one of the landmark surveys of power disturbances. Two Bell employees, Goldstein and Speranza, produced a study which was probably the most scientific and careful evaluation of the problem of power quality done to that time. Unfortunately, for those of us who are not mathematicians, they choose a statistical method called a *Polya probability density function* to describe their findings.

They, of course, had very good reasons for using this mathematical approach since Polya functions were used to create a set of tables that predicted, statistically, the number and duration of events that might be expected in the future. Had they merely been trying to show how bad the power was, we might find their results a little more intelligible.

Data was gathered from 24 Bell System data-processing sites for a total number of 270 monitoring months. At the end of that time, an analysis of the total number of disturbances measured showed that 87% were sags while only 0.7% were surges. Outages accounted for 4.7% of the total, and impulses represented 7.4%.

One thing that stood out as they assembled the data was that lightning-prone areas had no greater rate of impulses than did other areas. In fact, the power disturbance most often recorded during electrical storms was a sag. This is logical, however, since the power company places devices on the distribution line that momentarily divert lightning energy to ground by shorting the power line.

The study predicted that 50% of Bell sites could expect 25 sags of significance and 4 power failures annually.

The IBM Surveys

Perhaps the power-quality survey most-often referred to was the one undertaken by George Allen and Donald Segall of IBM. This survey was done in 1972, but IBM has done two newer studies since then. Several sites were monitored, for a total of 3312 monitoring days. The results are summarized in Table 3-2.

Table 3-2. Summary of the IBM Survey

Type of Disturbance	Number of Disturbances	Average Days Between Disturbances
Undervoltage	1569	2.1
Overvoltage	103	32.2
Outages	65	51.0
Switching Disturbances	2831	1.2
Impulses	1676	2.0
Total	6244	0.5

What do the results in Table 3-2 tell us? If we divide the total number of disturbances by the number of monitoring days, we get an alarming average figure. We can expect 2 events of one type or another every day!

IBM has since done two additional surveys; a small one in 1974–1975 and a comprehensive one in the 1980–1983 time frame. The more recent survey included 6827 days of monitoring and it covered 34 states, as well as Europe and Japan. This study showed that over the intervening years, power quality had deteriorated significantly.

The data collected indicated a wide disparity between different parts of the country. Even so, conditions on the whole were not favorable to reliable computer operations. One conclusion that has been reached from the survey is that an outage, or a low-voltage condition severe enough to interrupt computer operations, might be expected once a week. We could belabor the point by presenting a more detailed examination of power quality, but the facts given here speak for themselves. Utility power as it arrives at the building service entrance is often not compatible with on-going computer operations. While these studies may be interesting and compelling, most of us already knew that, for some time, a basic problem existed in one form or another.

Let me make one more point that might make the evidence a bit more dramatic where PCs are concerned. All of these studies were done at major data centers. These facilities are carefully engineered to give a large computer a very friendly electrical environment. If the power fed to mainframes is bad, imagine what the poor lowly personal computer has to put up with. We merely plug it into any convenient outlet, and it must take whatever comes down the line.

What causes these problems? Obviously, there are events that affect power once it leaves the generator. We will look at this issue from two perspectives—outside the building and inside the building.

Utility Grounding and Switching

Much of what was discovered during the surveys of power quality cited here had its genesis out on the power line. Strange things can happen to electricity between the generator and the user. Unintentional grounding, called *ground faults*, are perhaps the most common cause of sags in voltage. This unintentional ground connection can be caused by equipment failure, arcing, or animals that suddenly complete a path to ground. In desert communities, transformers typically display ground faults during rainy periods. The natural accumulation of dust inside the unit mixes with the moisture in the air to provide an unwanted path for current flow to ground. High winds can cause power lines to slap together. Arcing switches or arcing circuit breakers can flash over to ground.

Coastal areas are also subject to their own special kind of problems, due to the ravages of wind, salt, and spray. Then, there are the ever-present dangers of cars, kites, and ice. There are a multitude of causes that can cause ground faults. Note that ground faults do not always have to be direct shorts to affect the voltage relationships in a distribution system. Current leakage can occur through faulty components and this will affect the voltage. In the next chapter, we will devote some time to one of the most spectacular causes of ground faults—lightning.

All of these things that divert energy to ground will cause wide swings in power as it travels along the power lines. But a more subtle form of fluctuation is that caused by standing waves, which emanate up and down the line from the point of a fault. Standing waves are reflected back to their source when they encounter the end of the line. This reflection, back and forth, sets up an oscillation. The frequency of this "noise" is determined by the length of the line from the fault to the reflection point.

Utility switching causes this same effect. Of course, utility switching also causes a momentary interruption of power. There are many reasons why the utility might switch power lines. They might need to compensate for heavy loads on other parts of the distribution system, or switching might be necessary to bypass points of failure.

Another common reason for switching is power factor correction. Remember, we talked earlier about power factor as it related to power that was circulated but not used. Utility companies are not too excited about this since they charge their customers according to the wattage, or *real power*, used. Therefore, they will usually place a surcharge on the bills of those customers who have a bad power factor in their system. Often, utility companies will switch capacitors into the line to compensate for a lagging power factor. This switching causes several rather severe problems, not the least of which is a dropout of sufficient enough duration to bring down any sensitive equipment that is connected to the line.

All these disturbances, whether caused by switching or ground faults, can be coupled by the inductance and capacitance that exists between the power lines. We will look into these principles a little more later on.

Changing Loads (Outside the Building)

Some common power problems are heavy loads being switched on and off along the distribution system. Large motors, like those associated with building air conditioners, can cause damaging impulses when they are switched on and off. In fact, there are many reported cases where entire industrial neighborhoods have been affected by the switching on of AC units atop one building.

Arc furnaces are another traditional culprit. They draw huge amounts of current while reflecting distortions back into the line. The list goes on, but suffice it to say that any sudden shifting of the load on the distribution line will affect the quality of power delivered to neighboring facilities—a changing load will create sags, impulses, and noise.

Good and Bad News (Inside the Building)

The good news is that most personal computers are plugged into those circuits that are the farthest from the building electrical service. What this means is that impulses generated outside the building have a lot of building wiring to travel through in order to reach the PC. The resistance and the inductance of the wires have a cushioning effect that reduces the shape and magnitude of incoming impulses. Also, there will usually be one or two additional transformers placed in the line, especially in commercial buildings. The inductance of the windings in these transformers has a dampening effect on noise and impulses.

Every silver lining has a cloud, and here we find no exception. This same long path that can protect PCs can also cause a voltage drop. The voltage at the wall outlet might be significantly lower than the voltage at the building service. This may very well make the PC more vulnerable to sags. PCs use switching power supplies. They have a great tolerance for voltage swings, but, as a general rule, equipment will draw more current at lower operating voltages. This causes heating that might damage equipment. You can compensate for voltage drops by using transformers (with taps) to adjust for chronic low-voltage conditions. We will discuss the merits of transformers in greater detail in a later chapter.

Inrush Currents

As loads are turned on, they present an initial load to the power source that changes dramatically over a few seconds. Nearly all loads have power supplies with large filter capacitors or windings. These supplies drive motors or other energy-absorbing components that have an early heavy "demand" in order to reach some proper operating level.

Take a motor, for instance. A motor must produce an initial starting torque. The current demand of this initial inrush of power can be many times the steady-state running load of the device. This demand can last for as long as 10 seconds. An induction motor can easily draw five to ten times its running current for 3 seconds or more during start-up. To illustrate this, look at Fig. 3-5. Here we see a portion of the current sine wave of a common electric hand drill as it is starting up. Each additional sine-wave trace shows a decreasing demand for power. Finally, after a few seconds, the current demand flattens out to the steady-state running voltage at a level much lower. The inrush current of this device is so large that the full sine-wave trace was too big to get all of it on the oscilloscope screen and thus show a clear detail.

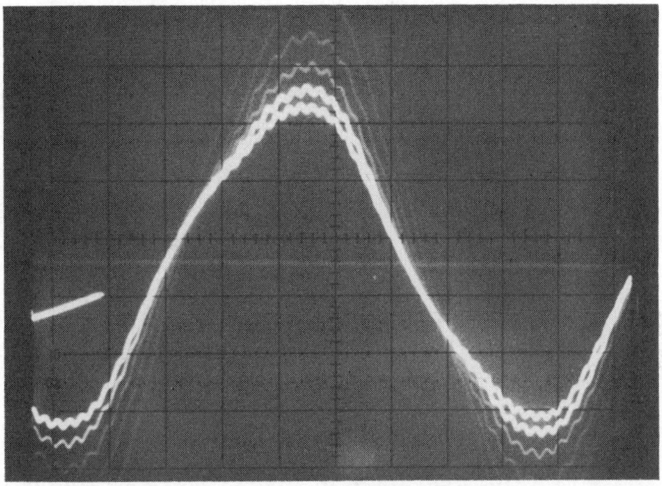

Fig. 3-5. The inrush current of an ordinary electric hand drill.

Switching power supplies, on the other hand, have a slightly different inrush characteristic. Most of the energy used by the power supply is held in a large capacitor. At turn-on, this large capacitor charges fully during the first half cycle. The inrush current during this brief period is large and can affect nearby equipment. Transformers have inrush needs that can be from five to fifteen times normal.

Inside a building, just across the hall or in the next office from a PC, there may be a device that cycles on and off. The inrush demands of the device can be such that it interferes with the current demand of the PC on your desk.

Step Load Changes

Inrush current could easily be classified as a step load change. But there are other events that produce step load changes that are not related to inrush currents. Elevators, for example, are already powered up and ready to operate when we step into them. Yet the amount of current demanded to lift a car full of people several stories upward can affect the power available all over the building.

Step load changes are heavy loads that cycle on and off. Elevators, copiers, and even coffee makers and microwave ovens are examples. This constant shifting of loads off and on causes voltage sags, noise, and impulses of a large magnitude. Several studies have been done and results show that such things as an oil burner—located in a residence—can produce a starting transient of up to 2500 volts. Commercial facilities can expect to experience impulses, caused by devices going on or off the line, of a magnitude of anywhere from 300 to 2700 volts.

Off the line? Yes, turning off a device can sometimes create a larger disturbance than that which is created when it is turned on. Any device with windings in it can produce extreme voltage transients when they are turned off. A transformer, for example, can produce an impulse in excess of ten times normal voltage when the power is switched off, especially when the load is a high-impedance load like power semiconductors. It is the collapsing field that induces this voltage into the secondary of the transformer.

Voltage impulses can be caused by switch arcing, fuses blowing, and breakers clearing. These aren't strictly what we would call step load changes, but they are an important source of undesirable disturbances within a building.

A good way to visualize step load changes is to think of a manufacturing plant. In back, there are huge machines stamping, pressing, and grunting—cycling one piece at a time. Meanwhile, in the front office, there is a local area network for the company's accounting department. The heavy cycling machinery may be placing such a high demand on building power that the computers may not see anything like a sine-wave voltage at all—just some distorted rise and fall of voltage waveforms, peppered with harmonic distortion, large impulses, and noise.

Power (Inside and Out)

There are plenty of gremlins to spoil our clean supply of pure repeating power sine waves. Outside the building, there are any number of events that can create perturbations, while inside the building we hold our breath every time a new piece of machinery is plugged into an outlet.

In succeeding chapters, we will discuss much of what we have commented on in more detail, as it relates to specific product technologies aimed at providing a cure for power problems. But before we do that, a little more background is required. What about power supplies—the things that convert AC into DC so the computer can use electricity which is at logic levels? And, of course, there is noise. We have referred to it a time or two. We must look more closely at noise and its specific impact on PCs. We will also talk in more detail about lightning, and will have a section on lightning arresters, as if lightning could actually be arrested. We will discuss grounding. There are three wires attached to that socket in the wall outlet. One of them is coded green and it's there for your health and much, much more.

4 Voltage Transients

So far, we have taken a look at electrical power and reviewed some of the basic laws of electricity. We have also established that there are a lot of undesirable things going on with that power. If we could summarize what those things are, we might put them into three categories.

Category one, we might call *outages*. By this, we mean a voltage excursion that is so low in voltage that the computer interprets the event as a complete loss of power and it goes down as a result. Of course, a total loss of power, like a blackout, would also fall into this category. This category will be dealt with extensively in later chapters.

Category two, we might call *slow-moving averages*. When we say slow here, we mean an event that lasts for longer than one half cycle. The term average refers to the RMS voltage during the event. These events might be either surges or sags. As we have seen by the evidence, a sag is much more frequent than a slow-moving surge. Voltage regulation to counteract surges and sags is sometimes, but not often, a concern in the PC environment. We will talk about this later and learn when we need voltage regulation and when we don't. This is important. Many users misunderstand the issues of this category and make uninformed buying decisions.

The last category, we will call *voltage transients*. These are momentary events of high magnitude that might be disruptive to operations or might even cause damage to equipment. Transients are sometimes called impulses or spikes. We would not call them surges since this is a misuse of the true meaning of the term surge. Voltage transients or impulses are extremely short-term events. This, as well as the following chapters, will build logically toward an understanding of transient suppression and power conditioning. More money is wasted in this area of the market than anywhere else. We will see why as an outcome of our study of transient voltage excursions and will learn how to protect PCs from them.

In order to more clearly discuss this subject, let's break it down into three more meaningful subcategories. These three subcategories are each variations of one another. They are: *lightning*, *static*, and *noise*. We will explore the cause and effect of these three phenomena. An understanding of each will prepare us to move on and see what some products are trying to accomplish in protecting our PC.

In a way, both lightning and static are forms of electrical noise. We might define noise as any undesired signal appearing in a circuit. But not all noise is the result of lightning or static. In this way, noise is a somewhat imprecise concept. But, as we shall see, it manifests itself in two distinct forms or modes. These modes are at the heart of the lore and the religion of protective product designs.

On the other hand, static and lightning are basically the same thing. Lightning is nothing more than an electrostatic discharge on a planetary scale. Static, as we typically think of it, can be no less destructive in certain circumstances. Well, let's try and sort this out.

Lightning

There are two kinds of electrostatic discharges that we call lightning. One is a discharge from cloud to cloud. The other is a discharge between earth and the clouds above. It might seem logical that the only type we need be concerned about, from a protective standpoint, would be the cloud to ground discharge. As a matter of fact, this is not always true. Obviously, the amount of energy which might potentially be injected into a power system by a lightning strike from above (to the ground) is significantly higher than a cloud to cloud discharge. But the amount of energy released during each kind of event is so enormous that even cloud to cloud discharges can damage equipment several miles away.

Let's take a look at how a lightning strike is generated. This will give us a clearer understanding of why precautions against lightning strikes must be taken. Scientists theorize that the lightning process begins when regions of the cloud itself develop differing electrical charges. As shown in Fig. 4-1, a cloud develops a positive charge at its base while the area above it takes on a negative charge. The buildup of charge between the two areas eventually leads to a discharge within the cloud itself. This process frees more electrons in the negatively charged region that might otherwise have been trapped in water droplets or ice particles.

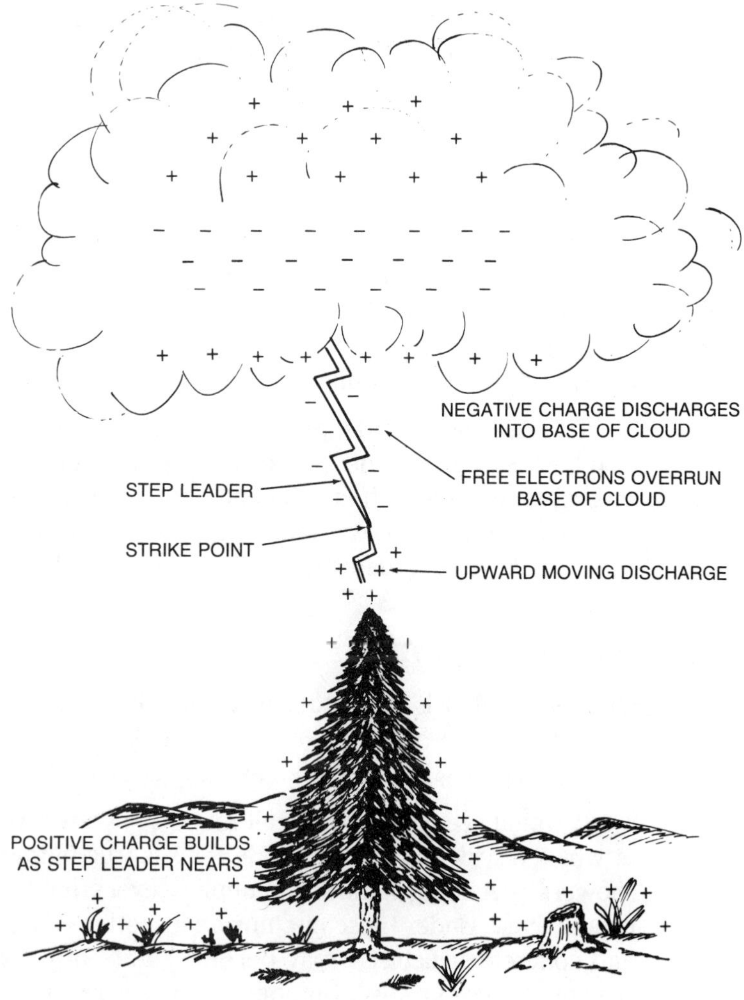

Fig. 4-1. The lightning process.

These free electrons overrun the positively charged base of the cloud, neutralizing its charge and continuing toward the ground below. It is estimated that this trip takes about 20 milliseconds. This trip is broken down into discrete steps less than a microsecond long, known as the *leader process*. Luminous, rapid steps of lightning, which are approximately 165 feet long, move toward the earth, one after another, with less than a millisecond separating each step.

As the step leader, which is made up of a large negative charge, moves toward earth, an opposite charge builds up on objects below. This opposite (positive charge) is especially large on objects that project above the surface of the earth, like trees, antennas, or tall buildings. Since the two charges are attracted to one another, the positive charge attempts to move toward the step leader.

This causes an upward moving charge to move toward the negative charge in faint luminous steps. Eventually, this results in a meeting of the two charges as they move toward one another. This meeting point is called the *strike point*. A channel for current flow between the earth and ground is now established. From the strike point, electrons move toward the ground with great violence. This creates the initial bright flash. This brightness moves up the channel, forming a return stroke. Electrons flow toward the earth as current and luminosity move skyward.

This does not end the process. New charges may exist at the base of the cloud, causing the whole process to repeat itself. In fact, this may happen several times in less than a second. The human eye cannot perceive these rapidly changing flashes, and we may see them as one very bright event. Scientists have recorded the whole process on film.

The Effects of Lightning

Of course, what is important to us in this whole process is the amount of current that flows in the channel. Peak stroke current averages about 20,000 amperes, but may it be as high as 270,000 amperes.

It would seem that some tall metal structures would be the likely point at which a strike would terminate. This is true but not always. The thundershowers preceding lightning dampens everything, increasing the relative conductivity. Under these circumstances, other objects, like trees, buildings, and concrete structures, may become sufficiently conductive to permit the flow of charges upward. But, because they are still insufficiently conductive to allow a large current flow without significant resistance, extreme heating and enormous mechanical pressures will result.

Some sources state that temperatures reaching 60,000 degrees Fahrenheit can occur after a few microseconds. Metal structures can be warped, and, of course, the current flow can create sparks between metal members that can ignite fires. Flammable material is a grave potential hazard. It is little wonder why lightning is the usual source of forest fires. Wooden buildings can sustain heavy damage since structural members might literally explode from the pressure of inside moisture turning to steam. Bark vaporizes on trees, bricks explode, huge blocks of concrete are demolished, and even the ground is sometimes furrowed for several hundred feet. Clearly, the effects of lightning are akin to the detonation of several hundred pounds of TNT.

Superheating of the type we are describing expands the air around the current channel, creating a shock wave. This expanding shock wave is the source of thunder as well as the cause of other widespread damage to the roofs of buildings.

The attractive forces that go to work when so much current flows can cause the fusing of parallel conductors and the squashing of hollow conductors. Large current flows exert a mechanical force as it travels down a conductor, similar to the flow of water through a garden hose. When this current flows through a wire that has tight bends in it, this mechanical pressure has a straightening effect. The bending force can be as high as 5000 pounds. It is recommended that ground conductors, which are meant to serve as a path for lightning-generated current, have no sharp corners.

Lightning Frequency

Fig. 4-2 is an isoceraunic map of the United States. This shows the mean annual number of days with thunderstorms. The numbers are recorded by each weather facility making a tally each time they hear thunder. Looking at the map, what we see is that the weather man in Tampa, Florida, hears thunder an average of 90 days each year. The weather man in Seattle, Washington, on the other hand, hears thunder an average of only 10 days per year.

This may seem like a funny way to calculate how often lightning will strike, but from this data, along with other information, a statistical inference can be made that will predict the probability of when a given building will be struck by lightning. Even the current-carrying size of the stroke can be predicted. This information can be used in designing the building and/or the protective equipment that would be used in providing protection from the effects of lightning.

This information on lightning-strike density, along with factors like the safety of building personnel, possible production losses, damage and repair costs, insurance premiums, as well as the cost of protection, are part of the decision-making process that determines the strategy for designing lightning-protective equipment.

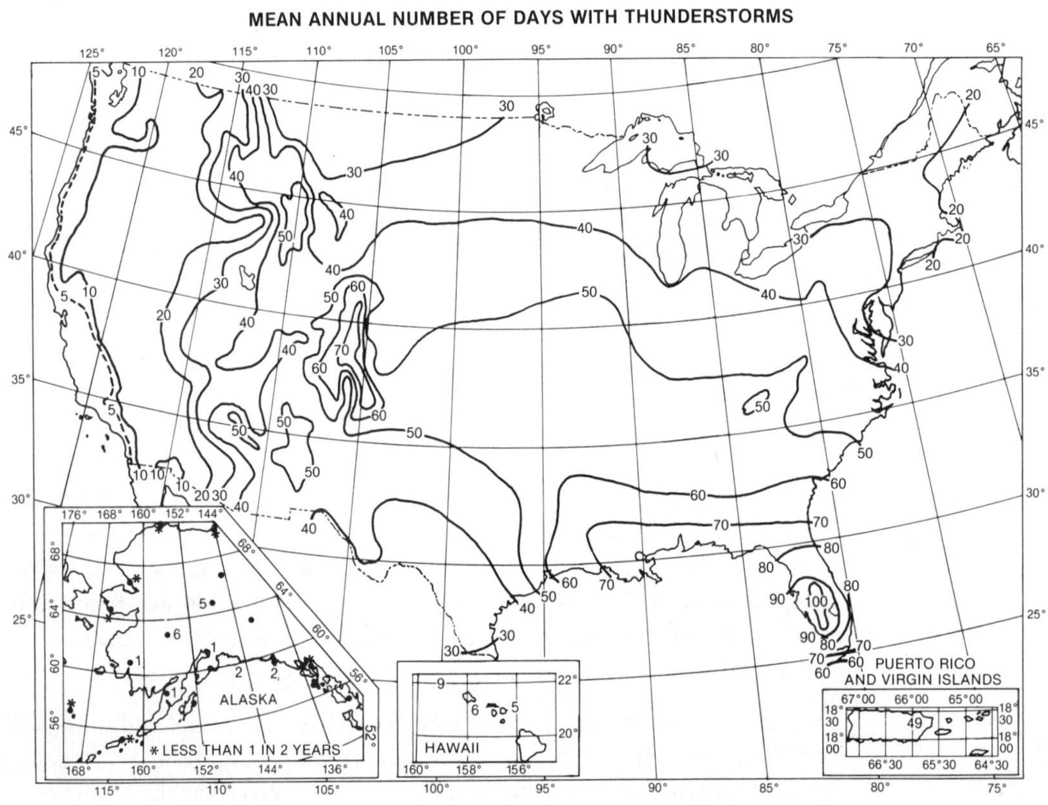

Fig. 4-2. Annual isoceraunic map of the United States showing mean annual number of days with thunderstorms. *(Courtesy National Weather Service.)*

Building Protection

You may be wondering what kind of strategy has been used to protect your building. Most buildings do not have protection built in as a design criteria. In fact, it is often the case that many building elements act together to direct lightning-generated energy directly into the building. To understand this hazard, let's look at what is commonly call a *lightning rod*.

There are three requirements for protection against a direct lightning strike that call for the use of a lightning rod. First, a conductor must be established that deliberately attracts the step leader. In other words, we want the lightning rod to be the tallest most-prominent point of the building, and not the piping, for example, of the building fire-sprinkler system.

Next, a low-impedance path to ground must be provided. What we mean here is that the lightning rod must present the lowest impedance path to earth ground. Remember, earth is the return path in the lightning circuit. We don't want a satellite dish to be the low-impedance path—not unless we want to direct massive amounts of current into sensitive equipment.

Lastly, the connection to the earth itself must be of low resistance. There are a variety of ways to accomplish this, with the most common being a copper rod driven into the ground. However, this should be dictated by practices which are common to your area, and which take into account the soil content, moisture, and other considerations that are beyond the scope of this book.

If care is not taken to provide a low-impedance path to ground, an action known as *side flash* may occur (Fig. 4-3). This can be prevented by providing two parallel ground conductors. At lightning frequencies, a ground conductor looks like an inductor. When we place inductors in parallel, the inductive reactance is greatly reduced. For this reason, two, and sometimes more, ground conductors are used.

The Electrical Effects of Lightning

Our primary concerns are the voltage transient that might be created by lightning and what we must do to prevent this energy from reaching the computer. There are a number of ways this might happen. Of course, a main worry is that lightning may strike the wire or wires feeding our building directly. If this should happen, enormous energy would appear on the line feeding the building. Some attempt has been made to measure this voltage. The highest lightning voltage recorded on a transmission line was 5 million volts. If that sounds impressive, consider this: The strike point was 4 miles up the line from where the measurement was made. Since the peak voltage

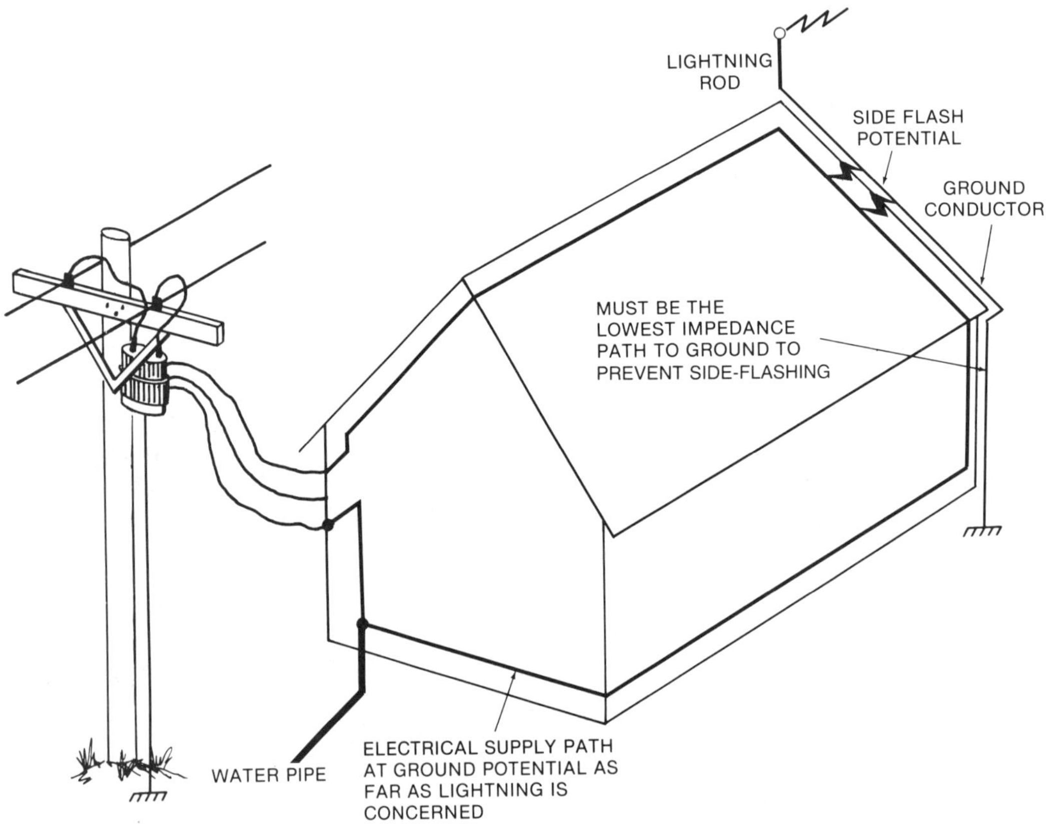

Fig. 4-3. Lightning may find a lower-impedance path by arcing to another conductor. This is called a *side flash*.

was reached in less than 2 microseconds, data indicated the voltage rose on the order of 10,000,000 volts per microsecond.

Another way that these impulses might reach the computer is via ground loops. When lightning seeks a path to ground, the potential between different ground reference points may be substantial. The resultant loop current can easily damage equipment. We will cover the topic of grounding and ground loops in detail later.

Induction is yet another way that lightning-generated energy might be injected into critical circuits. As large currents flow through conductors, the expanding magnetic field causes induced current to flow in nearby conductors that could then carry damaging impulses to computers. Even lightning discharges between clouds can induce transient-voltage impulses of several thousand volts in conductors that are several miles away.

We discussed side flashing earlier. This arcing can couple energy into data lines as well as power lines. It might seem strange that lightning would flash over to a current-carrying conductor. But, the voltages and currents that result from a lightning stroke are so large that lightning sees a 120-volt power line as ground potential.

Conductors can also act like antennas for radiated lightning energy and, thereby, can feed transient overvoltages into the power line. All these voltages have the capability of breaking down insulation, bridging the conductors of printed-circuit boards, and shorting the turns of transformers. Underground cable is a favorite path for lightning.

Obviously, the effects of a direct hit would be catastrophic to a PC. But this event would be infrequent. The effects of transient voltages caused by lightning many miles away are far more frequent. Ground-potential differences between points along the distribution system create surges in the power line. The firing of lightning arresters can create impulses as well as the inrush transient that follows momentary sags. Even remote strikes create huge fast-changing magnetic fields that have been known to induce impulses of several hundred volts into data links. All of this undesirable energy can damage equipment, confuse processors, and create disk errors even when the power is turned off.

So what are we to do? We will talk about the use of lightning arresters later in the chapter on "transient suppressors." For now, let us make the point that the potential damage from lightning is so great and the energy released is so powerful, that at or near the computer is the last place in the world to try and deal with it.

As alternating current increases in frequency, the current has a tendency to travel along the exterior surface of the conductor. This is called *skin effect.* Lightning is a mixture of very-high-frequency rapidly changing current. The physics of this is such that lightning tends to travel around, beside, and on top of the path it is following. Thinking that we can actually harness this energy and put it through some circuit in a box and, therefore, protect equipment from it, defies logic. There are places where we can deal with lightning effectively—they are far away from the computer!

Static

Static is short for "electrostatic discharge," or ESD. As we stated earlier, lightning is a form of ESD. But what we more commonly think of as static is that zap we get when we grab something metallic after walking across a carpet in the winter time. Most of us have a vague notion that the static charge came from movement and some kind of fuzzy material like the carpet. Many of us remember high-school experiments where a glass rod was rubbed with a certain cloth. The result was a charge that was built up on the rod and which could be discharged somewhere else.

In fact, this is called *triboelectricity*. The term comes from the Greek word *tribo* or *tribos*, meaning the action of rubbing. Triboelectricity, then, is an electrical charge that is built up by friction. The action of rubbing your shoes against a carpet creates a charge that is capacitively coupled to you through the soles of the shoes. You then carry this charge with you until it is either dissipated by discharging into the air or back to the floor, or, more likely, discharged through a low-impedance path much in the same way as lightning is discharged, like to a door knob or another person. In fact, the discharge may be so large that a spark may be visible for an instant.

It works like this. The two basic charged components of the atom are the *proton* and the *electron*. An electron carries a negative charge while the proton carries a positive charge. The proton is a permanent part of the atom in solid matter and will move with that matter. The electron is free to move from one atom to another as long as some energy is expended to move it. This energy might be thermal, chemical, or mechanical.

Static electricity is generated when two unlike materials are rubbed together and then separated. When the materials are in contact, electrons move from one material, interfacing with electrons from the other material. Meanwhile, the associated protons must stay behind. An attractive force is built up between the two materials as equilibrium is established. As the materials are separated, stray electrons produce a negative charge on the surface causing a potential difference between the two surfaces.

If the two materials are conductive, this potential difference will equalize before the materials are completely separated. In good conductors, the electrons can return easily during separation. In poor conductors, the electrons become trapped and cannot return. They remain and the charge remains. When the electrons come in close proximity with a good conductor, they move toward a discharge path. In most instances, the charge is sufficient to ionize the air that insulates it from its low-impedance path and the charge arcs across.

The speed of separation, the characteristics of the material, and the area of contact all have an effect on the possible buildup of a static charge. Perhaps the largest effect on the magnitude of the ESD is the relative humidity. Moist air is a much better conductor than dry air. Walking across the carpet in 10%–20% humidity might build up a charge of 30,000 volts.

The identical movement in 85%–90% humidity might build up a charge of less than 1000 volts. In low humidity, just raising one arm can generate a charge of 100 volts.

Gas, steam, or air passing through an opening can produce static. Chutes, belt drives, or conveyors can be a source of static. These charges can then be passed onto the operators who might then pass these charges to the PC they are operating.

What does this mean for PCs? As a static charge discharges into a conductor, peak voltage and current occur extremely fast—in picoseconds or nanoseconds. It is this rise time more than anything else that causes concern. Very fast rise times of high magnitudes, like 30,000 volts, produce an expanding magnetic field that can induce undesired current flow in nearby circuits. It is not unusual for a trace on a logic card to pick up 3 volts or more from an ESD traveling through a conductor 30 centimeters away. This undesired signal might be interpreted as data, causing soft errors in processing. These extraneous bits cause memory errors, pollute program results, and may cause an action to be taken, like the false starting of a disk motor. Suddenly you're in hyperspace—lost forever.

Damage to hardware can also occur. ESD has the capability to punch micron-size holes in the oxide of IC gates and cause junction or metalization burnout. Even if the ESD does not blow a chip, it may have stressed it to a point where it will have its life significantly shortened. A potential of 25 volts for 100 nanoseconds will destroy some memory chips and microprocessors.

The rise time of the ESD is affected by the position of a finger when it contacts a metal chassis. If the side of the finger touches, the rise time is significantly slower than if the tip of the finger touches. Fingernails create an even faster rise time, and a sharp instrument or tool is even faster. In an office of a dozen people, several hundred discharges of a potentially damaging magnitude may occur each day. Ironically, with the exception of JFETS and bipolar transistors, all semiconductors fail at 3 kilovolts or less. Our ability to detect or feel the static discharge in our own bodies starts somewhere around 6 kilovolts.

All of the preceding factors have been under observation by professional DP people for many years. Grounding wrist straps, special work surfaces, and protective packaging have been used by service personnel for many years. Mainframe operators have long been accustomed to using humidified air conditioning, ionizers, conductive floors and/or footwear, special clothing, and topical antistatic sprays. These techniques, however, are rarely applied in the PC environment. There are products on the market that plug into the safety ground conductor of the receptacle where the PC is connected. The operator is supposed to touch this device first before touching the computer, thereby dissipating any static charge. The principle of this idea is a good one in those parts of the country that experience chronic low humidity. The habit of touching some other metal surface before touching the PC is a good one. However, whenever possible, a far better approach is to encourage the use of carpeting materials that have a lower propensity for static buildup, as well as the use of humidification, sprays, and antistatic mats. If none of these precautions are taken, the PC is at the mercy of those charges carried by the operator.

Noise

Now, our discussion gets a little more relevant to the PC. Noise, as we described earlier, is a signal appearing in a circuit that is other than the desired signal. This may be the result of lightning or of ESD. More often, it is the result of other events happening in the environment. Certainly, lightning creates the kind of high-magnitude noise that we must ensure does not reach our computer.

As pointed out in the chapter on power quality, any number of things, both inside the building as well as outside, will produce unwanted noise impulses, along with surges, sags, and outages. Fig. 4-4 shows how noise might appear on a sine wave. We have turned on the cursors of the oscilloscope to show the magnitude of the sine wave and the relative magnitude of the noise impulse. Fig. 4-5 shows this same noise impulse, but it is photographed through a special filter that eliminates the sine-wave waveform and shows only the noise that exists above about 5 kHz.

It is not unusual for this magnitude of noise to exist on a sine wave (off and on) throughout the day. Obviously, we want only the sine wave to enter the computer. The noise is unwanted interference. Noise of a low magnitude will not bother our PC, but noise or impulses of a high magnitude can interfere with data processing or can damage internal components. Here, we are using the term noise interchangeably with the terms impulse, spike, and voltage transient. But, at some level, we might not consider noise an impulse or voltage transient. On the one hand, we have the constant source of low-level interference from a spinning motor with wearing brushes. We might call this noise. On the other hand, we have a huge voltage transient or impulse that is caused by lightning. We might call this a spike. The difference between the two is subjective, but their behavior in signal circuits is the same. Let's see how this works.

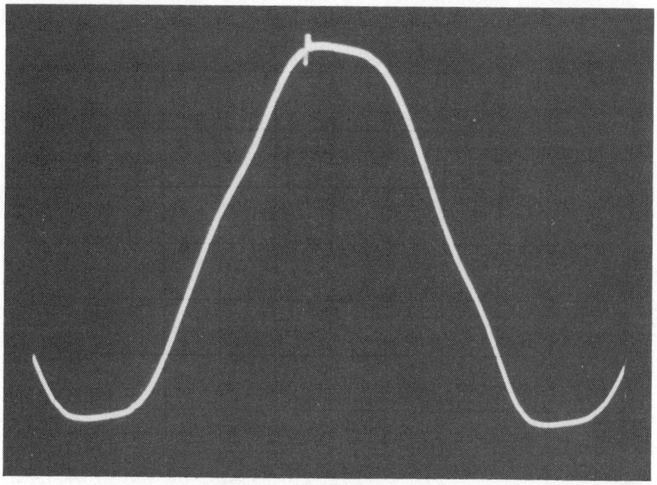

Fig. 4-4. A 60-Hz sine wave with noise riding on it.

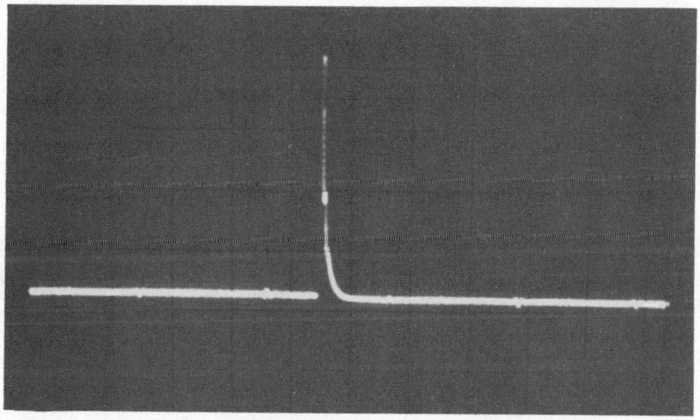

Fig. 4-5. Noise with the sine wave filtered out.

Noise in Circuits

Fig. 4-6 shows a simplified circuit diagram. Let's go through the circuit and identify each part of the circuit and explain what it is doing there. First we have our noise generation, which appears across terminals A and B. In the diagram, this looks like an intentional connection to a noise source. It is not. Noise enters a circuit in many different ways. What we are trying to do is to reduce this circuit diagram to something very simple to see something that is really the heart of this book. The noise generator might be lightning impulses coming down a power line, or a noisy piece of equipment, or an infinite number of noise sources such as are encountered in the environment everyday.

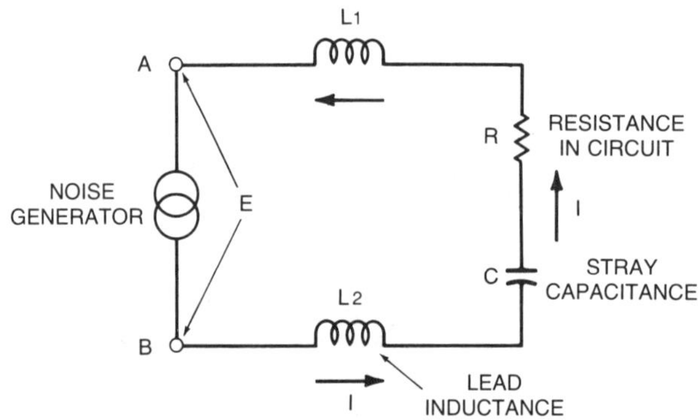

Fig. 4-6. A simplified view of noise in a circuit.

Take a look at L1 and L2. Unwanted noise in a circuit is going to have a high frequency, much higher that 60 Hz. As frequency goes up, the value of the inductance of the wires between components goes up. In other words, at 10 MHz, the noise signal may see a straight piece of wire as an inductive element of high impedance. We call this *lead inductance.* The value of R is a combination of the simple, purely resistive nature of the wire and the other components of the circuit.

Capacitance C, in the diagram of Fig. 4-6, is perhaps the most significant circuit element of them all. We are showing C as stray capacitance. What does that mean? At some noise frequency, two wires (or any other circuit elements) placed close together might take on a value of capacitance such that a noise impulse might see it as a conductive path. For instance, two tracings on a printed-circuit board might, at some frequency, have a capacitive value that completes a circuit between the two. These are unplanned and unexpected paths where high-frequency signals can pass with little impedance. This is called *stray capacitance.*

We also have a current, I, in the circuit. This is the current flow in the circuit. We have shown that current as flowing just one way, but the current could be flowing both ways if the noise signal alternates. The important point is that current flows in the circuit. Voltage E, then, is the voltage or electrical potential that the noise presents across the terminals of the circuit.

Now, we come to an important point. This is the circuit that the noise signal sees. The actual components that make up this circuit may be nothing like what is shown in our diagram, but because of the frequency of the noise, those circuit elements—ICs, boards, coils, wires, connectors, etc.—take on inductive and capacitive values.

Frequency

Let's clarify frequency. Fig. 4-7A shows an alternating noise signal. Notice that this is the kind of noise waveform that we might expect. It looks like noise, alternating rapidly up and down. Its frequency is dependent on the number of oscillations that occur over a given span of time. (Line voltage has 60 oscillations per second, so we call it 60-Hz, or 60-cycle, voltage.) If a noise signal oscillated 1,000,000 times a second, we would call it 1-MHz (megahertz) noise. Our signal in Fig. 4-7A shows a varying signal that may oscillate over a broad spectrum of frequencies.

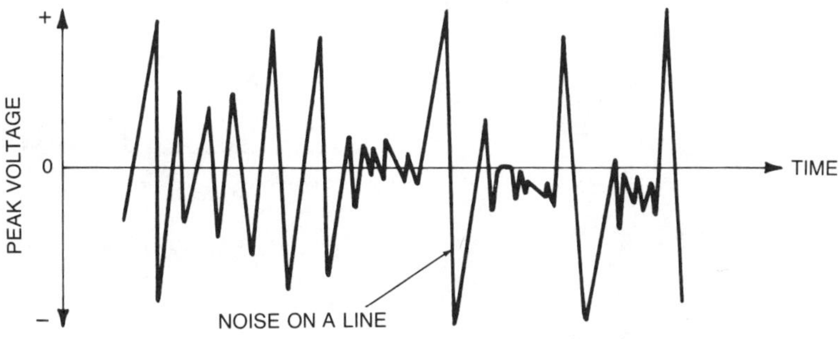

(A) An alternating noise signal.

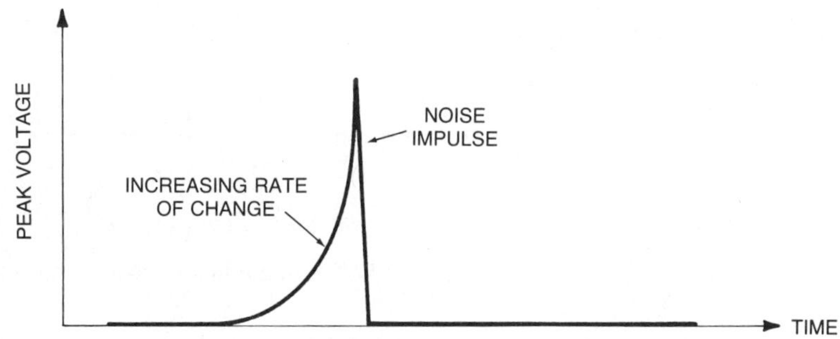

(B) A noise impulse.

Fig. 4-7. Two different concepts of frequency.

The noise impulse in Fig. 4-7B shows something entirely different. This is a single noise impulse. It might have been sliced out of the waveform shown in Fig. 4-7A. There is no oscillation occurring here. However, the face of the slope of the impulse is rapidly changing. Near the bottom of the slope, the rate of change is slow, while at the top of the slope the rate of change is extremely fast. If we wish, we can study the rate of change of the slope of a curve by using higher mathematics. But we don't need to do this to understand that the rate of change is synonymous with the term frequency.

If our noise impulse in Fig. 4-7B appeared across terminals A and B in Fig. 4-6, then capacitance C would appear to be a low-impedance path at some frequency which allows current to flow. Let's see how this works by simplifying our circuit even more in Fig. 4-8.

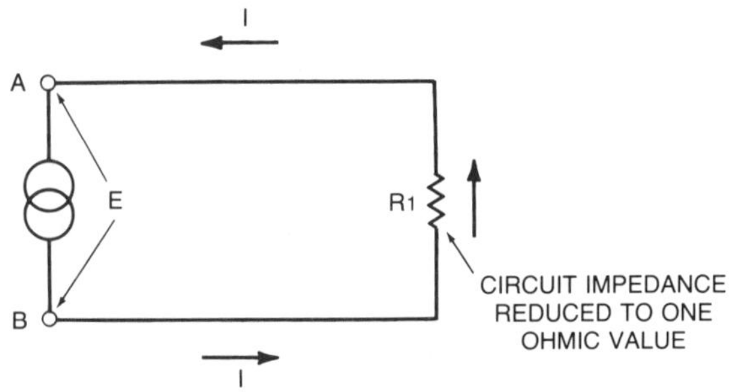

(A) A simple circuit.

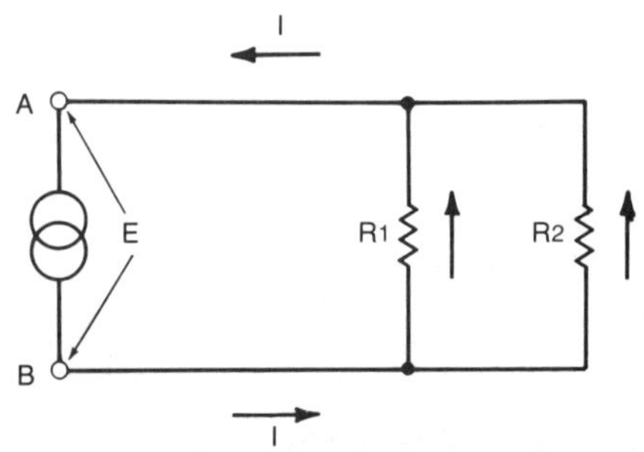

(B) Resistance in parallel.

Fig. 4-8. Simplified noise circuits.

Here we have two circuits. Let's look at the circuit in Fig. 4-8A first. At some frequency, a noise-signal potential appears as voltage E across terminals A and B. The very fact the this potential is present causes current to flow through resistor R1. The amount of current present depends on the value of R1, according to Ohm's law. (We might place a battery or a 60-Hz AC current across terminals A and B, and current would also flow in this simple circuit.) The point we are trying to make is that, at some frequency, a circuit like the one in Fig. 4-8A may suddenly appear when a noise signal presents itself to that latent noise circuit. This happens instantaneously. At some other lower frequency, the circuit quite literally might not exist as a path for current to flow, and our diagram would no longer be a valid representation.

What we are saying is that the components of a circuit designed to direct the flow of electricity in a certain way at one frequency may be seen as a completely different electrical path to a signal of a much higher frequency. We might never dream that a data cable can suddenly turn into a capacitor at some very high frequency, but it can. A power supply is designed to do one thing at 60 Hz, but, at 10 MHz, it looks entirely different to a noise signal. The physical characteristics of a material displays different properties as the frequency of a signal is increased. Wires become inductors, capacitors become wires, and coils disappear.

The circuit in Fig. 4-8B shows us that the noise current splits between the values of R1 and R2. The amount of current that flows in each is determined by their ohmic values. If R1 has a low ohmic value relative to R2, then more current will flow in R1.

This is a profound truth that underlies much of the discussion in this book. When we want to keep current away from something, we must give it an alternate lower-impedance path, so the current will flow through the alternate path. Inadvertently creating undesired signal paths is every engineer's nightmare, and they are not always easy to avoid.

Normal-Mode Noise

Noise as it appears on power lines comes in two varieties: *normal mode* and *common mode.* As shown in Fig. 4-9, normal-mode noise is noise that can be measured between the phase wire (or hot wire) and the neutral wire. Sometimes, the phase wire is called the "live" side of the line.

The root cause for normal-mode noise is usually heavy step load changes of the variety that we talked about earlier. Turning large loads off or on, or shunting utility power-factor correcting capacitors across the line, creates a ringing or oscillatory impulse. Fig. 4-10 shows the impulse created by a spinning motor or other such device, since we see the impulse appearing every one half cycle or 8.34 milliseconds. Fig. 4-11 shows this impulse on a shorter time base so we can see its typical waveshape.

Common-Mode Noise

Common-mode noise is a noise impulse that can be measured between the ground wire and the neutral wire, and at the same time is measured

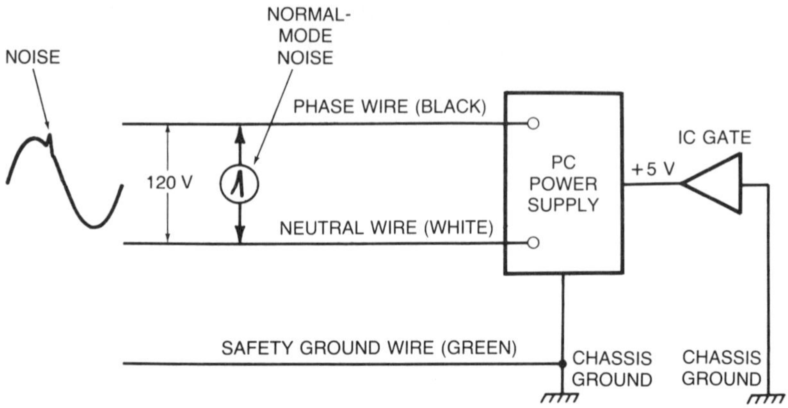

Fig. 4-9. Normal-mode noise appears between the phase wire and the neutral wire.

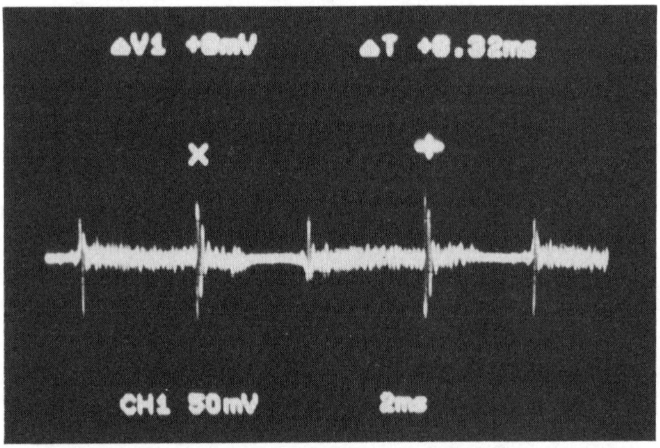

Fig. 4-10. A normal-mode impulse created by a spinning load.

between the ground wire and the phase wire. That is why it is called common-mode noise, since the impulse is common to both lines with respect to ground. This is shown in Fig. 4-12.

Common-mode noise is caused by such things as lightning and the tripping and reclosures of utility breakers. It is also caused by poor grounding techniques, ground faults, radio transmitters, time clocks, and machine tools. In addition, normal-mode noise traveling along a phase wire can induce noise in the neutral wire that can be detected as common-mode noise (Fig. 4-13). At times, this issue gets a little confusing. The important thing to remember about common-mode noise is that it is measured between the neutral and ground wires, even though the impulse is technically on both the live and neutral lines.

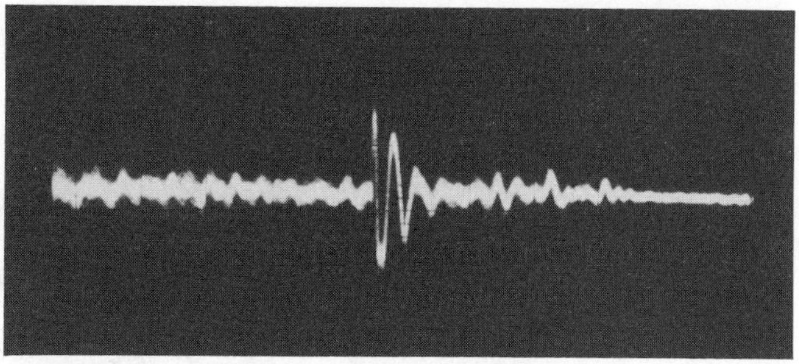

Fig. 4-11. The impulse of Fig. 4-10 enlarged for a better view.

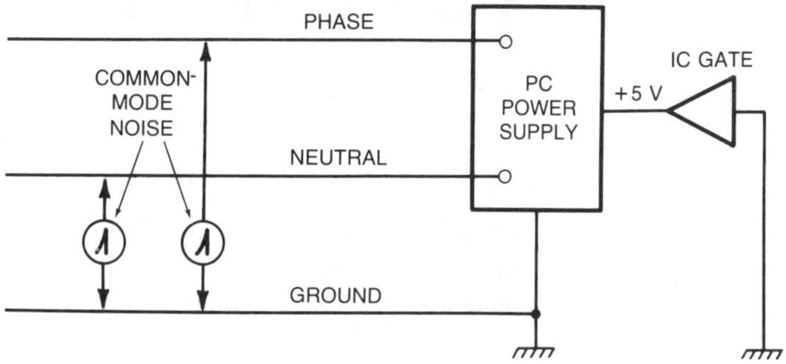

Fig. 4-12. Common-mode noise appears simultaneously between the phase wire and the ground wire, and between the neutral wire and the ground wire.

Noise about Noise

Noise is electricity just like the 60-Hz sine wave. Electricity, even one positive-going impulse, must follow the laws of electricity and flow in a circuit. What flows to a point also flows away from that point. Electrical energy doesn't just magically appear and disappear. The concept that electricity, even noise, moves in circuits or loops is so basic that we might forget it. We will discuss this more in Chapter 5, when we discuss *grounding*.

The point we made in Fig. 4-6, as well as in Fig. 4-8, is profoundly simple when we think about noise; it helps us understand what might at first appear to be complex. If a voltage is applied across an impedance, current will flow. If there is infinite impedance, no current will flow. If there is no potential across the impedance, no current will flow. The relationship we learned in an earlier chapter serves us well when thinking about noise: E = IR. Clearly, if the impedance (Z) is 0, then E = 0. If the impedance is some extremely high value,

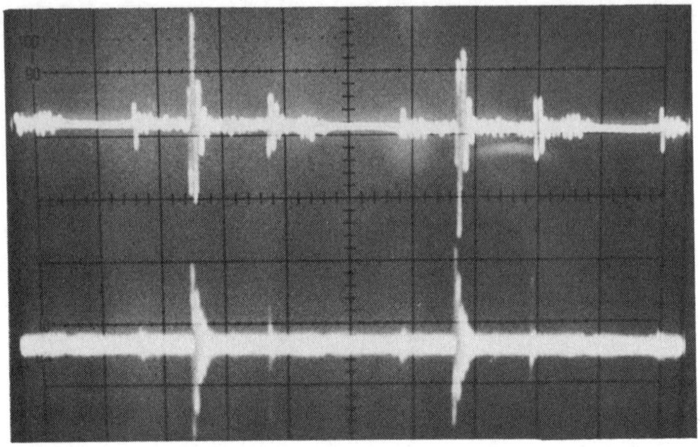

Fig. 4-13. These two traces show normal-mode impulses being induced in the wiring and converted to common-mode noise.

then I will be some minute value. If a noise potential, E, appears across an impedance that is not extremely high, then an increasing current, I, will flow as the impedance decreases. Note: Normally, the letter "Z" is substituted for the letter "R" when we talk about impedance instead of a pure resistance.

5 Grounding

Every time we flush the toilet at my house, the waste water flows into a cesspool. The cesspool is constructed of cleverly aligned brick which gives the support of a hard structure while allowing the water to gradually leach into the soil around it. Someone, somewhere along the line, must have picked up on this as an analogy for electrical grounding. Unfortunately, the analogy is totally false.

And yet, what a concept! Imagine being able to drive a copper rod into the ground, and having the moist spongy soil greedily gobbling up unwanted noise and voltage spikes that have invaded the wiring of our home or office. The ground becomes the repository for unwanted electricity—a path of no return for the gremlins looking to garble our granules and deceive our data. Let the ground hogs worry about the stuff.

Unfortunately, like many fantasies, this scenario has no—repeat—no basis in fact. The opposite is sadly the case. Misbegotten beliefs about "ground" are a common source of the problems that bedevil computer operations. Let's throw a grenade and explode this myth once and for all. From an electronic standpoint, earth is not ground.

Since the early days of electrical power distribution, the earth has been used as a ground return path for lightning, fault current, and other utility-related occurrences. Proper earth grounding is important in the construction of buildings, swimming pools, and overhead power lines. But what these techniques do is use the earth as a grounding path. This is logical when we remember that lightning uses the earth as part of a current path.

But earth grounding does not have the magical capacity to absorb electrical energy. A path for electrical energy? Yes. A sponge that soaks it up? No. Computers run fine in outer space or aboard planes. The Space Shuttle does not drag a ground wire behind it that is connected to the earth. So just what the heck is this grounding?

Safety

Fig. 5-1A shows a safety hazard. The ground wire has been eliminated from the circuit, and fault current could flow from the equipment cabinet to ground through the first person who touches it. In Fig. 5-1B, we see that fault current will flow through the extremely low-impedance path of the "safety ground," thereby tripping the circuit breaker. If we think about Ohm's law, we will see why this happens. Remember "E," or voltage, will equal resistance (R) times current (I). If the resistance is very low, maximum current will flow. The impedance of the ground wire is such that enormous current flows through in an instant, thereby tripping the breaker. A human body, on the other hand, has a high resistance, and through a high resistance, less current will flow. But there will still be enough current to cause death, while possibly not being sufficient enough current to trip the circuit breaker. That's why it is so important not to use radios and hair dryers in the bath tub. Since these devices do not have a ground wire, and the water itself provides an alternate path, the only current path is the most dangerous path.

Fig. 5-1 clearly shows the advantage of proper safety grounding. Safety must not be sacrificed in any wiring scheme. That is what proper installation of the green wire (in electrical wiring) is all about. But let us leave safety aside for a moment so we can talk a little theory. As the discussion continues, however, safety grounds (those green wires) will pop up again.

Floating Grounds

Let's imagine a power system that is not referenced to an earth ground. In fact, let's imagine that it is referenced to a 20,000-volt power line. What? How can we do that? Fig. 5-2 shows what this might look like. For many, this might appear to be the first step into the twilight zone. But this deceptively simple drawing shows a very important concept.

The computer has no idea that it is at 20,000 volts with respect to the

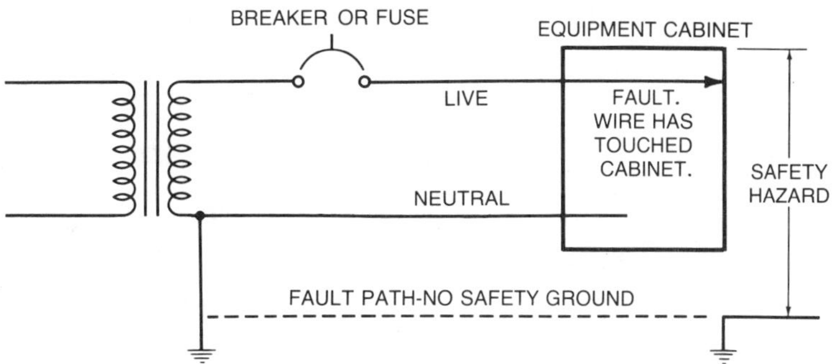

(A) A potential safety hazard exists should someone close the fault path by touching the cabinet.

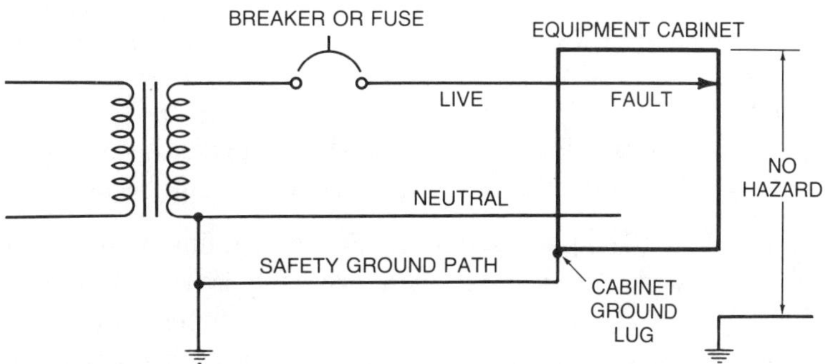

(B) Fault current will flow through the safety ground, tripping the breaker immediately. No touch hazard exists.

Fig. 5-1. Two potentially dangerous circuits.

earth. It only cares about what its relationship is to ground. In this case, we have assumed that the computer is using a standard type of power supply that converts 120-volt AC power into usable DC power for the logic circuits. As long as the power supply sees this voltage, everything will operate normally. The logic circuits will be referenced to ground the same way. No problem.

Think for a moment. Let's take a mental journey. Take the diagram off the page and put it inside an aircraft. We will assume that our working computer is flying from New York to Los Angeles. On the way, we fly through a variety of storm systems and clouds. Because of this triboelectrical effect, the structure of the plane picks up a charge of 20,000 volts with respect to the earth. Even though we are aware of this, we find the computer working just fine.

When we land, our plane keeps its charge because it is insulated from earth by rubber tires. Unfortunately, the ground crew forgets to equalize this buildup of electrical charge through the use of a metal strap or chain,

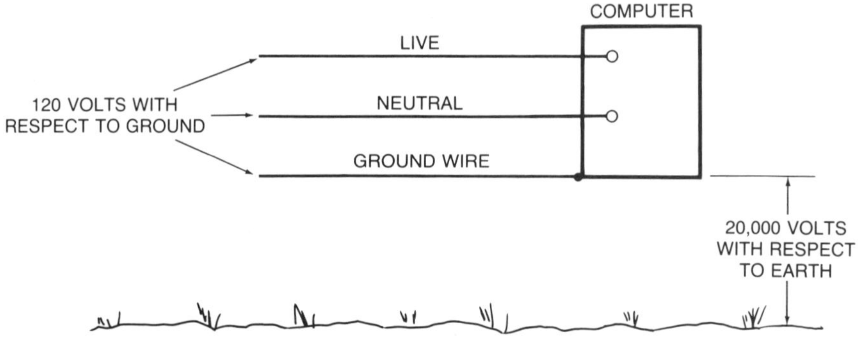

Fig. 5-2. This computer is fed by a system that floats with respect to the earth. As long as the voltage relationships do not change with respect to ground, the potential between ground and earth might be most any value.

and the first passenger off the plane dies a horrible death as the charge passes from the off ramp to the tarmac through his body. But that's another story.

The point is that the PC worked fine no matter what its grounding system was referenced to. There are safety issues here that we are obviously ignoring. But the point applies to many other types of equipment that are around us and in use every day. Consumer electronics, like stereos, TV sets, and VCRs, are not connected to even a safety ground. They are what's called *double insulated.* We know this because the round ground-wire prong on the power plug is missing. This means that the chassis of the device can float with respect to the building's power ground. The touch-voltage danger does not exist because of the double insulation.

We might ask, why don't we have a floating ground for our PC if all of this is true? This is a good question and we will answer it as the chapter progresses. For now, let's frame another question while we are on the topic of other electronic devices. Why do manufacturers recommend that the chassis ground of a record player be tied to the chassis of the stereo amplifier? The answer to both of these questions has something to do with a technique called *single-point grounding* or *signal referencing for equalization.* Let's see what this is all about.

Single-Point Grounding

Every building has a built-in floating ground. Fig. 5-3 shows this in simplified form. This is a safety precaution that equalizes any potential differences

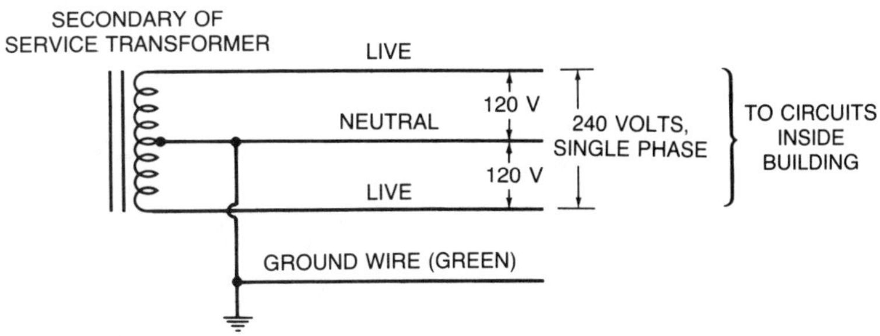

Fig. 5-3. The service transformer has the neutral-to-ground bonded on the secondary. This point allows everything connected to it to be referenced to this single-point ground.

between neutral and ground. If we look at Ohm's law, we can determine that no voltage can exist between ground and neutral because of this bonding. If there is no resistance, there can be no voltage drop. So now, even if the power ground varies with respect to some other grounding point somewhere else, the power system for the building is properly referenced to a single point.

This is a point of vital importance. We can reestablish this neutral-to-ground bonding point anywhere we desire by simply placing a transformer at the desired location. This is consistent with the National Electric Code and proper safety practices. A good way to visualize this is to think of the PC as a boat (Fig. 5-4). If the neutral and ground are tied together, the computer's ground potential floats with the nearby power-ground single-point reference. If, however, we tie the boat to the ocean floor by referencing our PC ground to some other point with respect to the power ground, we may find ourselves bailing water.

Let's expand this concept a bit further. Fig. 5-5 shows the electrical distribution of a typical personal computer system, with CPU, printer, modem, etc. Each of these devices might have its own power cable. At 60 Hz, each device's chassis is at zero potential with respect to the others because they are all tied to the neutral-to-ground bonding point of the building service transformer. Because of this, the entire group of devices float together with respect to ground. This means that voltages are equalized between cabinets. The happy consequence of this is that we don't get a severe shock when we touch two cabinets at once.

Grounding Noise

Single-point grounding is a valuable tool in the fight to keep unwanted signals or noise from getting into our PC system. But it must be applied

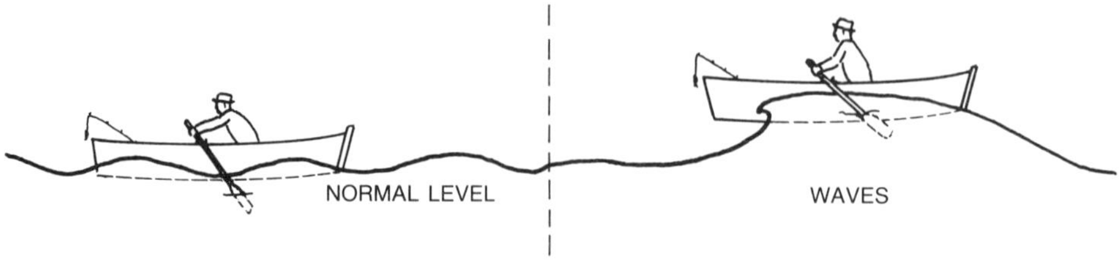

(A) Our boat is referenced to the top of the water and therefore floats on the waves.

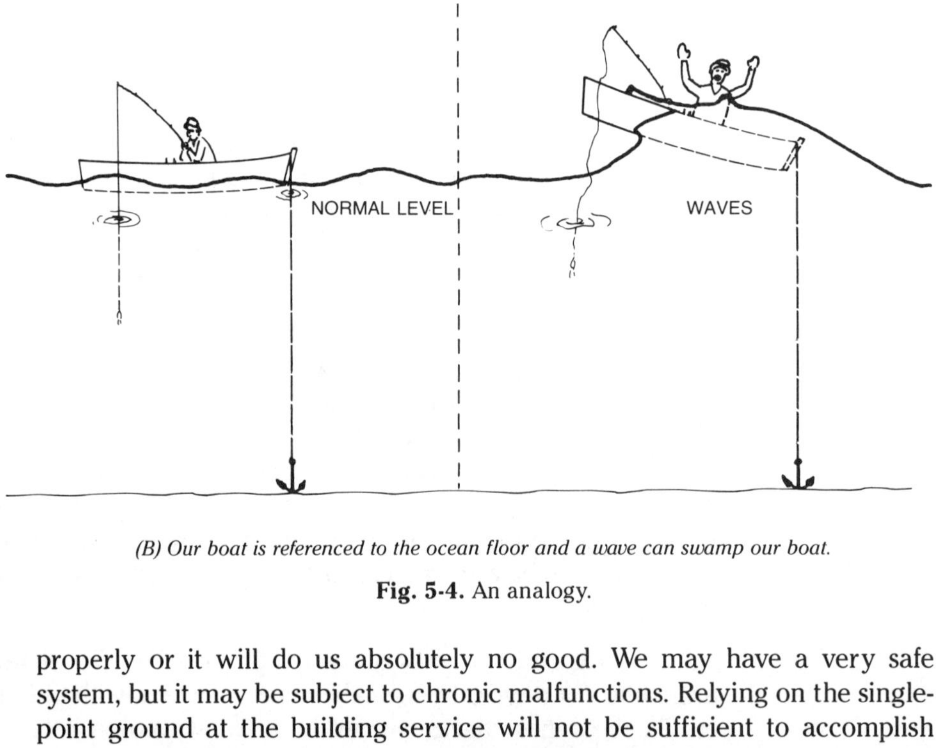

(B) Our boat is referenced to the ocean floor and a wave can swamp our boat.

Fig. 5-4. An analogy.

properly or it will do us absolutely no good. We may have a very safe system, but it may be subject to chronic malfunctions. Relying on the single-point ground at the building service will not be sufficient to accomplish what we want. The goal of any critical computer installation, whether it be a PC or a mainframe, should be a noise-free environment.

You will notice we use the term, "Power Frequencies." Of course, it is no mystery that the frequency of power is 60 Hz, or 60 cycles per second. At noise frequencies, something much different happens. We touched on this in an earlier chapter, but in the context of grounding, we ought to look at it again.

At the frequency of power, the current path is only through the resistor, but at 10,000,000 cycles per second, the circuit acts totally different. The resistance has stayed the same, but the actual wire in the circuit, or what

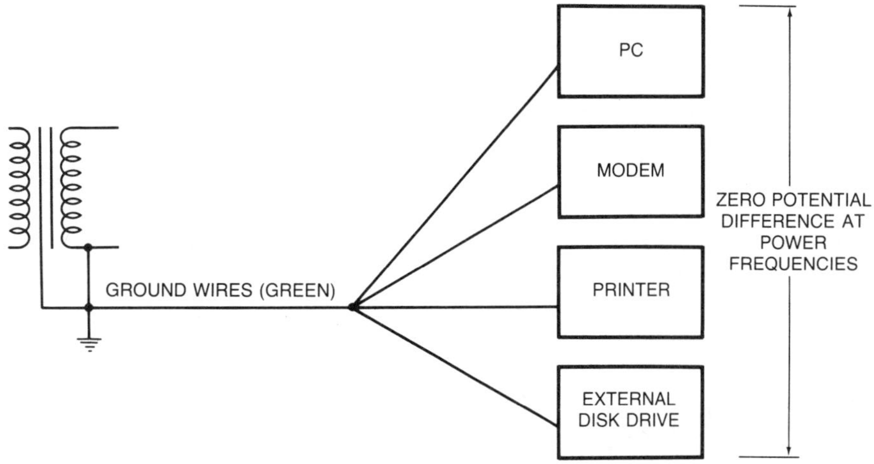

Fig. 5-5. Since each device is ultimately tied to the single-point ground, they float together.

are called the *leads* of the resistor and capacitor, have become inductors of some value. That's right. Straight wire will behave at noise frequencies just like a coil of wire does at power frequencies. The capacitor which appeared to be an open circuit at power frequencies has become a short circuit at noise frequencies. If it is truly a short circuit to the 10-MHz signal, nearly all the current will flow through that path. An experienced electronic student would have seen that the lead inductance in the circuit of Fig. 5-6B has added a large amount of impedance to the circuit. This is illustrated in Fig. 5-6.

Let's concentrate on the concept of lead inductance. Look back at Fig. 5-5. There is one electrical path that we did not show. That path is the path that data must take between each item of the system. Fig. 5-7 shows us this concept both in block form and as a circuit. We still have our single-point ground. At power frequencies, the green wires are at a much lower impedance path and the cabinets still float. The little tiny ground wire that runs through the printer cable is a high-impedance path and very little ground current will flow in it.

However, at noise frequencies, the path through L1 can become a higher impedance path if the ground wire is unusually long. In our diagram (Fig. 5-7A), this noise has two paths to choose from. All that wire running clear back to the neutral-to-ground bonding point of building service transformer looks like a high value of inductive reactance. The shorter path

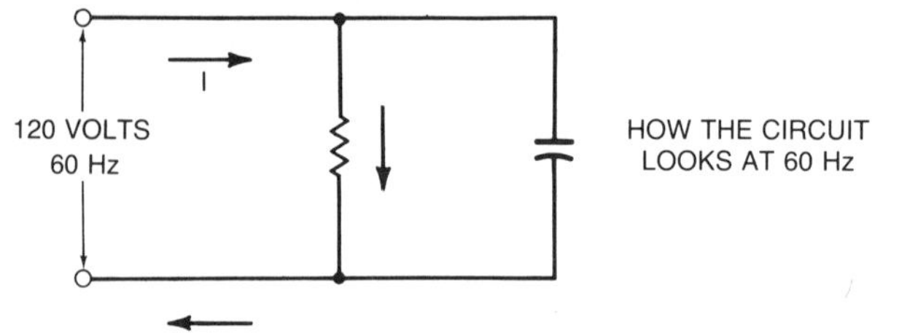

(A) Circuit at 60 Hz.

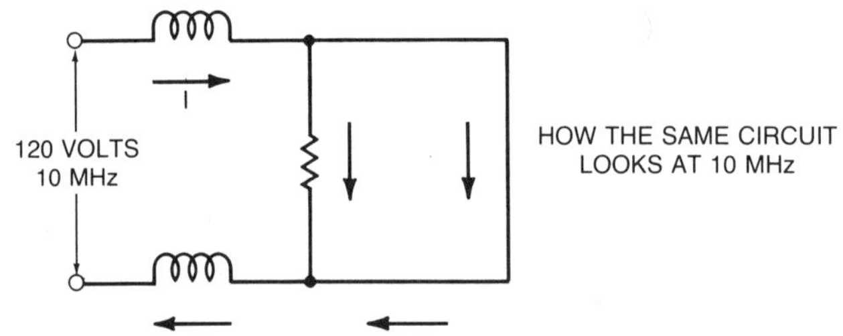

(B) Circuit at 10 MHz.

Fig. 5-6. At 10 MHz, the circuit elements appear totally different from what they are at 60 Hz.

through the printer cable to the CPU may be of nearly equal or lower impedance and, therefore, will carry some of the noise. The fact is that even if the power ground path were a lower impedance path, some current would still flow in the printer cable. This unwanted current can couple signals into nearby wires, which might be interpreted as data—causing print errors. To prevent this, the power ground system must be held to an extremely low impedance.

Let's consider the voltage drop across the inductive reactance. At power frequencies, the low impedance of the wire will have a low voltage drop across it. As frequency goes up, the value of "Z" goes up, and the "E," or voltage drop, across the inductance increases. This voltage offset appears as a noise voltage between the two cabinets.

How do we equalize the voltage and provide for an alternate current path? There are a couple of things we can do to keep noise from using data lines as a return path. One thing we could do is tie the chassis together with an additional ground bonding strap. This ground strap should be short and wide. Because of the skin effect at higher frequencies, a braided copper strap has enough cross-sectional area to present a much lower impedance path than a data cable might.

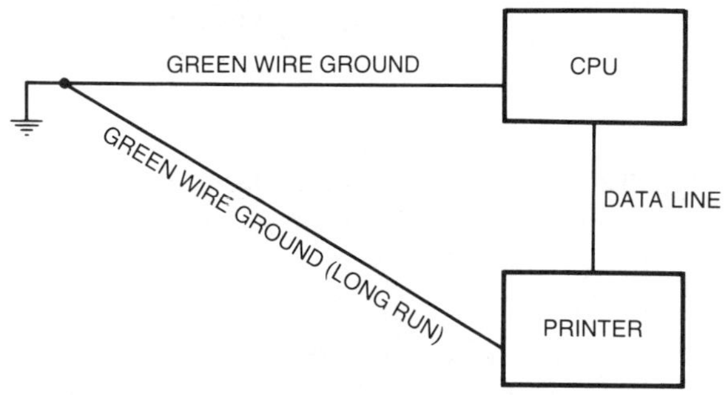

(A) Block diagram.

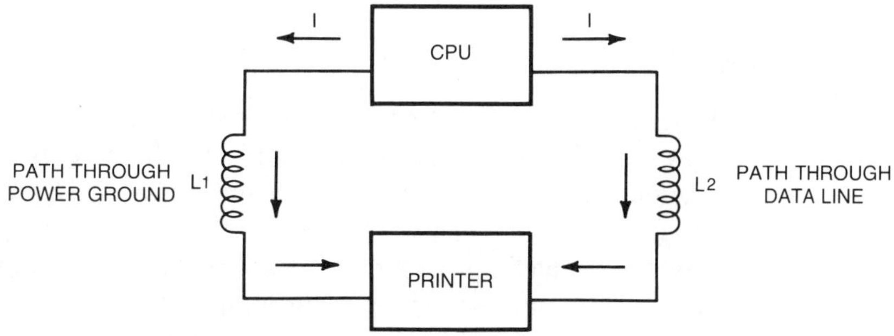

(B) Circuit schematic.

Fig. 5-7. If the path through the power ground is at a higher impedance than the data line, then more ground-noise current will flow through the data line.

This alternative might be somewhat cumbersome. Who wants to drill holes in modems that have no grounding lugs? Another alternative is to buy a power strip. Most of us already use power strips just because we need the additional receptacles to plug things into. But we also gain the benefit of using a single-point ground that is very near the cabinets. This serves to equalize voltages between all of the devices plugged into the power strip. The short lengths of the individual power cords, themselves, are impedances too small to worry about. And at noise frequencies, everything plugged into the power strip is floating without respect to the single-point ground at the building service.

Two points must be made here. First, we are not talking about those power strips that have surge suppressors built into them. We will cover those later. We are talking about a simple power strip with multiple outlets, that is all. Secondly, while a power strip will equalize noise voltages between cabinets through their respective power grounds, this does not always make them immune to any noise that might appear between ground and neutral or between ground and the line. But it is a desirable goal to equalize any potential differences between the PC and any peripheral so data communication cabling remains free of interference.

Remember our floating boat. Computer chips that process signals are expecting to see a logic level with respect to ground. If we present the chip with an offset voltage to look at, in addition to the logic signal, the intelligence is no longer floating above ground but may be swamped out as the ground-noise impulses rise and fall. If this offset voltage is large enough, it may exceed the breakdown voltage of the data communication chip itself and will bridge the insulating barriers within the chip causing its destruction.

Shielding

Whenever we think of keeping data communication wiring free of unwanted interference, we are likely to think of *shielding*. The common wisdom is that a shield will prevent noise from being coupled, either capacitively or inductively, to the wire or wires carrying the intelligent signal. By shielding, we mean the practice of wrapping a mesh of wire around an inner conductor, or, in some fashion, the enclosing of conductors with some other conductor. Coaxial cable and wires run inside a metal conduit are examples of this.

The unfortunate fact is that as frequency increases the "shielded" effect starts to disappear. Fig. 5-8 illustrates this effect. We see that a noise impulse can be capacitively coupled between a water pipe and the shield of a conductor, and the shield and the conductor become a low-impedance path at some noise frequency.

Curiously enough, current flowing in our water-pipe illustration induces an opposite current flow in both the shield and the conductor. However, the induced flow in the shield sets up an induced flow of its own in the conductor (Fig. 5-8B). These two currents are 180° out of phase and will tend to cancel or "buck" each other. But, some residual noise current will be left from this imperfect cancellation. This "bucking" process does not help with capacitively coupled noise, however.

We might be tempted to solve both of these problems by grounding one end of the shield. Of course, in normal practice, the shield would be terminated at the chassis of the computer on one or both ends of the cable. Grounding only one end of the cable adds an additional problem to the situation, as we can encounter standing waves, unwanted resonances, and

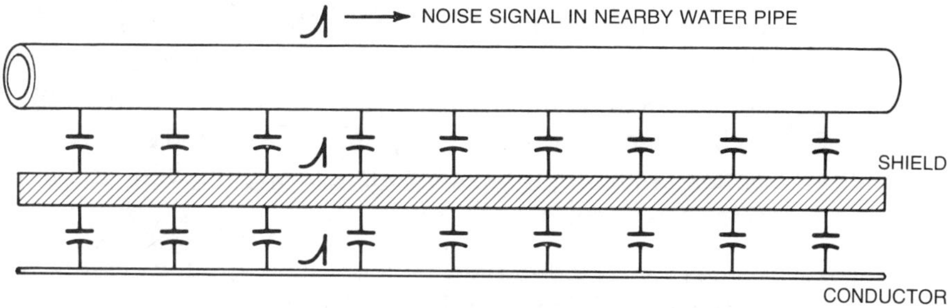

(A) Noise is capacitively coupled into the conductor.

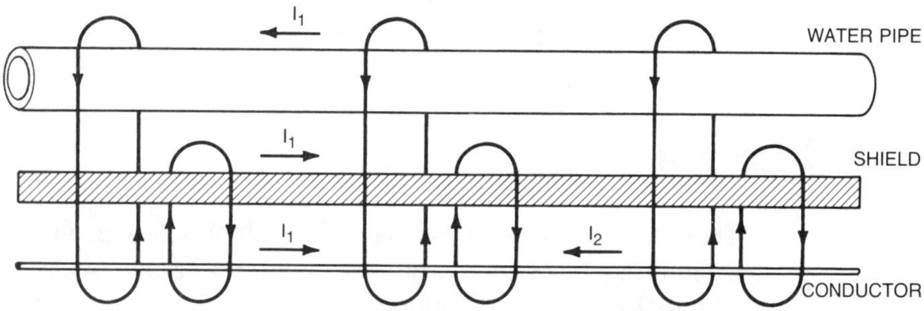

(B) Two induced currents are "bucking" each other and cancel in the conductor.

Fig. 5-8. Noise coupling versus shielding.

hot spots that are caused by the actual amplification of signals (at multiples of the signal's quarter wavelength). A detailed discussion of why this happens is beyond the scope of this book. There is a simple answer, however. Ground the shield at both ends. If the cable is very long, don't hesitate to also ground it at multiple points along its length.

What we are attempting to do by using this method is reduce the ground-lead lengths, so as not to present a high-impedance path to a noise signal. It is much more desirable to give the noise signal multiple short paths which complete a loop circuit, than forcing it to appear along the entire length of the cable. In actual practice, this is seldom done because of misunderstandings about ground-path impedances, and it is sometimes a difficult solution to implement. The typical response to a data-cable corruption problem is usually to lift one or both grounds so that the ground noise cannot reach the chassis of the affected equipment. Of course, this often makes the problem worse since the shield has no path to ground and acts as nothing more than a capacitive coupling device. The use of multiple bonding points to a common ground plane, like building steel, is usually the answer. One creative solution, using this idea, is to ensure that every equipment chassis connected by a data cable is also connected to the same column or building steel member. This is a more practical way of equalizing the potential differences between PCs or terminals that are scattered throughout a building. Then there are baluns, traps, and filters available as well, that can be used to help solve these problems. And there is always the option of finding the noise source and eliminating it, but this may be easier said than done.

As we stated earlier, multiple short grounds connected from the shield to the ground plane can help reduce the problem of noise being capacitively coupled into a shield. This technique is the formation of a *ground loop*. The use of ground loops in grounding shields is one of the few instances where ground loops are beneficial. Usually they cause problems, as we shall see.

Ground Loops

There are a number of ways that we might define ground loops. Basically, a ground loop is formed when a potential difference exists between any two places that are, by definition, at ground potential. Let's start with a simple diagram of this. Fig. 5-9 illustrates a simple ground loop. In the drawing, we are using a ground rod to make a point, but the loop could be formed by any two grounds of differing potential. Fig. 5-10 shows this as a schematic.

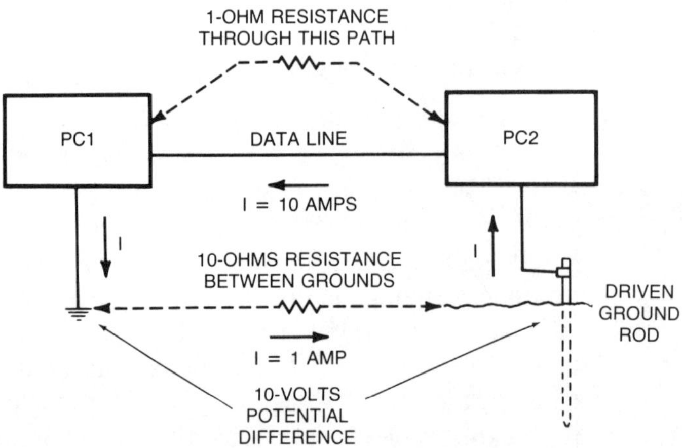

Fig. 5-9. A potential difference appearing across the two separate grounds will force current to flow through the data line.

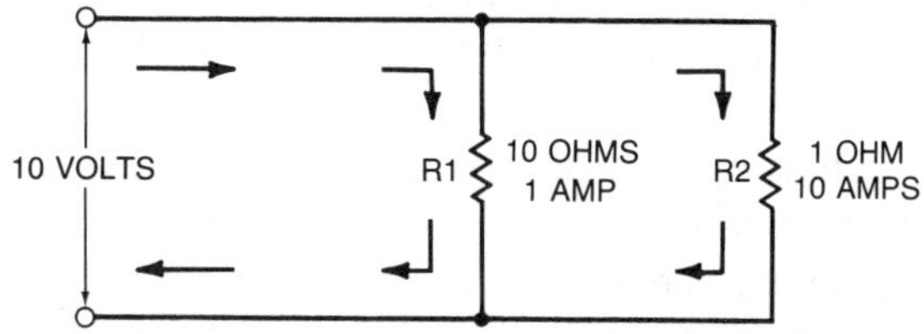

Fig. 5-10. This is a schematic of the sketch shown in Fig. 5-9. Here we see R1 as the resistance between the two grounds. R2, then, is the resistance through the chassis of the two PCs and the data line.

There are a number of important points to be made about these diagrams. First, if we had one ground connected to each PC, there would have been no loop current flowing since voltage cannot develop across a near-zero impedance. The obvious solution to this problem would be to get rid of one of the ground connections.

This tells us something about ground loops. A ground loop may be formed when there are two or more different ground connections in a circuit. This circuit might be also formed between boards inside a PC or in a local area network.

Another point to be made is that driven-rod earth grounds are never appropriate as a solution to ground noise. They are a source of ground noise! However, there are situations where a driven-rod ground is appropriate, like on the secondary of a building transformer, for example. But, to arbitrarily bond a ground plane to a driven rod just for the sake of the *cesspool effect* hazards the potential of degrading system operations by injecting unwanted ground currents.

Notice that, consistent with Ohm's law, the bulk of the current is developed through the path of least resistance, or lowest impedance. We are assuming that whatever is generating the noise voltage between the grounds is capable of delivering the full flow of current we find from the calculations. (This energy is called a *joule,* which is a unit of energy of work that is related to wattseconds.) But, the noise source might not have enough kinetic energy to release a current flow of the kind we might expect, or, possibly, the current flow might only last for nanoseconds or picoseconds. Also, we are using Ohm's law here in its simplest form. For the sake of simplicity, we are not taking a number of complicating factors into consideration. Nevertheless, the flow of anything like 10 amperes of current through the chassis of a PC and a data line is surely a disaster. It will clearly override data signals, break down insulation, or induce sufficient energy into nearby circuits to cause hardware failure.

We have presupposed the values of voltage, current, and impedance. The fact is that the voltage and current are not the only concerns here. The voltage drop caused by the impedance of a ground loop can cause serious problems. A noise voltage offset of several hundred or several thousand volts is likely in the real world. Impulse values that large are injected into signal circuits only as they appear across high-impedance differences in the circuit. This may hold the current to small fractions of an ampere. But any current bridging a microcomputer chip will ruin it, whether it causes a puncture hole that is a micron in diameter or the total destruction of a circuit board.

We might attempt a solution to this problem by adding a grounding strap to equalize the potential of the two cabinets. By doing so, we divert some energy away from the data line by providing a lower impedance path for current to flow. We could calculate this addition by adding another parallel branch in Fig. 5-10 to see what current would flow through this bonding strap. This approach will not reduce the voltage appearing across the data line, however. Our calculation, using Ohm's law, would have to assume that the noise source was capable of delivering additional current. The reason for this is that in a parallel circuit, the voltage appears simultaneously across each parallel element. Our bonding-strap solution, however, might be able to divert enough current through its low impedance to significantly reduce the exposure of the data line to unwanted current flow.

A better way to think of this is to think in percentages. In Fig. 5-10, a much greater percentage of noise current will flow through the path where impedance is expressed as 1 ohm than through the 10-ohm path. If we add a low-impedance bonding strap, the percentage of energy flowing in the data-line path will be significantly reduced. This is nothing more than a substitute type of single-point grounding.

To summarize this, remember that whenever there is some impedance existing between two points, voltage can appear across these points and current can flow. When it comes to grounding, it should be a goal to hold all grounds to the same potential by not allowing this impedance to develop. Any impedance between two differing points along the ground plane should have a significantly lower impedance than the alternative paths that could divert current through sensitive circuits.

Maybe now we can see why computers do not have a two-pronged plug on their power cords. If our PC is to communicate with the outside world, we must have some way to reference the signals between devices. Like the example of a stereo amplifier and a turntable, we cannot allow the grounds of two devices to move independently of one another, or we will develop noise voltages that interfere with the desired signals.

Loops Due to Wire Length

Ground loops can also develop because of the sheer length of a circuit wire. As frequency goes up, the inductive reactance of a piece of straight wire begins to increase. The flow of high-frequency current sets up a magnetic field that induces an opposing current in the wire. This has the effect of raising the overall impedance of the line to high-frequency noise. At power frequencies, we have no problem plugging a PC into a power outlet that terminates at the power source 50 to 200 feet away. This distance, however, looks like a resistor of high value to a noise signal of, say, 10 MHz. Some of the things that may contribute to this are loose conduit fittings, ground terminations that are not tight, or small-sized ground conductors. Typically, we would not expect normal "green-wire" grounds to show much impedance at any frequency, as long as the length(s) of the power cord(s) are reasonable. But common-mode noise problems are usually caused by a combination of things that work together to develop excessive voltage drops.

Fig. 5-11 shows how this might work. Because of the long run of wire from the grounding point of the PC and the entrance of the neutral wire into the PC, a voltage drop occurs across this impedance. This voltage simultaneously appears from neutral-to-chassis ground and may find current paths through the stray capacitances that exist in connectors and along phenolic-board traces, or worse yet, across ICs. If no stray paths are found, obviously the PC will float on the common-mode noise and no harm will be done. The detrimental effect of common-mode noise to a single PC, where no ground loop through an external device exists, is the subject of some controversy in the industry. Will it float or will it be affected? There is evidence to support both notions. And some equipment designs are more immune than others.

There is disagreement about the ability of long neutral-to-ground loops being able to develop significant noise voltage. Many experts contend that the sheer size of the wires is enough to present low impedances, even at high noise frequencies. And yet common-mode noise voltages do cause processing errors and equipment damage. There are always those locations where strange unexplainable things are happening. The solution almost always is found through proper bonding, single-point grounding, or the elimination of ground impedances.

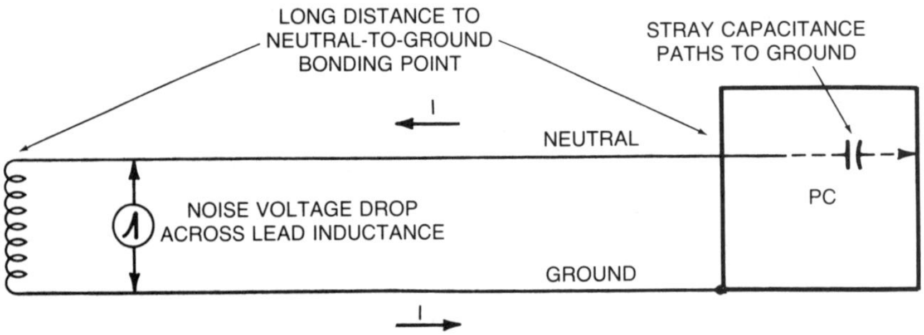

Fig. 5-11. Because of the high impedance of the connecting wire, a ground loop is formed with the neutral wire. Thus, loop current may find a path through the stray capacitive paths that exist inside the PC.

Naturally, had the lead length been shorter, with good integrity, no ground loop would have existed. Just because the neutral and ground wires are bonded at power frequencies does not guarantee they are bonded at noise frequencies.

Any time that ground wires have excessively long lengths, we can expect ground-loop currents to flow or high offset voltages to be present. This is the case with one of the most commonly misunderstood devices, the *IG* (isolated ground) *receptacle*. They are those receptacles having the funny orange plastic faceplates. They are misused more often than driven ground rods. Fig. 5-12 shows the construction and application of an IG receptacle. When the IG receptacle is installed according to the *National Electrical Code (NEC)*, the ground pin must terminate at the appropriate power-source transformer. On its way there, it must not bond to any enclosures, including the enclosure for the receptacle itself. Enclosures are bonded with a separate wire, or sometimes with the conduit. In effect, this method uses the conduit as the safety return path for fault current. This is a poor idea because of its reliance on the tightness of mechanical fittings and the continuity of the metal, which might be broken if used with plastic fittings or PVC.

If the power-source transformer were placed close to the computer devices, IG receptacles might be a reasonable idea. This is usually not the case, especially where PCs are concerned. Often the IG wire does nothing more than act as an antenna for noise, which is impressed upon its lead inductance. While the enclosure ground must go the same distance, its multiple bondings, with enclosures, can act as a noise return path for loop currents which might otherwise appear as common-mode noise at the PC. In addition, the IG receptacle method forces equalization to occur along the entire distance of the IG path. Safety grounds will come together either at the nearest receptacle enclosure or at the nearest panel board.

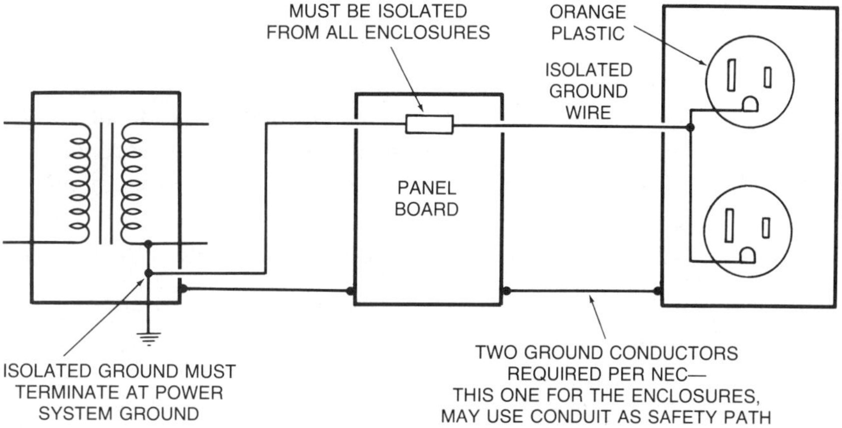

Fig. 5-12. The isolated ground receptacle, when installed according to the NEC, must terminate the ground pin at the power source and must not touch enclosures.

Another typical problem is the proper installation of the IG receptacle itself. There is much misinformation about how the receptacles are to be installed, and, in addition, many electricians have no understanding of signal referencing to begin with. Often times, signal lines are mistaken for dedicated lines, a branch circuit dedicated to the computer. But, this doesn't necessarily mean it has an isolated ground. The manufacturers are to blame for much of this. Some of the printed material that accompanies the receptacles shows the isolated ground wire going off to a driven-rod ground or to a water pipe. This is a violation of the NEC and a safety hazard. IG receptacles are not a substitute for proper grounding of computer equipment.

While we are on the subject of the *National Electrical Code* (NEC), it might serve to point out that the code allows a smaller wire to be used for the safety ground than for the phase and neutral wires. This is a mistake from the computer's point of view. As noise frequencies increase, the inductive reactance of wire increases. All things being equal, a larger wire has considerably less inductive reactance than one of smaller cross-sectional area. It is recommended that green-wire grounds be selected that are at least the same size as the phase wire to ensure a low-impedance path to ground.

Some Final Comments

Earlier, we made the point that common-mode noise is noise that appears between neutral and ground and between the line and ground. We can see from the previous discussion that ground loops create common-mode voltages. As it is assumed that we want to keep noise out of signal circuits, the elimination of ground loops as a source of noise would seem to be desirable. The main principle behind this goal is equalization of voltages along the ground plane. If logic signals are tied to the ocean bottom, as in our earlier example, they will be swamped as the unreferenced ground level sweeps above the signal level. Circuits that are referenced to a ground at zero potential, with respect to one another, float on the ground plane no matter what its relative voltage might be in relation to some other ground.

This gets tricky as the frequency of noise increases. The electrical behavior of various components change, causing a divergence from safety grounding practices. While not sacrificing safety, we must see that impedance differences do not exist at noise frequencies.

Let's look at this another way. Fig. 5-11 shows us a ground loop formed by the long loop of wire that runs from neutral to ground. Let's imagine for a moment that this bonding point is infinitely short; that right—short. If this distance is infinitely short, it has zero impedance at any frequency. If $E = IR$ and $R = 0$, then E must equal 0.

Now, let's imagine what happens as the loop gets longer. As the loop gets longer, two things begin to happen. The likelihood that noise will be impressed, either by direct physical contact or by capacitive or inductive coupling, increases. Also, the impedance of the wire to that noise signal increases, thereby creating a larger voltage drop across this impedance. As this happens, this signal voltage appears as a potential difference between the PC's chassis and the neutral wire.

We might not be too concerned at this point since our ground loop might still have basically a short-circuit value of impedance. If current were to flow, it would surely flow through the neutral-to-ground circuit rather than through a data-communications cable or telephone line. At some point of increasing length, we reach values of loop impedance that cause damaging amounts of current to flow through the wrong paths. Meanwhile, the voltage appearing across the ground loop increases. This might exceed the breakdown voltage of the microcomputer chips or power transistors that are in parallel to the voltage drop, thus creating some new current path and destroying components in the process.

Imagine that the lines get even longer, so that, to the noise signal, the neutral-to-ground circuit has a very high value of impedance. Now other alternative paths that might exist inside the computer look to have a much lower impedance than does the power ground path. If a path were ever found, such as through a data line or through stray capacitance, then damaging current will flow through this unwanted path. As the neutral-to-ground connection moves further away from the computer, these problems grow worse. The value of the "length" impedance is enough to create a disruptive ground loop all by itself.

Hopefully, this mental journey has shown why low-impedance ground paths are so important, and why a short single-point ground is the only way to connect power to a computer system. The goals are to equalize chassis, prevent ground loops from developing, and keep the noise current away from the signal circuits by reducing the coupled voltage that appears across them. Low-impedance grounds should be short and thick. Even lengths over four or five feet can be a problem at high frequencies since these represent quarter wavelengths.

The basic themes that are laid out in this chapter will be touched on many times in the chapters to come. We will find that sometimes, as in local area networks, there is little choice but to live with ground loops. But there are products and strategies that deal with this problem.

Grounding is like religion. Everybody believes ardently in it, but everyone has their own doctrine that support those beliefs. The subject of grounding can be confusing and controversial. We have tried to lay out our discussion in a way that is consistent with the advice of experts in the field.

Let's summarize by restating a few tips:

1. Whenever possible, connect devices to a single-point ground.
2. Attempt to equalize potential differences between cabinets through single-point grounding, using a power strip or supplemental ground straps between the cabinets.
3. Keep ground connections as short as possible in order to make the ground path a low impedance path.
4. Keep the neutral-to-ground bonding point as close to the computer system as is practical.
5. Use large conductors for green-wire grounds to ensure a low lead impedance, and avoid reliance on conduit as a ground path because of its tendency toward loosening, rust, and corrosion.

6 PC Power Supplies

It may come as somewhat of a shock to some that electronic circuitry like that found in a personal computer uses DC power. The role of the power supply is to convert the incoming AC power to DC power at the logic voltages used by the internal circuitry of the PC. It is the power supply that is tied directly across the 120-volt AC line. It is the front end of the computer's power structure.

Over the last few years, there have been major changes in the technology behind the design of power supplies. Interestingly enough, the technology of some power products have not kept up with these changes and, as we shall see in a later chapter, some of those products are no longer appropriate for the newer PCs that are on the market.

There are basically two different kinds of power supplies found in modern computer equipment: the linear power supply and the switching power supply. The *linear-type supply* was popular for many years after World War II. We will discuss its design characteristics shortly. More recently, the *switching power supply*, often referred to as the *switch-mode power supply*, appeared in computer equipment. These two different types of power supplies take radically divergent approaches to converting AC power into DC power. Their unique behaviors and needs are the focus of this chapter.

Principles of DC Power Supplies

Most microprocessors and other associated electronic circuitry need one level of voltage from the power supply, +5-volts DC. Other common voltages that may be required are +12 volts, −5 volts, −3 volts, and +10 volts. For simplicity, we will use +5 volts in our examples. Clearly, 120 volts is larger than 5 volts so a transformer will be needed to step the voltage down to the 5-volt level. Next, we must worry about how to convert alternating current to direct current so our +5 volts will be usable by the logic circuits connected to it.

Rectifiers

Alternating current, as we have seen, moves in two directions. During a portion of the cycle, it moves in a positive direction. Then it turns around and moves in a negative direction. This change of direction is not consistent with what we want to feed to logic circuits. To correct this changing of direction, a device called a *rectifier* was invented. It consists of one or more diodes arranged in a circuit so that current can flow in only one direction.

Fig. 6-1 shows a diode rectifier in action. Notice that when the anode is positive with respect to the cathode (Fig. 6-1A), the diode is forward biased and current will flow. But when the voltage polarity reverses, the anode is negatively biased with respect to the cathode (reverse biased), and no current flows. The result is a pulsating output that is unidirectional. This is not pure DC, but at least the direction of current flow does not change.

There is a small problem with this arrangement. Fig. 6-2 shows the output waveform of the rectifier. Notice that every negative-going half cycle is missing. Because of these missing half cycles, our rectifier is called a *half-wave rectifier*. Unfortunately, the output voltage of this type of rectifier is only 0.45 times the input RMS voltage. Also, the half-cycle effect makes it necessary to have a transformer with a VA rating that is 40% higher than the VA of the load. Obviously, these characteristics make the half-wave rectifier extremely inefficient.

Intuitively, we might expect to discover another design that would overcome these inefficiencies, and which would rectify the full sine-wave waveform of the input. In this case, our expectations are correct. We simply modify the circuit slightly, add another diode rectifier for the missing half cycle, and we have a *full-wave rectifier*. Fig. 6-3 shows this design.

During one half cycle, diode D1 will be forward biased and diode D2 will be reverse biased. This will cause current to flow from the center tap,

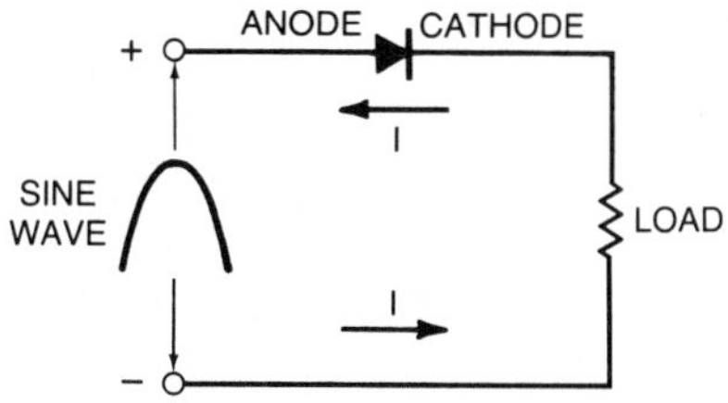

(A) Forward biased, current flows.

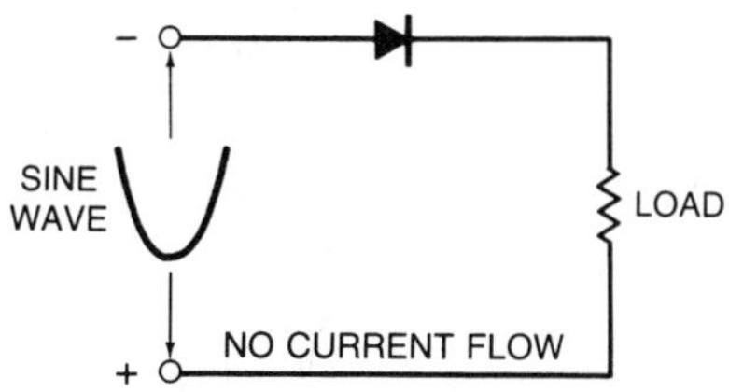

(B) Reversed biased, no current flow.

Fig. 6-1. Current flow through a diode rectifier.

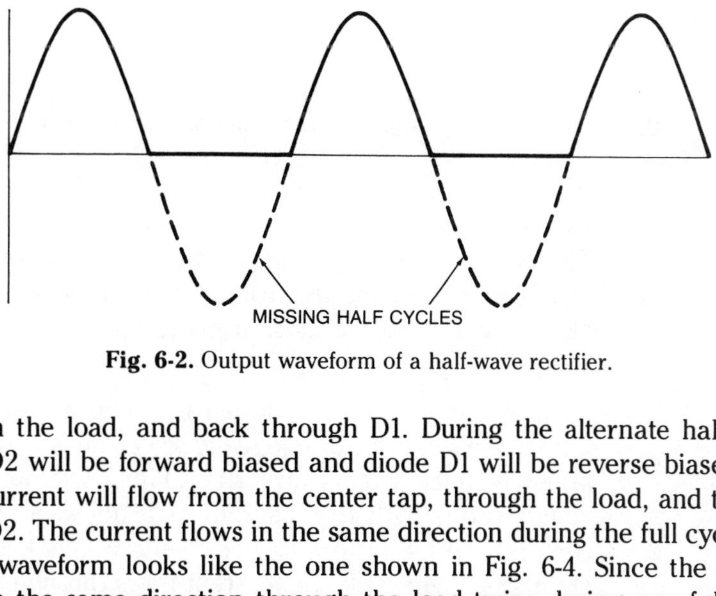

Fig. 6-2. Output waveform of a half-wave rectifier.

through the load, and back through D1. During the alternate half cycle, diode D2 will be forward biased and diode D1 will be reverse biased. This time, current will flow from the center tap, through the load, and through diode D2. The current flows in the same direction during the full cycle. The output waveform looks like the one shown in Fig. 6-4. Since the current flows in the same direction through the load twice during one full cycle, there are two humps per cycle in the output waveform.

The average output voltage from this type of full-wave rectifier is 0.90 times the applied RMS input voltage. By comparison, this makes the

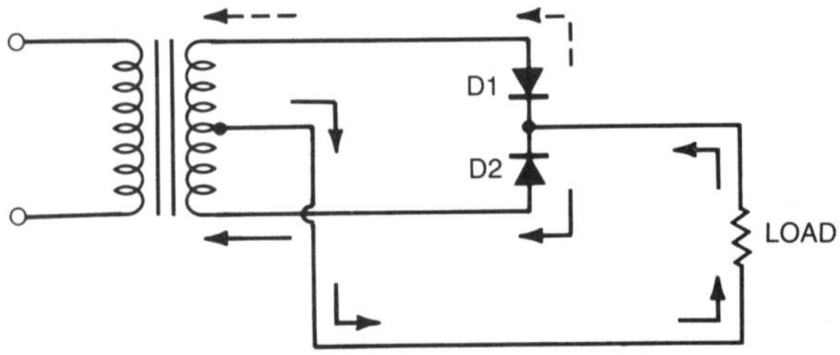

Fig. 6-3. A full wave-rectifier circuit that uses a center-tapped transformer. For one half cycle, current flows through diode D1. In the next half cycle, current flows through diode D2.

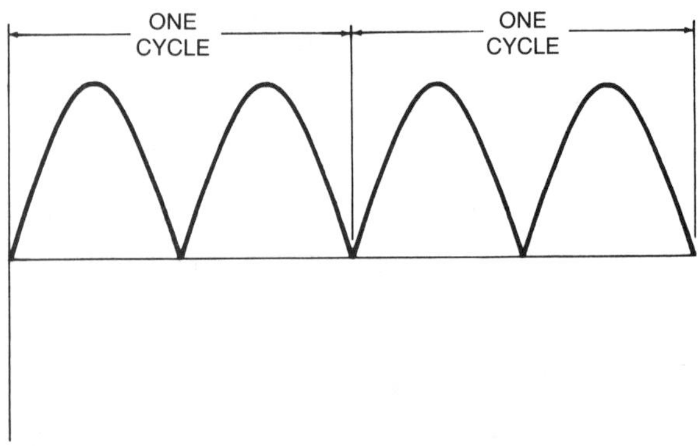

Fig. 6-4. The output waveform of a full-wave rectifier.

full-wave rectifier twice as efficient as the half-wave variety. You might ask yourself, why would any design engineer ever call for a half-wave rectifier? The half-wave rectifier allows the use of certain designs that call for rectification without the use of a transformer. Often times, consumer-electronic devices are made using this kind of design—for the sake of cost, weight, and size.

There is yet another design that can be used without a transformer. That is the *full-wave bridge rectifier*. For now, we will discuss the use of the bridge rectifier with a transformer. Fig. 6-5 shows a bridge rectifier. We can compare this with the diagram of a full-wave rectifier and see that the center-tapped transformer has been swapped for two additional diodes. During one half cycle, the current flows through diodes D1 and D2. During the next half cycle, the current flows through diodes D3 and D4. Another thing to notice is that although the output waveform of the bridge is basically the same as that of the full-wave rectifier, we are now using the entire secondary winding of the transformer to produce the desired voltage.

Therefore, the design considerations used with the transformer is different due to the differing turns ratios and power ratings.

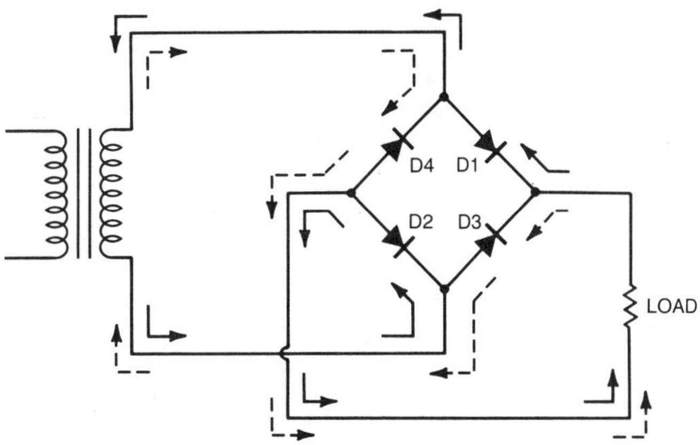

Fig. 6-5. A full-wave bridge rectifier.

The Sine Wave

You may have wondered by now about the relationship between various voltage measurements of the sine wave. We've used the term RMS or root-mean-square. Later in the book, we will talk about peak voltages or peak-to-peak voltages. Fig. 6-6 shows how these different terms relate.

Filters and Regulators

So, now we have an output waveform that looks like a bunch of humps (Fig. 6-4). This is called *pulsating DC*, and as such is still unusable by our personal computer. *Filtering* is the next step toward producing a clean, ripple-free DC. Fig. 6-7 shows the bridge rectifier with a filter section and voltage regulator added. Fig. 6-8 shows the output waveform after filtering.

The output of a full-wave rectifier (Fig. 6-7) has a 48% ripple component. As we might expect, the frequency of this ripple is twice the line frequency, or 120 Hz. By selecting the proper value for capacitor C1, we can fill in this ripple. Capacitor C1 will charge to a value equal to the peak of the voltage magnitude. After the peak has passed, C1 will begin to discharge back into the circuit. The net affect of this is to fill in valleys between voltage humps (Fig. 6-8). Resistor R1 is what's known as a *bleeder resistor*. Its purpose in the circuit of Fig. 6-7 is to drain the charge of the capacitor when the power is turned off—to eliminate possible shock hazards.

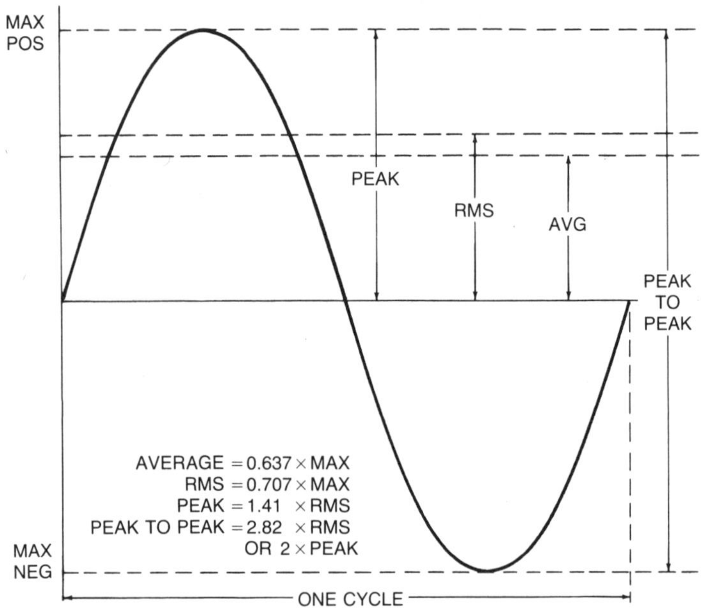

Fig. 6-6. Sine-wave relationships.

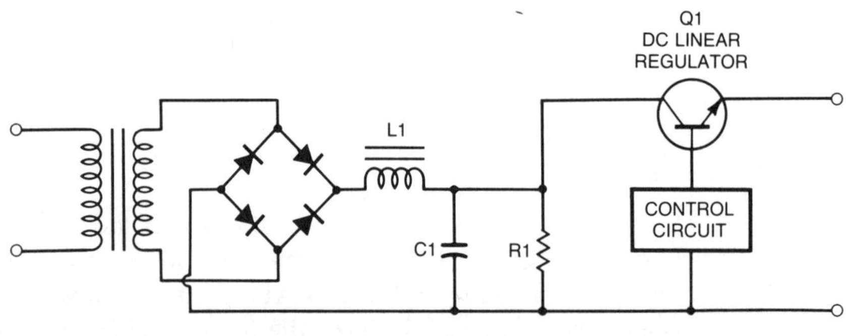

Fig. 6-7. A bridge rectifier with a filter section and voltage regulator added.

Inductance L1 is a coil of wire wound around an iron core. This is known as a *choke*. If we select the proper value of inductive reactance, at the ripple frequency, the choke will oppose the flow of ripple current.

A voltage regulation section is then added. Most often, this will be a series-pass regulator. A *series-pass regulator* is a series-connected transistor (Q1) that varies its voltage drop to keep the output voltage at a constant level. This is known as *linear regulation* and is where that type of power supply gets its name.

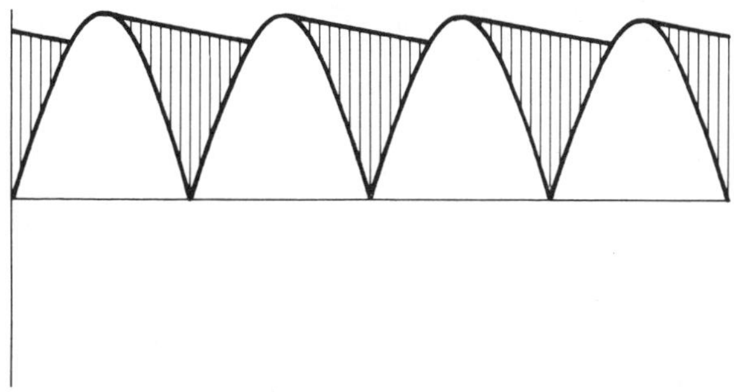

Fig. 6-8. Output waveform of Fig. 6-7 rectifier circuit, after filtering. The discharging capacitor fills in the area between voltage humps and smooths out the waveform.

Linear power supplies have the disadvantage of being both large and heavy, because of the 60-Hz transformer. They are also inefficient, operating at around 50% for the typical 5-volt supply. This means they give off significant heat. Also, linear supplies are voltage sensitive. The linear voltage regulator can compensate for only small voltage excursions. Beyond that, it may cause system failures or even shut the system down. Its internal ride-through time is about 10 milliseconds on the average.

Switching Power Supplies

Fig. 6-9 shows the schematic for a *switching power supply*, sometimes called a *switch-mode power supply*. A switching power supply is 70% efficient, is smaller, lighter, and cooler, and has a ride-through on the order of 20 to 40 milliseconds. Let's take some time and see how this circuit works. We must point out that there are a variety of designs and variations to this concept. We are only concerned with the design principles involved.

In Fig. 6-9, we see a number of circuit elements that we have seen before. The first of these is the bridge rectifier. Notice that it is connected directly across the power line. During alternate half cycles, current flows and charges capacitor C1. Next, we see an inverter circuit made up of transistors Q1 and Q2. These two transistors conduct when they are turned on by the *pulse-width modulation* (PWM) control circuit. For the sake of simplicity, we have drawn this circuit as a box.

When either transistor Q1 or Q2 conducts, current flows through the high-frequency transformer and through the full-wave rectifier. The choke and capacitor filter the ripple current and we have 5-volt DC output for our logic circuits.

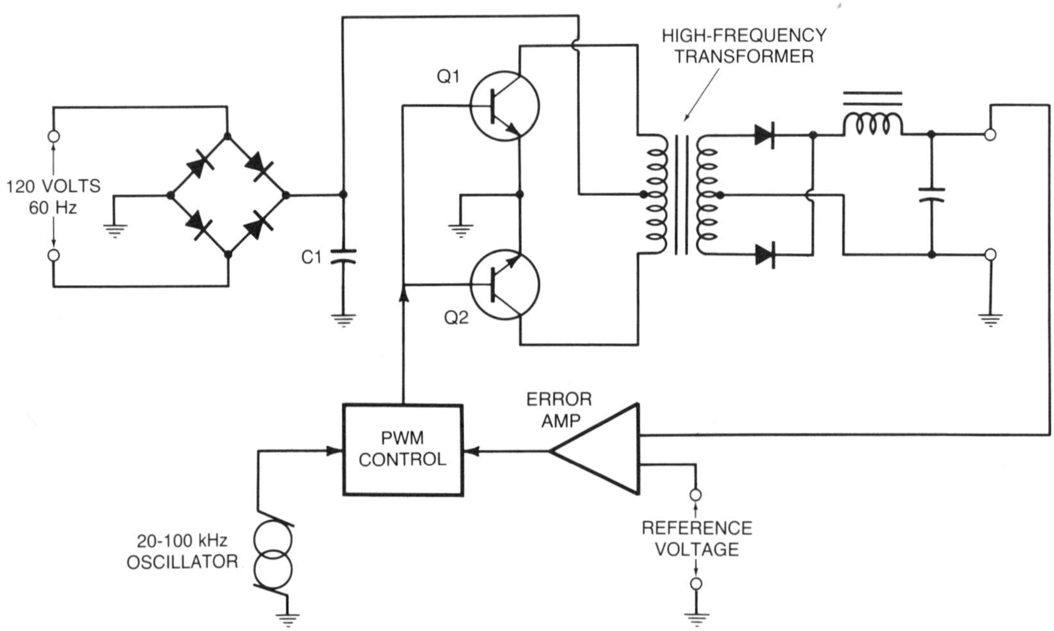

Fig. 6-9. The circuit of a switching power supply.

At the output of the power supply, the circuit takes a sample of the voltage and compares it to a reference voltage. If the output voltage is too high or too low, an error amplifier tells the PWM control circuit to vary the amount of time that transistors Q1 and Q2 are turned on. In other words, what is happening is that the timing of current flow through the inverter controls the voltage across the final stage of the power supply.

We have shown a 20- to 100-kHz oscillator. The oscillator frequency is fixed for any given switching power supply. But designs are in use that use differing rates—from tens of thousands to hundreds of thousands of cycles per second. The trend more recently has been toward faster switching rates.

The switching power supply is current hungry. The amount of current drawn from the line during any given half cycle is largely dependent on the charged state of capacitor C1. Fig. 6-10A shows a photo of the voltage and current sine wave of a switching power supply. Clearly, the bulk of the current is drawn at the peak of the voltage sine wave. This is, from a power standpoint, the most unique feature of this design. The capacitor gulps large amounts of current in short pulses twice every cycle. Meanwhile, the switch is chopping the conduction of current flowing from the rectifier and capacitor into thousands of chunks every second.

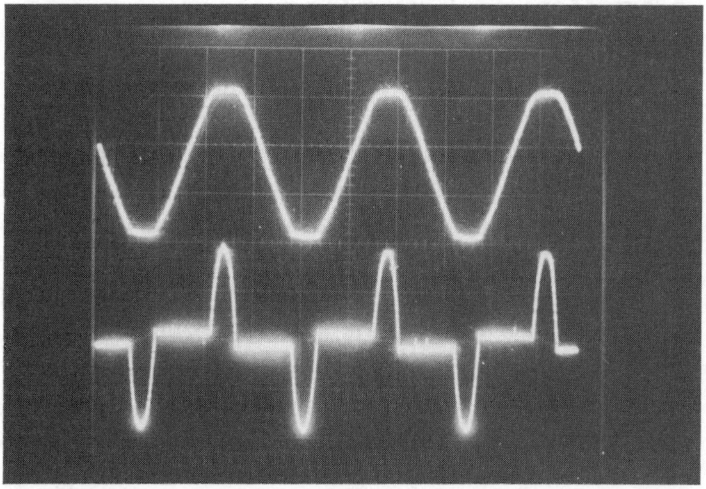

(A) Voltage and current waveforms of a switching power supply.

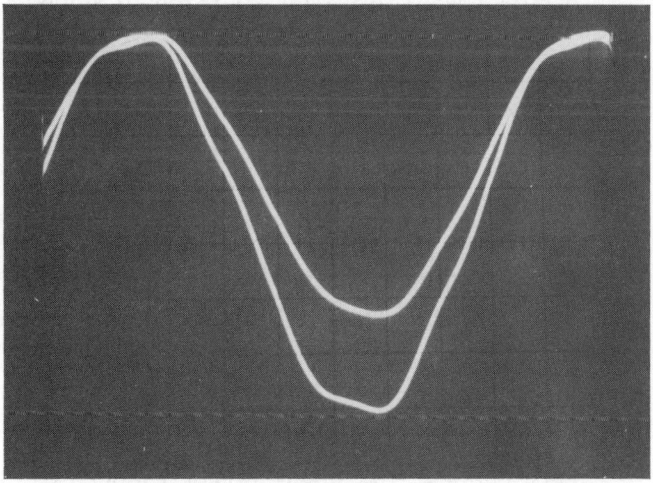

(B) Voltage and current waveforms of a linear device.

Fig. 6-10. Power supply waveforms.

The net effect of this action is the extremely fine correction of voltage variations at the output. The input voltage, since the supply is mostly current sensitive, can swing from 85–90 volts to 130–140 volts. The previous discussion shows why a switching power supply is so popular among PC power-supply design engineers.

Noise and Power Supplies

Since this book is about computer power problems, it would seem logical to question the ability of a given power supply to handle both normal-mode and common-mode noise. Let's review what we mean by noise. Noise is any signal in a circuit other than the desired signal. Noise has many sources and many magnitudes. When we say noise in the context of power supplies, we are talking about repetitious or transient impulses that appear across the terminals of the supply. These may be large enough to do actual damage or can interfere with the data processing.

Fig. 6-11 reminds us of what common-mode and normal-mode noise is. Normal-mode noise can be measured between the line and neutral. Common-mode noise can be measured from line to ground or neutral to ground. From this, we see that common-mode noise must appear on the line and neutral at the same time. Often we hear the term *ground noise.* This is common-mode noise that appears on the ground side as measured from the line and/or from neutral. Usually this voltage is measured simply between neutral and ground.

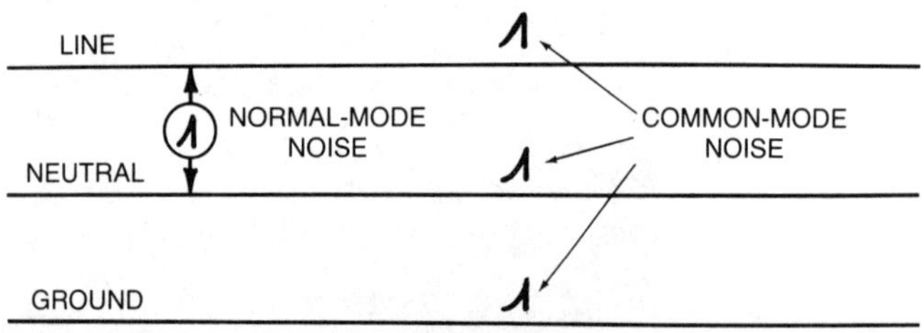

Fig. 6-11. Normal-mode noise appears between the line and neutral. Common-mode noise appears between ground and the line and neutral.

Noise in Linear Power Supplies

Let's consider the linear power supply first. Fig. 6-12 shows the same diagram that we used earlier. Notice that across the input, we have put both normal-mode noise (the little impulse in the circle) and common-mode noise (the impulses on both line and neutral).

In a later chapter, we will take up the subject of transformers in greater depth. For now, let's take a simplified look at the common-mode noise that is

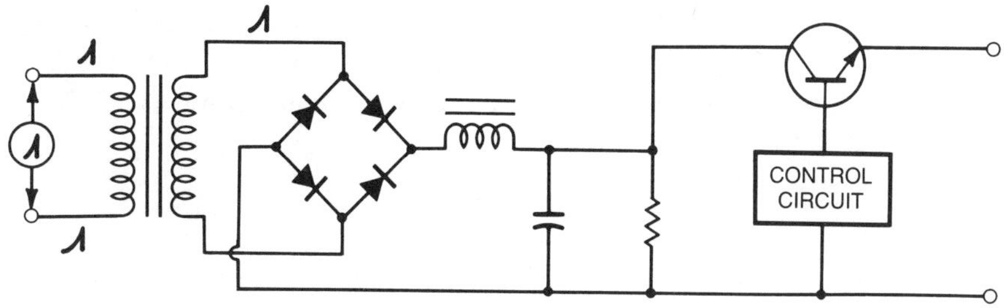

Fig. 6-12. Noise across the transformer windings of a linear power supply.

simultaneously appearing across the primary of the transformer. These impulses are 180° out of phase and will cancel each other out. For reasons we will explain later, this is an imperfect process and there isn't a complete cancellation. The resultant of this is a normal-mode impulse that appears on the secondary of the transformer.

In other words, the common-mode impulses that move toward the center of the transformer primary winding cancel each other to a large extent. What is not cancelled is transferred to the secondary and appears as a single normal-mode impulse. From this, we can see that linear power supplies are nearly immune to common-mode noise by virtue of the transformer input to the power supply.

What about normal-mode noise? Clearly, if an impulse of sufficient magnitude enters the power supply on the live side, damage will be done. However, we must remember the components that would be subjected to the impulse first. The first line of defense is the transformer. Transformers of the type used in linear power supplies have almost no ability to attenuate normal-mode impulses. The inductance of the windings can change the waveform of the impulse, but the overall magnitude will be unchanged.

The next line of defense is the bridge rectifier. If the polarity of the impulse is not in phase with the conduction of the rectifier, the impulse will not be able to pass through; it will be dissipated as heat if this voltage finds a leakage path through the components. If the magnitude of the impulse is large enough, it could exceed the junction breakdown voltage of the power diodes. This would take a lot of joules of energy.

The filter section and voltage regulator are rugged components designed to handle the stress of both high currents and heat. They have large energy-absorption capacities. In short, the linear power supply is well able to handle all but the most destructive normal-mode impulses.

Noise in Switching Power Supplies

What about switching power supplies? Fig. 6-13 shows the diagram we used earlier along with normal-mode and common-mode impulses. Notice that we have added a block in the circuit called "Logic."

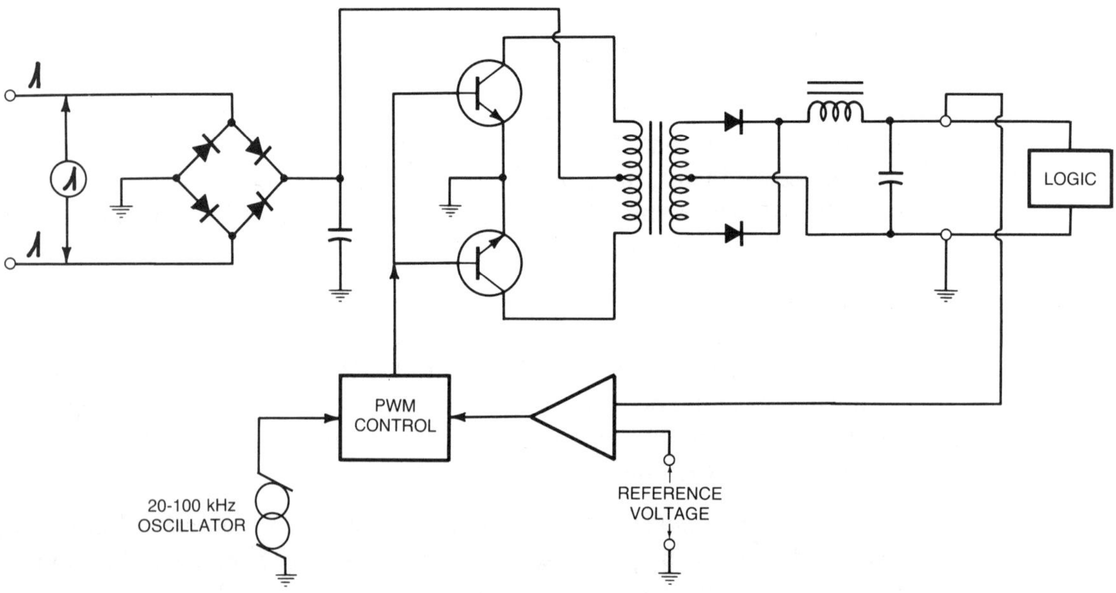

Fig. 6-13. Noise across a switching power supply.

Let's start with normal-mode noise. Normal-mode noise is trying to complete a path from line to neutral. As it tries to find this path, it appears across the terminals of the power supply just as it did in the previous case. And, again, we see that those components which are well able to absorb this energy will block the path of normal-mode noise. Unless the magnitude of the noise is high enough to break down power diodes and capacitors, normal-mode noise will have little effect on the PC.

Common-mode noise is another matter. While normal-mode noise is trying to complete a path from line to neutral, common-mode noise is trying to complete a path from neutral to ground or from line to ground. While the power supply would be the first casualty from normal-mode noise, this is not necessarily the case with common-mode noise.

A PC's susceptibility to common-mode noise is a highly controversial subject. In order for damage to be done, a voltage must appear across a component that is high enough to break down whatever insulation there is, so that a current path is established. As we stated in our chapter on "grounding," unless this path exists, we would expect the PC to float with respect to any noise appearing between line or neutral and ground. This current path would almost certainly be through the power supply.

The debate that rages concerns the probability that noise could flow through the high-frequency transformer, or through other paths which are made up of stray capacitance. If it could, then, obviously, common-mode voltages would appear between logic ground and the supply-voltage pins. In some systems, there are decoupling capacitors and other methods which attempt to isolate logic ground from power ground. Most PCs have these two ground systems tied directly together.

Electricity behaves in strange ways, and high-frequency noise can find coupled paths that designers might never have dreamed of. The high-frequency transformer is designed to pass a signal that, by its nature, is like a noise signal. The probability that unwanted noise would see this transformer as a coupling capacitor is high.

All components have some inherent leakage current. The output electrolytic capacitor changes characteristics dramatically as frequency increases. A switching power supply is a tightly packed circuit. In fact, space is at a premium, which is one main reason why the industry moved in the direction of the switch. But, ever since the switching power supply's inception, stray coupling has been a problem. And, stray coupling is not confined to a neat band of interference. Low-frequency as well as high-frequency noise can cause problems. No one can design around such a broad range of potential noise.

Two things are clear regarding switching power supplies and noise, however. They are much more vulnerable to common-mode noise than they are to normal-mode noise, and a damaging common-mode impulse will be magnitudes smaller than a damaging normal-mode impulse.

Switching Noise

It may have occurred to you that all this switching between 20 kHz to 100 kHz just might generate some noise. The fact is that noise from the power supply, as well as the clocks inside the logic, is a problem for PCs. That is why PCs are now subject to strict requirements from the FCC, due to their tendency to emit EMI. EMI stands for *electromagnetic interference.* In recent years, it has replaced another term which had essentially the same meaning—*radio-frequency interference* or *RFI.*

In Fig. 6-10, we saw the rather strange current sine wave of the switching power supply. This waveform is made up of odd harmonics which are reflected back into the line. This harmonic content can appear as noise on the input of other devices.

A PC, then, is a source of EMI from both its clocks, and from the oscillator and inverter in its power supply. And it's a source of noise to other devices connected along the same line. Let's take this a step further. In Chapter 2, we made the point that in a three-phase system, the current of each phase adds algebraically to a vector sum of 0. Odd harmonics, however, actually add mathematically. But the difficulty does not just stop there. The current needs of switching power supplies, along with a lagging power factor, can further unbalance a transformer. It is not uncommon to see neutral currents higher than the sum of the three individual phase currents, when the load is that of many switching power supplies.

This type of circumstance is not unusual. In fact, it is typical. Now, power lines become like antennas. The switches are sources of multiple kinds of noise. And the neutral line carries large amounts of current. If we add a simple ground loop, we have a receipt for constant soft errors, excessive power-supply heating, and the eventual breakdown of solid-state components.

Beyond Power Supplies

What is beyond power supplies? Why, logic, of course—the little computer chips scattered all over the motherboard. Those integrated circuits are the ones we see pictures of all the time. You know, the little black speck sitting on the end of someone's finger?

We've made a big deal out of the ability of an IC to withstand noise voltages or induced currents from ground loops. The fact is that the PN junctions of an IC cannot hold back more than a few dozen volts, and usually substantially less. Current flows that are in excess of a few dozen milliamperes (thousandths of an ampere) cannot be tolerated.

The reason for this is not surprising when we consider the size of the circuits. A typical gate inside an IC is on the order of the width of a human hair. A half dozen or so gates might easily fit into the period at the end of this sentence. The distances between current-carrying paths are measured in microns (one millionth of a meter, or 1×10^{-6}). A distance of a few microns between the logic voltage supply and ground is typical. It is these tiny distances that make IC chips so vulnerable to the high-energy impulses coming through the power supply or discharging through the chassis, especially the common-mode potentials.

Noise immunity is another factor. Noise immunity is the chip's ability to distinguish data from noise. For TTL-type ICs, this is only 400 to 500 millivolts, or roughly $^1/_2$ volt. For the more rugged logic families, this can be as high as 3.2 to 6.5 volts, but this better immunity often comes at the expense of operating speed. Of course, a chip is most vulnerable to noise when it is in transition from one logic state to the next. This is why soft errors can seem so bedevilling. The noise impulse must occur at exactly this transition time of the chip and in such a way that the noise event actually interferes with the chip.

Well, the time has come to do something about this. The remainder of this book will be devoted to those technologies that solve power problems. The next three chapters will consider devices that deal with high-energy transients, both common mode and normal mode.

7 Transient Suppression Devices

There are a number of transient suppression devices on the market today. By this, we mean the discrete components that are the primary defense against damaging voltage impulses. We are not yet talking about the product that is commonly called a *surge suppressor*. Clearly, surge suppressors contain transient suppression devices, but an understanding of how the components themselves act upon the transient impulse is vital in the understanding of the products that use them.

IEEE 587 AND ANSI C62.41 STANDARDS

It turns out it is much easier to design a product to suppress something if you have some notion of what that something is. *Transient suppression* is no exception. It would be very difficult to design a component or assembly of components to act upon an impulse unless the designer had some idea as to the characteristics of the impulse. This is where the IEEE 587 standard and ANSI C62.41 standard come in.

IEEE stands for the *International Association of Electrical and Electronic Engineers* and is often referred to as "eye triple E." ANSI stands for the *American National Standards Institute*—called "anssee." These groups have come up with a description of what an impulse in a low-voltage (120-V AC) circuit might look like. This is based on a lot of research, interpolation, and field experience. Fig. 7-1 shows the famous IEEE 587 "ring wave." This is also referred to as ANSI C62.41, but we will ignore the politics of transient voltages.

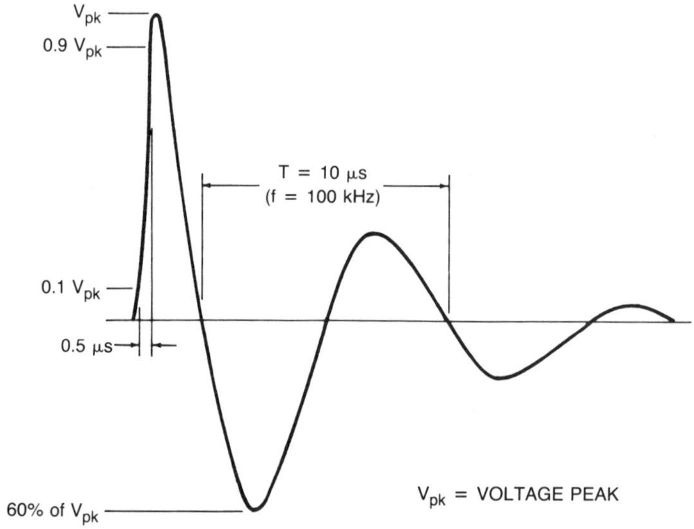

Fig. 7-1. IEEE 587 0.5-µs, 100-kHz ring wave.

Description was only one priority for the working group that took up the subject of transients. The other priority was to establish the ring wave as a standard for testing. The ring wave is not the only waveform that the group of engineers came up with. But the common household or office convenience receptacle falls into the ring-wave category. Based on research and testing, the ring wave has been born out as a reasonably good likeness of the typical impulse that might appear in those electrical outlet locations where PCs are to be found connected.

The wave (Fig. 7-1) is expressed in percentages—0.1 of the peak voltage, 0.9 of the peak voltage, and so forth. So what is the peak voltage? IEEE makes an attempt to predict what the peak voltage might be. This is reasonable since not every event is going to release exactly the same amount of energy; but experience has shown that they do tend to fall within certain boundaries. The IEEE standard says that since building wiring is known to experience insulation breakdown and sparkover at 6000 volts, we can expect events of no greater magnitude than 6 kV. Notice also that the standard predicts that each peak in voltage oscillation will be 0.6 of the previous peak. This describes an oscillating event that gradually dissipates.

The oscillating nature of the wave, plus the possibility of 6-kV peaks, are critical criteria for evaluating equipment. When a product claims to meet

IEEE 587 standards, or when the product literature advertises that the device will withstand repeated hits of a 6-kV IEEE 587 ring wave, you can be sure that the manufacturer is aware of proper engineering design criteria. More on that later.

ANSI and IEEE have addressed two other waveforms. We find them shown in Fig. 7-2. It is not terribly important to master the significance of these waveforms since they describe what an impulse might look like at the building service entrance. These impulses are unidirectional, as opposed to being oscillatory like the ring wave. The impedance of the building wiring will cause one to literally become the other.

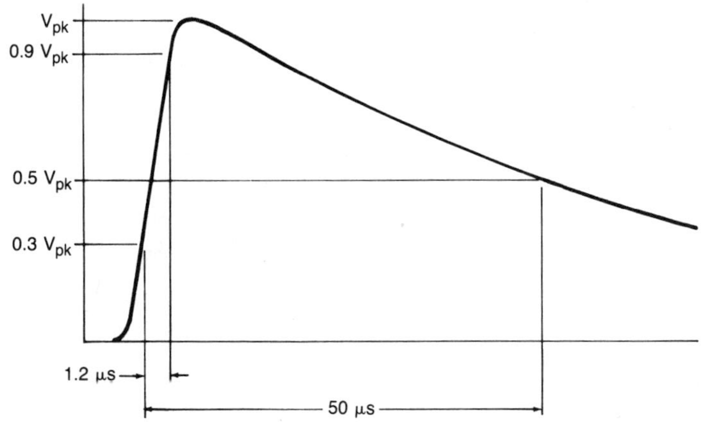

(A) Voltage waveform.

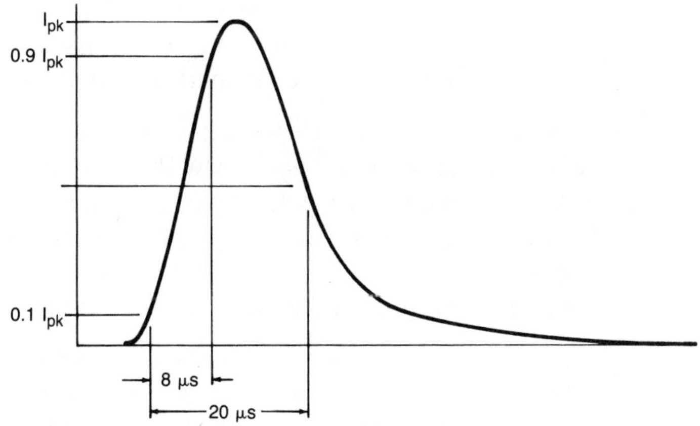

(B) Current waveform.

Fig. 7-2. Unidirectional (ANSI C62.41) waveshapes of outdoor and service entrance impulses.

Another reason why we should not be too concerned about these particular waveshapes is that they are to be found only at the building service entrance. PCs are connected to the line at such a point that the characteristics of the impulse waveshape have changed considerably. We are not just restating our previous point. A product designed for the unidirectional waveshape should not be used in conjunction with a PC. A manufacturer who would do this is using improper design criteria.

Furthermore, the place to deal with the unidirectional waveshape is at the building service entrance, not anywhere else. We will talk about these devices briefly in a few moments. But, let's clarify this discussion further by asking what kinds of events produce this unidirectional impulse? The answer is: Major events that occur along the power distribution system. Lightning would be the most common event.

Thus, *lightning arresters* are the most common device that we think of when it comes to keeping this enormous release of energy away from sensitive equipment. As we shall see, lightning arresters, as a form of protection for computer equipment, are not only an inappropriate application of technology to a problem, but they create a silly sense of security for the user.

Filters

Transient suppression devices come in two basic forms. The first form is made up of Ls and Cs. Sounds like alphabet soup, but what we are really talking about are *inductors* and *capacitors* arranged in a circuit, with that circuit being used to block or attenuate the propagation of high-energy noise into the critical load. Shortly, we will talk about another kind of suppression device—*diverters*.

Remember from an earlier discussion that we mentioned the subject of resonance, and we talked about how the reactance of a capacitor or inductor changes as the frequency of the signal applied across it changes. This property of coils and capacitors makes them ideal for the purpose of blocking certain noise frequencies. But, we are not going to get heavily involved in the theory behind this. Let's just consider a simple two-element filter (Fig. 7-3).

In this case, we want to permit the normal 120-volt AC line current to flow to the "critical load," but we don't want the noise that might appear between the line and neutral to enter the load and cause problems. At some frequency, we know that the coil (L1) will develop a high impedance. This type of coil or inductor is commonly called a *choke*. So, we select this choke to have a particular reactance at the noise frequency.

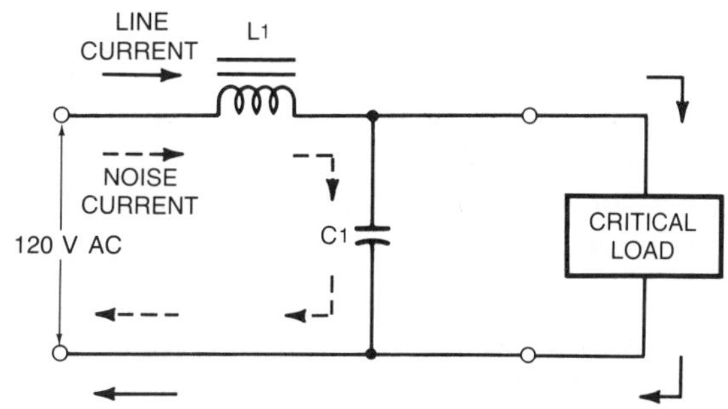

Fig. 7-3. A two-element filter using a coil (inductor) and a capacitor.

As noise tries to pass through the choke, an opposing current builds up that is 180° out of phase to the noise. This opposition to the noise current attenuates the noise and dissipates its energy as heat. But just to make sure, we have chosen capacitance (C1) to have a low impedance to the noise, so it will see the path through C1 as a virtual short circuit, while the line current will see it as an open circuit. Thus, any remaining noise is given a path away from the load. This kind of filter is called a low-pass filter because it passes low frequencies while attenuating the higher frequencies.

It may have occurred to you that building a filter for all the various frequencies which might be considered noise would be very difficult. And, in fact, it is. It is far easier to design a filter to block a certain narrow band of frequencies than it is to build one that must work well over a broad band. This is one of the problems with filters. We will see this again in a later chapter. However, a well-engineered filter can be a power problem solver. The effects of a filter on that band of noise to which it is most closely tuned to is indeed dramatic.

Diverters

If we look back at our filter circuit of Fig. 7-3, we might be able to make the argument that the capacitance (C1) does more diverting than attenuating. And we would be correct. There are several additional devices that perform this same function and which are designed to handle varying degrees of energy. We will look at each device, one at a time. Then, the stage will be set to take a look inside of those products in which they are used. Diverters are divided into two more categories: *crowbars* and *clamps*.

Crowbars

A *spark gap* is the driving concept behind all crowbar-type devices. But before we find out how a spark gap becomes a *crowbar*, let's think for a moment about the definition and use of a crowbar. When we wedge an iron (construction-type) crowbar between iron, wood, or cement materials, there are periods of time when we apply more and more pressure. Finally, the materials give and separate, and our leverage pays off. Crowbar-type electronic devices that use spark gaps work in much the same way. Pressure in the form of a voltage buildup appears across the spark gap. When enough force (electromotive force) is applied, the gap ionizes, forming an electrical path.

The typical crowbar-type device in present use is a gas tube. Inside a sealed chamber, electrodes are placed in close proximity. This gap is filled with a special gas that is selected for its ionization properties. If the gas tube is connected between a line and ground, high-energy impulses will cause a high voltage to appear across the terminals of the gas tube. At some point, this potential will ionize the gas and a spark will bridge the spark gap, allowing energy to flow to ground. This is exactly how a lightning arrester works.

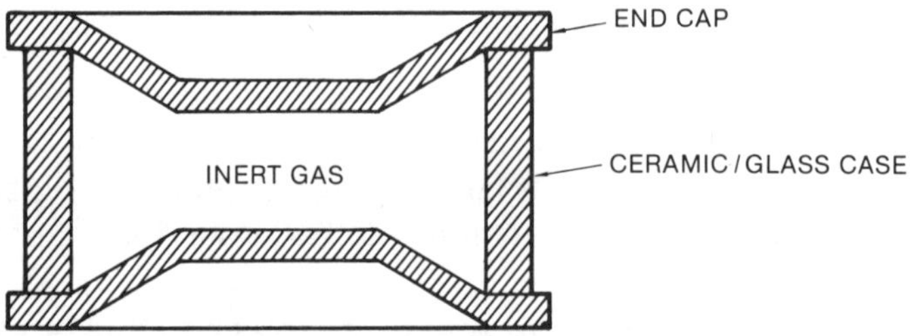

Fig. 7-4. The gas-surge arrester, just one gap-type device, has electrical parameters that are a function of gas pressure and content, gap distance, and electrode size, content, and mass.

From the standpoint of a PC, there are a couple of inherent problems with crowbar devices. The first problem you may already have guessed. It is called the volt-time response. This refers to the amount of time it takes for the voltage buildup to trigger the arc mode of the gas tube. Typically, this is in the millisecond range. The problem is that during the initial rise time of the impulse, no protection is being offered the PC.

Ionizing the gas inside the tube is not a perfect process. This leads to varying voltage levels that might be needed to fire the device—sometimes higher, sometimes lower. Lower voltage ratings are difficult to produce with consistency due to the small gap that must be manufactured. The gap- or arrester-type device is well suited to handling large amounts of energy, far better than handling small amounts of energy.

After the high-energy impulse has dropped below the device's firing threshold, the gas between the electrodes of the tube may remain ionized. Thus, a path to ground would remain, causing power to continue to flow away from the load. In other words, power from the steady-state voltage source will follow the path of the impulse. The clear result of this is a temporary power outage. Due to the nature of the device itself, it will often cause an outage or a significant sag as a result of its operation. At some point during the sine-wave period, the device will extinguish itself. It is not unusual, however, to find the hot gas and electrodes reigniting during the next voltage peak.

Still another problem for PCs is that the functioning of a gap device can cause an impulse of dangerous magnitude to occur. Arcing, sparking, and firing are not the kinds of events we would typically encourage near a computer. Also, the functioning of the gap device may couple energy into other conductors, which might direct this energy into some sensitive equipment. Remember that earlier we mentioned the importance of designing products in anticipation of impulse waveshapes. Crowbars bring this issue into focus. The unidirectional waveshape is usually an event of high magnitude moving in one direction. This type of transient is ideal for a gap device. The much-lower-magnitude ring wave and its characteristic environs do not match well with the functioning of spark gaps. A ring wave calls for a different approach. Gas-discharge tubes are useful for the high-current type of waveshapes found at the building service entrance. They are not as effective when used to protect low-voltage, low-impedance circuits.

Clamps

Now we come to the good stuff. *Clamps* are the most common devices used in protective circuitry. They come in two basic varieties: *zener* or *avalanche diodes* and *metal-oxide varistors (MOVs)*. The two discrete components have differing properties, but overlapping functions. We will look at avalanche diodes first.

Avalanche Diodes

"Diode" is a term we have heard before. It is at the very heart of the rectifier circuits we discussed earlier. Remember that it has an anode and cathode, and when properly biased will allow current to flow. When it is reverse biased, no current will flow.

This is where the *zener* or *avalanche diode* stands alone from other types of diodes. Yes, it is true that when it is reverse biased, no current will flow. But this is only true to a point. That point is called the *breakdown voltage*. What this means is that at some reverse-bias voltage, the internal PN junction of the diode breaks down. Now, we don't mean it breaks down physically and causes some kind of harm to the junction. What breakdown means in this context is that the physical behavior of the electrons suddenly change, allowing current to flow across the PN junction. This action is due to special doping of the semiconductor material during the fabrication process. Fig. 7-5 shows this at work. When the voltage across the diode reaches the breakdown magnitude, current flows through the diode. The diode acts as a voltage divider and a low-impedance path. The bulk of the noise current then flows through the diode.

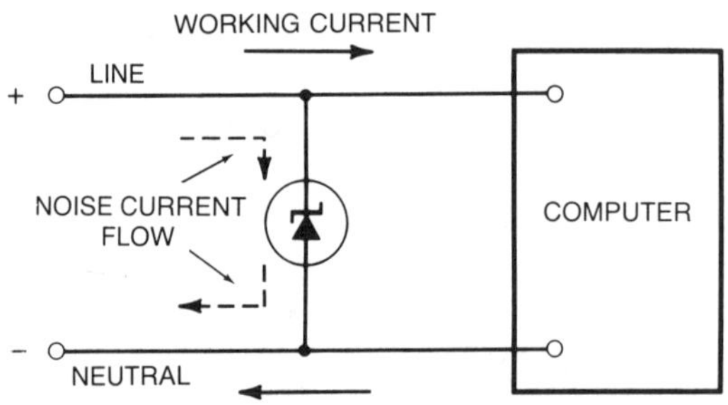

Fig. 7-5. When the noise voltage potential reaches the breakdown voltage, the zener diode becomes a low-impedance path.

Two unanswered questions may still be hanging in the air at this point. The first relates to Fig. 7-5. We have shown polarity signs at the input of the circuit. If we assume an alternating current source, clearly then, the diode would only protect during the half cycle when it is reverse biased. We have not shown the complete protective circuit for simplicity's sake. The answer to having protection when the polarity is reversed is to put two diodes back-to-back.

The other question may be as to why are zeners called avalanche diodes? *Avalanching* is the process of charge carriers (which are accelerated to a high velocity by the buildup voltage applied to the device) colliding with valence electrons. This all has to due with the physics of the crystalline structure of the P region, the N region, and the junction between the two. These valence electrons collide with more valence electrons, producing a snow-balling effect—thus the term, avalanche. This process generates a nearly instantaneous high-current flow across the junction, thereby creating a low-impedance path. Holes are involved in this process also, in the same way.

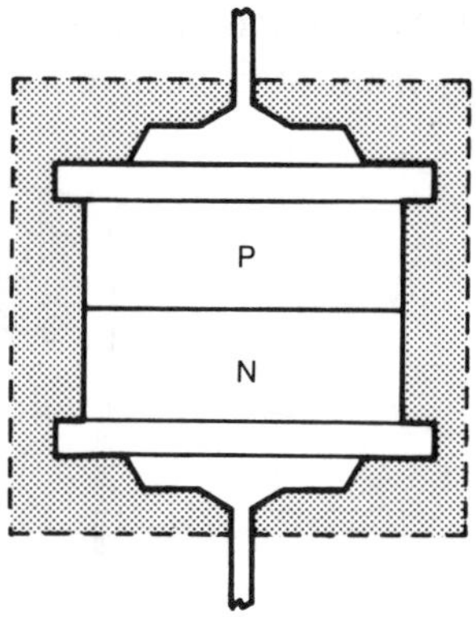

Fig. 7-6. Zener diodes are constructed using a large-area PN junction which has been affixed between two heat sinks to protect the junction during impulse conduction.

We are now going to leave the zener diode, but we will talk about its relative advantages and disadvantages later. We want to wait and compare it to the next device being discussed. Comparison between the two devices will make the benefits and weaknesses of each stand out even more clearly.

MOVs

As we stated earlier, MOV stands for metal-oxide varistor. *Varistor* is an amalgamation of the words variable and resistor. A varistor is a variable resistor. This should give some clue as to its operation. Although different in construction, MOVs are voltage-dependent devices which operate in a fashion similar to back-to-back zener diodes.

The origin of the MOV is a story as serendipitous as the discovery of penicillin. Supposedly, the electrical properties of silicon-carbide grains were discovered when a grinding wheel accidentally became part of a circuit on a disorderly workbench. For years after, varistors made from silicon carbide were formed in the shape of tiny grinding wheels. It seems the fabrication of varistors is as much an art as it is a science.

Modern varistors are made of zinc oxide, along with bismuth, manganese, cobalt, and other metal oxides. The structure of an MOV is a matrix of zinc-oxide grains bonded together in such a way that the boundaries of the grains have the characteristics of a PN-junction semiconductor (Fig. 7-7). Like the zener diode, these junctions block the conduction of electricity at low voltages and allow conduction at higher voltages.

Fig. 7-8 shows a varistor at work. While the voltage applied by the transient has much to do with the operation of a MOV, the current affects its clamping voltage to some degree. The important fact about varistors is that they clip off the voltage impulse at a certain level and conduct the impulse current away from the sensitive load.

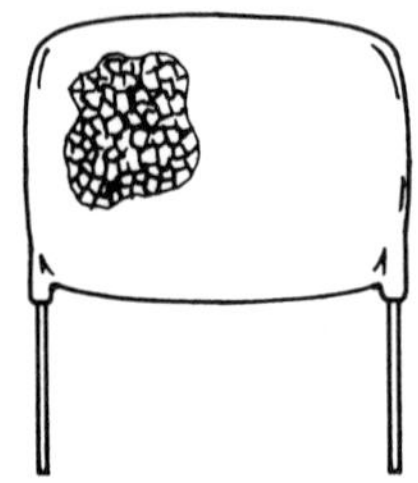

Fig. 7-7. The structure of an MOV is a matrix of zinc-oxide grains bonded with a bismuth material.

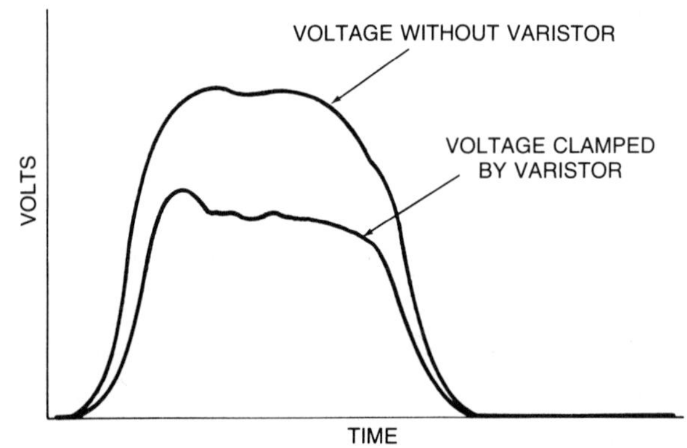

Fig. 7-8. Diagram showing a varistor-clamped voltage impulse.

Zeners and MOVs Compared

So, which device is better, a zener diode or an MOV? During the period of impulse conduction, large amounts of power are absorbed by the device. This might last from only nanoseconds to milliseconds, but current flowing through resistance creates heat. The life of the suppressor is dependent upon how it tolerates heat—can it dissipate the heat before the heat damages the crystalline structure that is doing the work.

Junction burnout has long been a problem where zener diodes are concerned. The PN junction must have a way of directing heat away from it. MOVs, on the other hand, distribute heat evenly throughout the device and are inherently better able to withstand energy over repeated numbers of events. The manufacturers of zener diodes are aware of this and have developed products that compete favorably.

Zener diodes have an offset advantage to the heating problem. They have lower clamping voltages. Obviously, lower clamping voltages mean that less current will be allowed to flow to the sensitive load. There is some argument that zeners have a faster response than MOVs, with the response time of some zeners being claimed to be on the order of one picosecond. This is labeled as theoretical. MOVs are rated at down to 500 picoseconds.

Other considerations are leakage current, aging, and capacitance. All of these are points of contention between manufacturers, and each manufacturer has developed design strategies to alleviate technological weaknesses.

It is natural for each manufacturer to think their device is by far the most effective in all cases. The fact remains, however, that most designers tend to think of the MOV as a more rugged device at higher energies, while the zener diode is a much more versatile device in low-power circuits. It is for these reasons that MOVs are used far more often in transient suppression products for personal computers.

MOVs at Work

Let's take a closer look at the clamping action of an MOV as it might appear in a surge protector type of product. The typical MOV would be rated to clamp voltages above 130-volts rms. This is an important rating. The 130-volts rms means that impulses will be clipped above 184-volts peak. (130-volts rms times 1.41 equals 184-volts peak. Normal AC power is 120-volts rms or 170-volts peak.) One might be tempted to subtract one from the other and conclude that the impulse might be limited to only 14 volts.

Of course, this might be true if the impulse occurred right at the peak of the sine wave. But, as Fig. 7-9 shows, if the impulse occurred at the negative peak, the impulse might have a magnitude of 368 volts. In fact the manufacturer's specification for this particular device claims this voltage to be as low as 340 volts. These values will vary slightly depending on the varistor and the impulse current and waveshape, but the principle we have illustrated is an important one.

Another important consideration is that negative-going impulses are not clipped. As was shown earlier, many impulses seen inside a building have a ringing waveshape. We have no guarantee that every transient event will be positive in polarity. The vast majority of damaging events, however, have

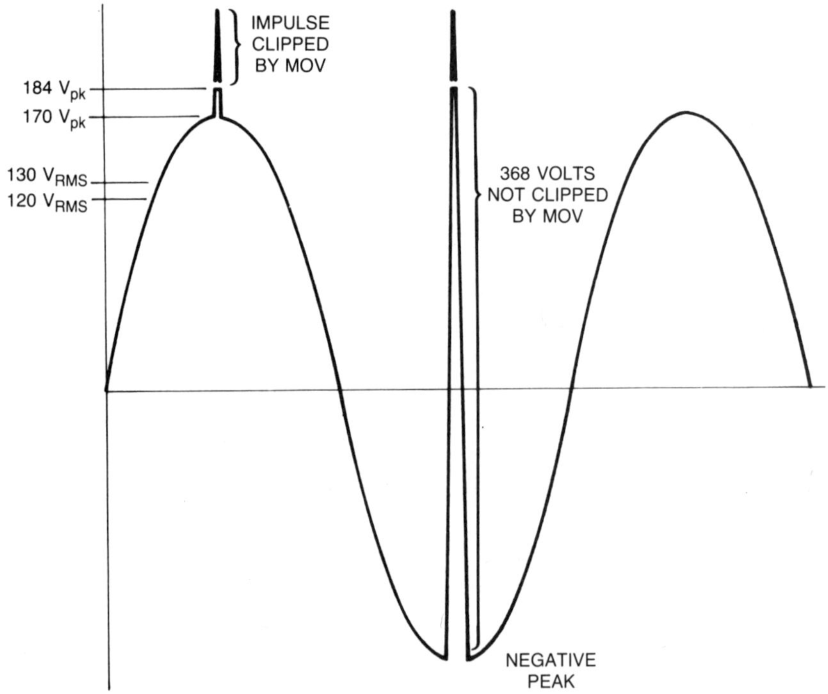

Fig. 7-9. How an MOV clips impulses.

their beginnings as positive, unidirectional impulses. This does not mean that energy which is coupled, reflected, and induced will always meet this neat scenario, and will allow the suppressor to act as if it were operating under laboratory conditions.

MOVs in Circuits

Like avalanche diodes, MOVs are connected to the computer in parallel. This allows the MOV to act as a low-impedance path. Undesired currents are short-circuited through the MOV, keeping the currents away from sensitive circuits.

In Fig. 7-5, we saw how a zener diode might be connected across a load, from line to neutral. But we know that there are actually three wires connecting our PC to the outside world. How might this effect the connection of transient suppressors across the lines? Fig. 7-10 shows three alternative connections, and will be our introduction into the next chapter on Surge Suppressors. We see three distinct options for connecting MOVs across lines. Let's explore each and see what we might accomplish in the way of protection.

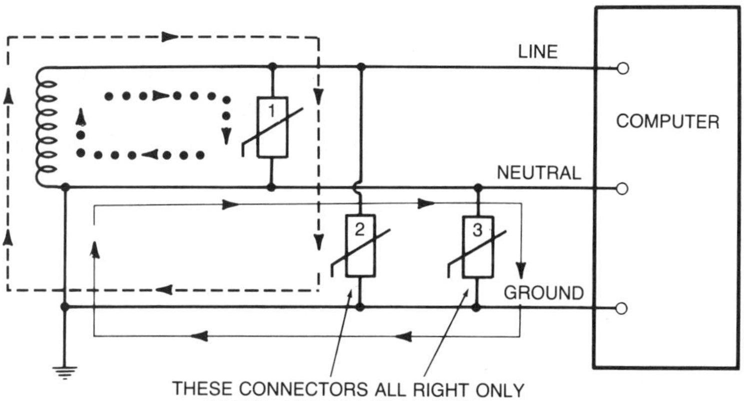

Fig. 7-10. How MOVs can be connected to protect a PC.

MOV 1 is connected between line and neutral. We might remember from an earlier discussion that normal-mode noise appears from line to neutral. Clearly, what MOV 1 will do is provide a low-impedance path to complete the noise circuit from line to neutral. By diverting the impulse current through the MOV, we are protecting the power supply of the PC.

MOV 2 is placed from line to ground. If it were used without MOV 1, no protection would result unless the impulse was of the common-mode variety. In that case, we would need MOV 3 since common-mode noise appears between both the line and ground, and neutral and ground. If the event were normal mode, MOV 2 would not be activated because it would not see any voltage differences from line to neutral.

Obviously, MOV 3 is needed to complement MOV 2, and form total common-mode protection. As we will see in the next chapter, many design engineers think of the ground wire as a pipeline to the electrical cesspool, and the use of a single MOV from line to ground is not uncommon. Electricity, even transient voltage impulses, travels in circuits. We can see that the neutral-to-ground terminals of the computer are connected across the current path flowing through MOV 3. This current will cause a voltage drop across the impedance of that circuit. We can see there is no alternative path for this current should the computer somehow bridge the gap from neutral to ground. All of this voltage will appear across the stray capacitance of the various components and boards inside the PC. And, of course, if a ground loop is present, we may have unseen paths that lead through boards, buses, and cables before returning.

Using all three MOVs is the most desirable design. This gives protection from both normal-mode and common-mode events. However, the let-through voltage of an MOV is far too high, possibly by several hundred volts, to really provide common-mode protection. And, as we shall shortly see, if we use an MOV from line to neutral, we must have them from both neutral to ground and from line to ground. Why? Because MOV 1, while it absorbs some energy, converts one form of noise to another. Let's move on to Chapter 8, and we shall see this process in action.

8 Surge Suppressors

As an introduction to this chapter, let's take a few moments to talk about terms and how we go about defining things. By now, we know that the term "spike" is a slang term for a positive-going impulse. We have used the term "noise" rather loosely and have defined it as any signal other than the desired signal. We have also talked about noise impulses, with a *noise burst* being made up of many individual impulses. The term "transient" had been used. Even in industry literature, the term "transient" is used interchangeably with the term "impulse." But, strictly speaking, a transient is not an impulse. Transient is a word that describes the fleeting nature of an event. It passes. It comes and goes. It is transitory.

So with that backdrop, we come to the term "surge." We have described a surge as an rms voltage higher than the standard limits. The term *rms* (root-mean-square) is the key. Use of the word *mean* (average) implies more than one measurement. Clearly, a transient voltage excursion is a single event. High-energy impulses that are only nanoseconds, microseconds, or milliseconds in length are not measured in rms voltage. They must be measured in relationship to their peak voltages, waveshapes, and rise time.

A surge describes a sine wave, or series of sine waves, that exceed standard values. This means the top of the waveform curve exceeds normal instantaneous values. A half cycle, for instance, lasts 8.34 milliseconds. Impulses are almost never longer than a dozen or so microseconds. An impulse and a surge are vastly different events. So, it is with this semantical incongruity that we tackle the subject of *surge suppressors* or *surge protectors*. These are devices that are designed to protect equipment from high-energy impulses rather than surges. But that is not the only difficulty.

We are in the last half of the book now, and the remainder of the book will focus on specific product technologies and applications. Surge suppressors are the first of many devices that we will investigate. But we must be wary. We are in the world of PCs—consumer products. This means that packaging is as important as protection. It means that price is as important as performance. It means that persuasion is important to perceived value. To put it bluntly, there is more smoke and mirrors sold under the guise of protecting computers from lightning hits and such than in any other area of the industry. Why? Because the world is full of folks who think nothing of spending $2000 for the latest whiz-bang computer and, then, will start haggling over a $10.00 surge strip to protect the whole installation. You get what you pay for, as we shall soon see.

In this chapter, we are going to start with the simple and move toward the more complex. It will be impossible to cover every combination of components used in the various products on the market. We will not attempt to deal with the wild claims of some companies or the outright fraud of others. What we will do is arm the reader with enough understanding of the principles behind product designs that intelligent choices can be made.

Simple Surge Suppressors

A simple surge protector comes in one of several forms. But at the heart of the device is usually one and only one component—an MOV. Currently, this product appears in three incarnations. The first of these is the surge strip that we are all familiar with. This is a multi-outlet power bar. The second form of the same basic product is the single-outlet device that is plugged into the wall ahead of the CPU. The idea behind this form is that one of these units would be required for each of the pieces of equipment that needs protection. The third form of this product idea is the receptacle itself. Special receptacles can now be purchased so that surge suppression can be built right into the wall.

With a few exceptions, the only active component installed inside these products is a single MOV that is connected between the line and neutral. Fig. 8-1 shows an oscilloscope display of an impulse from a test generator. It traces a 900-volt impulse (between the line and neutral). Fig. 8-2 shows how the top of the same impulse has been clipped off (or clamped) by the MOV. It is this action of the MOV which diverts potentially damaging energy away from the load. Fig. 8-3 shows how this appears in a circuit diagram.

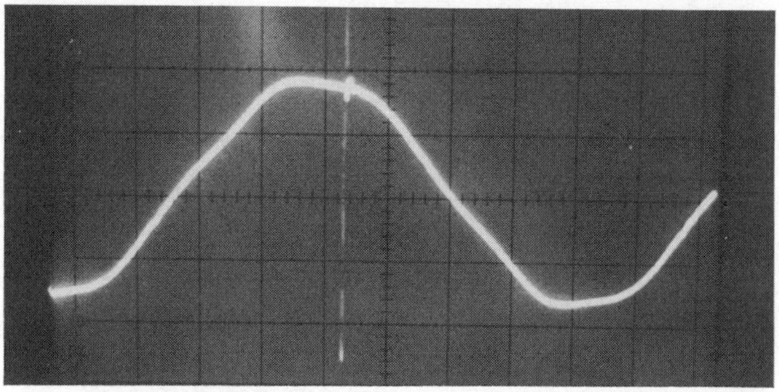

Fig. 8-1. In this photo of a 900-volt impulse, we see that the magnitude of the impulse is great enough that the peak of the pulse goes off the top of the screen.

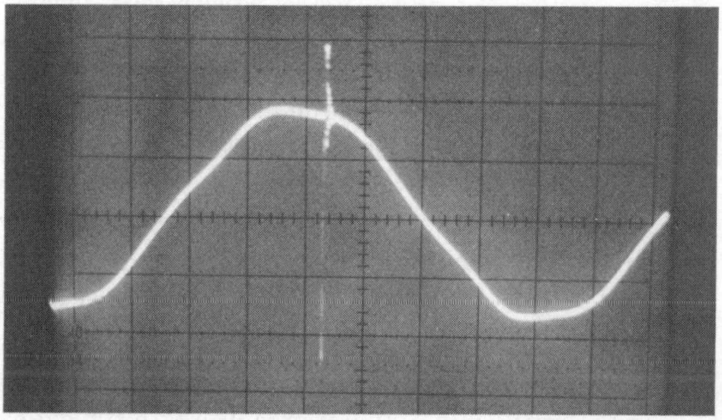

Fig. 8-2. With the insertion of an MOV between the line and neutral, the 900-volt impulse is clipped off or clamped.

A Test for Surge Suppressors

We mentioned that we used a test impulse voltage of about 900 volts. There is a good reason for this that is vitally important to the proper application of this product. At various points throughout this book, we have made reference to the kinds of power disturbances we might expect at various locations in a building. That is why there are different stages of protection required, depending on the size of the event we might expect.

The MOV used in most surge suppressors is designed with the rationale that lightning arresters have been installed in accordance with the activity in the area. In addition, there seems to be a common misconception that surge protectors will stop most anything that comes down the line, and if they don't, they are no good. Let's put this into some orderly perspective.

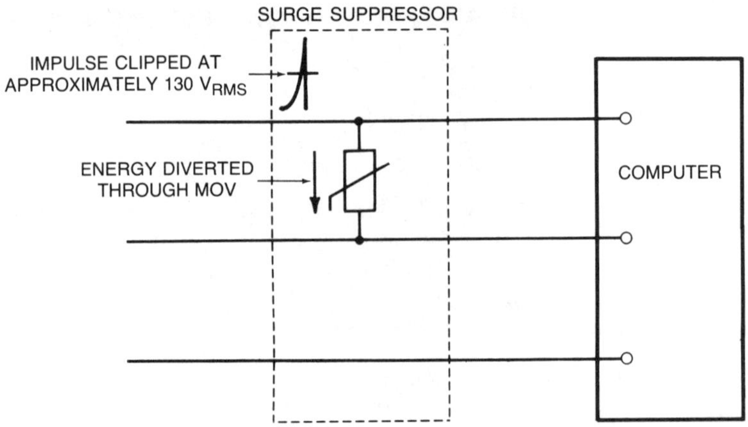

Fig. 8-3. How a simple surge suppressor works.

The IEEE 587 standard talks about 3000- or 6000-volt test impulses as does the new UL 1449 standard (discussed in the next chapter). Naturally, it would seem to be desirable to test products to these standards to see if they work. We couldn't agree more! A recent magazine article that compared surge suppressors found that the typical 6000-volt, 200-ampere impulse showed no significant difference between products. Why? The only component reactive to this type of energy in most of the products tested was the same MOV manufactured by the same company.

The testers evidently didn't suspect this so they increased the amperage of the impulse to 500 amperes. Here's a typical example of what happened to one product.

> . . .produced excellent results through the first half of the tests, clamping 6-kV spikes down to as low as 60 volts. Then, poof—the unit croaked. We were not impressed.

The unit croaked because the MOV inside the device finally gave up its life after handling repeated hits (about 192 in this case) of energy that possibly were in excess of its specified ratings. Actually, the performance described was very good and would have done exactly what the owner bought it for. The surge suppressor that took all those 6000-volt, 500-ampere hits before it "croaked" was priced at less than $40.00. That's an incredible performance for the money. Tests need to be designed that properly reflect the design differences between products, not just the survivability of the same type of MOV from one product to another. We believe that the new UL 1449 standard does this.

It is for these reasons that we choose the more realistic level of about

900 volts for our tests. We wanted to show the performance characteristics of differing technologies, not blow up black boxes. As we will see in this and later chapters, this test is just as dramatic at 900 volts as it is at 6000 volts.

MOV Failure Modes

For an investment of under $40.00, we should be happy to see our simple surge suppressor give up its life. Considering the alternative, $40.00 is a small price to pay. When we say give up its life, we mean the MOV has failed, and MOVs always fail "short." This means that as they fail, they become a short circuit as the peak current capability of the device is exceeded. Current beyond this failure level will cause the leads of the device to melt or will cause the casing to explode.

This short-circuit characteristic is an important advantage as well as a major disadvantage. It is an advantage in that surge current will continue to be diverted away from the computer as the MOV fails. It is a disadvantage in that once this failure has taken place, most simple products have no way of warning the user that the protection is no longer available.

There are many MOV-based products plugged into sockets all over the country that have long ago given up what measure of protection they were designed to give, but have no way of telling their owners. Meanwhile, the user has a false sense of security and continues to use them.

How can we take care of this problem? A properly selected fuse, placed in series with the MOV, can trigger a status indicator to annunciate the failure of the MOV. Without this indicator, it is impossible to tell if the MOV is still operational without opening the case of the product. Beware, however—there are many products on the market that have some sort of status light which has nothing whatsoever to do with the health of the MOVs or any other internal suppression device. The additional circuitry needed to provide the user with this information increases the price of the product. Suffice it to say, most simple surge suppressors have no status indicator. Without this feature, the device is useless and a waste of money.

Noise-Mode Conversion

We have shown that the typical positioning of an MOV in a simple surge suppressor would be from the line to neutral. Let's take a few moments to consider the implications of this.

As the MOV conducts current through the line-to-neutral noise path, a noise voltage drop occurs that is in parallel with the neutral and ground wires. Fig. 8-4 shows this in simplified form. It almost appears as if the MOV has clipped off a large part of the impulse and has placed it on the neutral wire. Strictly speaking, this is not exactly what happens, but the net effect amounts to the same thing, due to the relationships between impedance, current, and voltage. The MOV is driving current through an impedance that is seen to drop from neutral to ground.

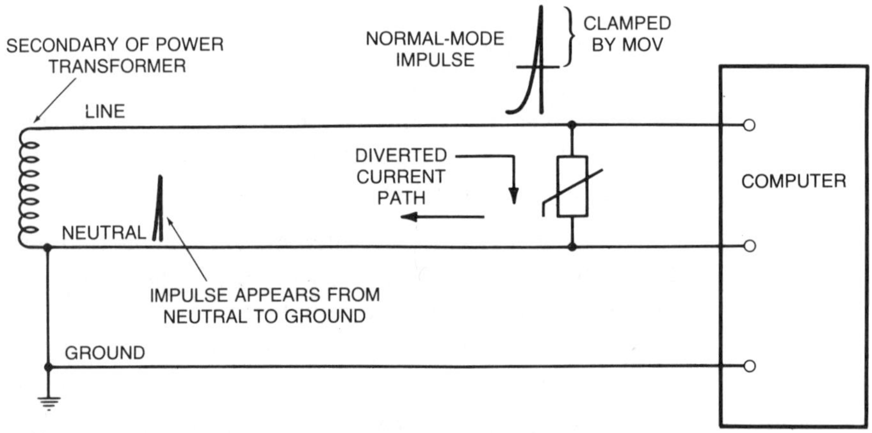

Fig. 8-4. Normal- to common-mode conversion as created by a surge suppressor.

This conversion action has taken a normal-mode impulse and, by diverting it through the neutral-line impedance, created a common-mode impulse. The MOV has literally converted normal-mode noise into common-mode noise. Fig. 8-5 shows a display of our test impulse appearing in the normal mode, while we see nothing in the common mode. Fig. 8-6 shows what happens if we insert a surge suppressor into the line. The common-mode impulse that is created may be either smaller in peak voltage or larger, depending on the impedance of the lines and the current of the source.

We are now back to the controversy of grounding. If we are convinced that the PC is immune to common-mode noise, then we have no real concern with this scenario. If, on the other hand, we worry about the vulnerability of the chips inside the PC to common-mode offsets, then we might just rather risk the power supply rather than the logic circuits. More on this later. Suffice it to say that surge suppressors, by their designed action on normal-mode noise, will generate common-mode noise.

If we refer back to Fig. 7-10, we see that an MOV in position 2 will also divert energy away from the normal mode. This can create even larger voltage drops because of the added impedance of the ground line, which is not a part of the noise path. It is almost as if the designers forgot that the

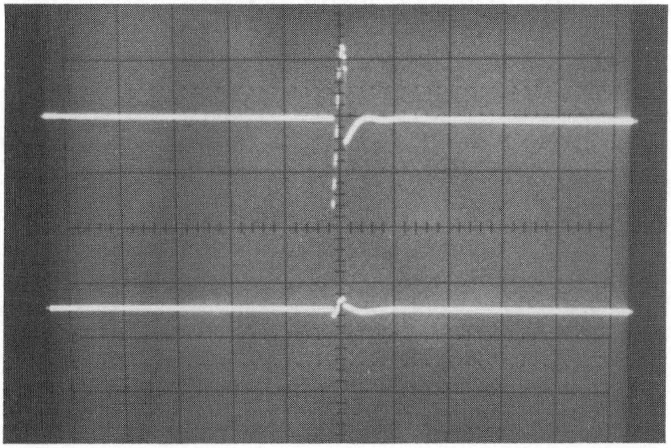

Fig. 8-5. The test impulse appears in the normal mode without a surge suppressor.

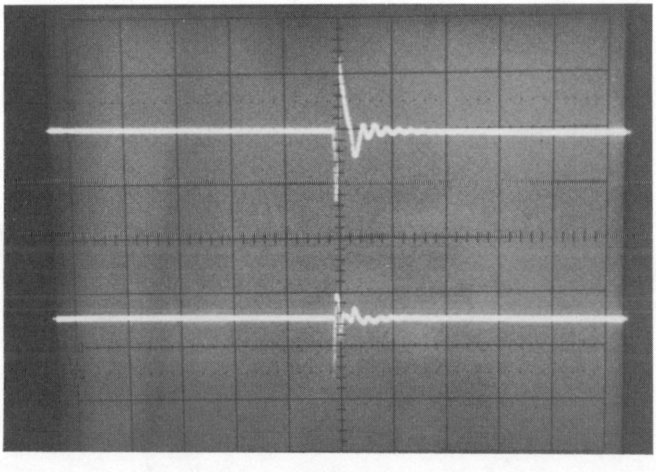

Fig. 8-6. The addition of a surge suppressor has created common-mode noise.

neutral and ground wires come together at some point. However, if MOV 2 were combined with MOV 3 (in Fig. 7-10), we have some very useful protection. We will talk about that later.

The Anatomy of a Spike

The simple surge suppressor we have been describing typically retails for under $20.00. By adding more components, we can do more things to eliminate the potentially harmful effects of high-frequency noise and high-energy impulses. Before we see what these additional components are, let's take a closer look at the impulse itself.

We have mentioned frequency here and in other places. But where noise impulses are concerned, there are really two aspects of frequency. One, we are already familiar with. That is the *rate of oscillation of a signal.* The power waveform has a frequency of 60 Hz because it oscillates back and forth 60 times a second. A noise frequency of 10 MHz oscillates 10 million times a second. If we were concerned about a certain band of noise frequencies, we would design a filter to block those frequencies. We discussed this earlier.

There is another aspect of frequency, however, that we need to explore. It is the *rate of change.* In other words, how fast is a given thing changing at any given instant. A drag-race car has a varying rate of change in acceleration. During the early stage of a race—the first few seconds—the rate of change is slow. Then, as traction with the road is established and the rpm's of the engine build, the rate of change in acceleration dramatically increases. Seconds later, the dragster reaches its peak acceleration and the rate of change slows. Fig. 8-7 shows what a graph of this action might look like.

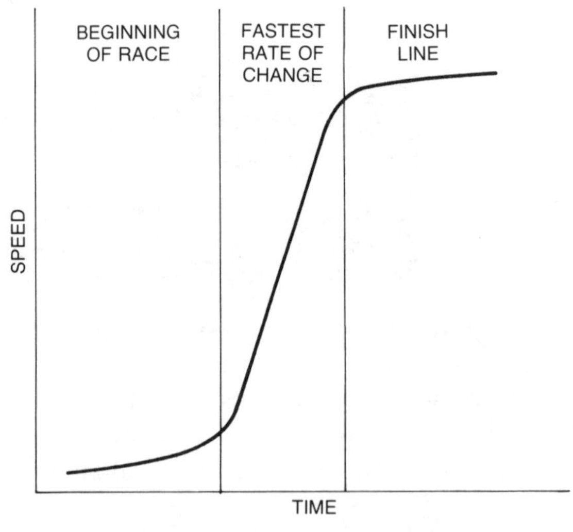

Fig. 8-7. What a graph of acceleration might look like during a drag race.

Bear in mind that the actual speed of the dragster is increasing throughout the whole race. The rate of change is what we are getting at here. At some point along the curve, we see that the frequency of change is far different than the frequency of change at other points. Fig. 8-8 shows what a high-energy impulse might look like. Notice that it has differing rates of change, or frequencies. This can be defined by plotting the instantaneous slope of the curve. The steeper the slope of the curve, the higher the frequency of change in voltage.

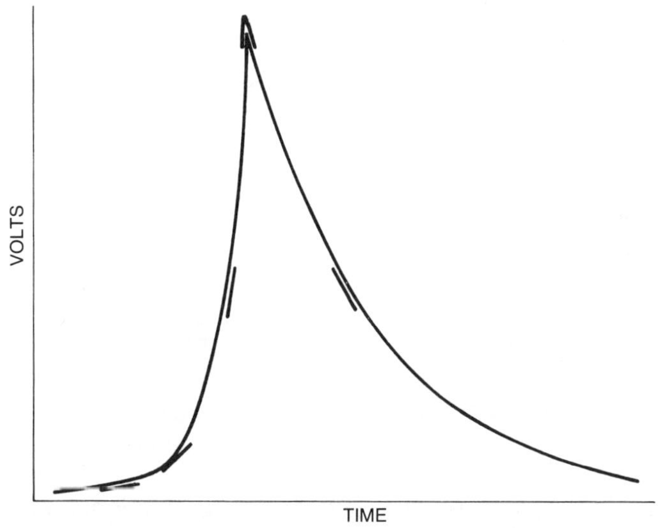

Fig. 8-8. The waveform of an impulse has many instantaneous rates of change, or frequency components.

By now, you may be able to see where this discussion is heading. A transient voltage impulse contains many frequency components. Usually, it is the fast rise time or high-frequency components that can be the most troublesome. They are the parts that find strange paths of previously nonexistent inductance and capacitance inside computers. It is the high-frequency components of the impulses that do the damage. Obviously, it would be nice to change the shape of the impulse so as to reduce as much as possible its high-frequency nature.

This can be done two ways. One way is to divert high-frequency noise through capacitors. Another way is to slow down the impulse by forcing it through an inductance which will set up a bucking effect that is counter to the impulse current. Through the use of chokes or coils of wire, the shape of the wave can be rounded out, stripping away many high-frequency elements of the impulse—those elements that encounter high impedance at frequencies that match those of the choke.

Hybrid Circuits

We have discussed the relative strengths and weaknesses of both the MOV and zener diode. In general, MOVs are better able to handle high-magnitude, high-energy impulses while zener diodes have lower breakdown voltages. These characteristics can be used to advantage in a surge-suppression product to create a barrier to the propagation of damaging events. Fig. 8-9 shows us a hybrid circuit that combines diverting elements with blocking elements. It also combines high-energy handling with low breakdown voltages.

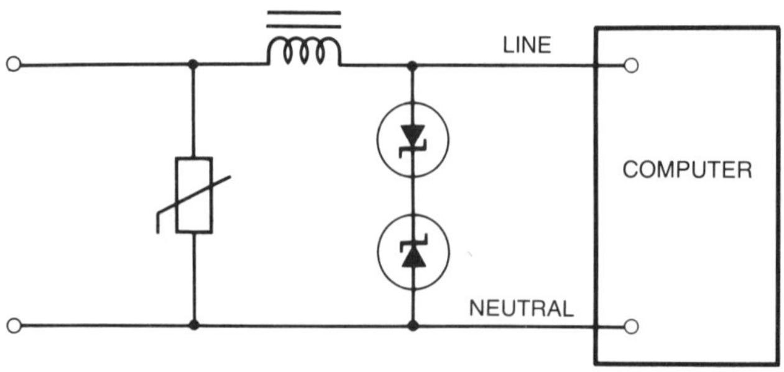

Fig. 8-9. A hybrid circuit combines the advantages of MOVs and zener diodes with a choke for more protection.

A MOV is the first stage of protection. It has a somewhat slower reaction time than the zener so some of the fast-rising initial slope of an impulse might pass through during this extremely short interval. However, the MOV is not going to allow much more than a peak of about 400 volts to pass through after its clamping action. Its large current-handling capability diverts most of the energy away from the sensitive load.

Next, the choke will present a nearly open-circuit reactance to those high-frequency components of the front slope of the impulse that make it past the MOV. The impulse current generates an opposing current due to the current being induced by the choke's own magnetic field. Much energy is blocked by the choke and is dissipated as heat.

The energy impulse that remains is rounder, slower, and lower in magnitude. Now that the impulse has been knocked down to size, the diodes can clean up what is left, as well as that which made it through before the MOV was activated. We should note that both MOV manufacturers and avalanche diode makers have various models that might suffice in our circuit. But our point, here, was to use the advantages of different technologies to accomplish some unique form of protection. And, in fact, this type of design is often used in commercial surge protectors.

However, a note of caution is now appropriate. Hybrid designs were discussed in my earlier book, *Computer Electrical Power Requirements*, as they related to large systems. A hybrid design can be constructed by using a gas-discharge tube as the first stage and, then, using the building wiring as the inductive cushion or choke. But, as we have stated earlier, gas-discharge tubes function in such a way that their effects can be nearly as disruptive as the spike that might trigger them. This is especially true in the PC environment since events are of a smaller nature anyway.

There are tiny, little, gas tubes on the market that work just as well as the large ones. But, again, solid-state transient-voltage devices have far more desirable characteristics. Yes, there are gas tubes used in many consumer surge protectors, and the literature furnished with them gives the illusion that some protection against enormous events is available. The question is, "Do they represent the highest level in design sophistication?" The belief is that because of the device's high current-handling capability, they are a good first stage of protection. Usually, they are placed in circuits along with MOVs and chokes. But because of their response time, other devices usually deal with the impulse long before the gas tube can operate. The response time of the three devices we have discussed are: zeners first, MOVs second, and gas tubes last. Gas tubes may very well take a relatively unimportant impulse and, by arcing to ground, create a damaging, fast, rise-time transient. This action should never take place near the computer's grounding point.

Total Protection

By now, we have some idea about how different elements might be used to construct a product. We have discussed the transient suppression devices themselves. We have talked about the use of capacitance and inductance, both as they apply to filtering and as they are used in the hybrid-circuit concept. We have also talked about normal- to common-mode conversion. Before we see how the various elements come together to form some of the more sophisticated product types, we need to talk about one more thing—common-mode protection.

One of the points we have emphasized several times in this book is the vulnerability of microcomputer-based products to noise associated with logic ground. As we have stated, this is one of those grey areas of controversy and folklore. In fact, if we all got on an airplane and flew to Europe, we would find a philosophy of grounding that might make no sense whatsoever. The laws of physics don't change from one continent to another, but the practical application of electrical practices and terminology are so different that we might think so. Of course, after we had learned the European system, it would make perfect sense from a scientific point of view.

How does this discussion apply to surge suppressors? We have shown that the simple surge suppressor is a common-mode noise generator. We may feel warm and fuzzy knowing that a high-energy impulse has been diverted; it has been prevented from damaging our power supply. But, most people have no idea that electricity travels in circuits and that diverted energy can enter the logic circuits through stray capacitance or ground loops.

So what can be done? Fig. 7-10 shows how all three MOVs might be applied to divert both normal- and common-mode noise. Remember, common-mode noise is a voltage that appears common to the line and neutral with respect to ground. In Fig. 7-10, we see that MOV 1 will take care of diverting the normal-mode noise, a voltage measured from line to neutral. MOVs 2 and 3 are needed for common-mode protection. Either one will operate if the common-mode voltage appearing across them exceeds the threshold of the MOV.

MOV 2 alone doesn't help much. It's a poor choice for normal-mode protection and it leaves the neutral line untouched for common-mode protection. MOV 3 is a good choice to use in combination with MOV 1 since it will divert energy from the neutral line that is routed there by MOV 1. In essence, MOV 3 bonds the neutral and ground lines together, providing common-mode protection, and thereby eliminating the impedance in the neutral-to-ground loop. MOV 2 can be added to further divert common-mode voltages. But, before this happens, the MOVs will let enough voltage appear across the PC's circuits that processing errors or actual chip damage may occur.

In less expensive surge suppressors, we might find only MOV 1 or MOV 2—sometimes both. The solution for total protection is the use of all three MOVs. Now, no matter where the voltage appears, there is a device that can be a short circuit for excess energy.

The use of three MOVs for total protection is the exception not the rule. Most of the simple surge protectors not only generate common-mode noise when they operate, they offer no common-mode protection.

Complex Surge Circuits

Now we come to the real effective products, which have had some true engineering thought put into their design. These products often cost in excess of $100. Fig. 8-10 shows an example of what the circuit of one might look like. This is just one example. There are any number of combinations that might be just as effective. What we are attempting to show here is the combination of all the elements we have talked about so far.

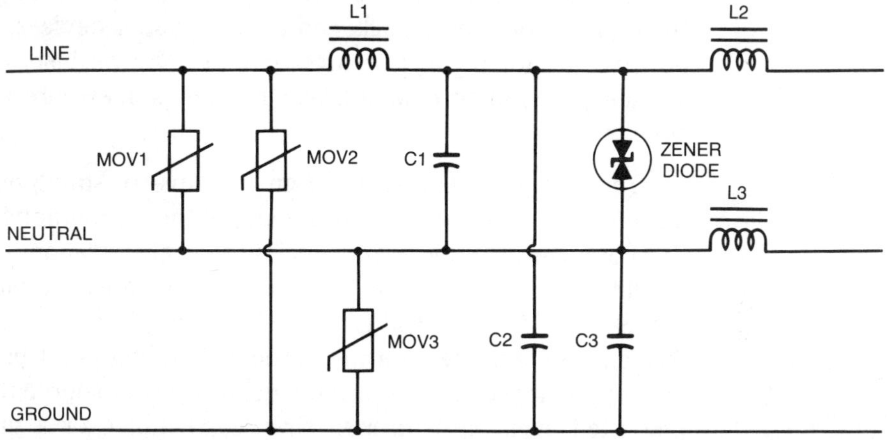

Fig. 8-10. What the schematic of a complex surge-protector circuit might look like.

Let's analyze this circuit as it might react to a very fast impulse as it appears across the surge suppressor. In terms of surge suppression, the zener diode would be the first of the devices activated. Its fast response time would begin conduction of the impulse as soon as the impulse's voltage reached the zener's breakdown voltage. Next, the MOV would be activated, and the bulk of the current would flow through these components.

Meanwhile, inductance L1 and capacitance C1 are stripping away the high-frequency components of the impulse's leading edge. Inductance L2 is a choke that blocks the flow of noise toward the load. In practice, we would probably not see both L1 and L2 in the circuit. The filter section might be constructed of just one choke on the line. Also, MOVs 2 and 3, along with capacitors C2 and C3 and coil L3, have been added for complete common-mode protection.

Two Additional Points

For the sake of simplicity, we have left a few things out of the circuit shown in Fig. 8-10. These missing items do not affect the operation of the circuit, but they are essential. Fuses or circuit breakers and status indicators must be used for complete product utility. If the MOVs have shorted out, or somehow given up their life, we must have some indication that the unit needs attention. It does no good to spend $100 on a product that can't tell you when it has done its job and must be repaired or replaced. After all, it's the computer we are worried about. The surge-suppressor manufacturer must design his product with this worry in mind also.

Another fact that must be highlighted before we move on is that not all surge protectors come packaged as multi-outlet devices. Some come packaged with wire pigtails or lugs so they may be inserted at the building service or mounted near a breaker panel, somewhere upstream from the computer.

This is a very good idea from a couple of standpoints. First, it takes advantage of the inductive cushioning of the wiring between the panel and the computer. At high frequencies, this presents an impedance that is roughly equivalent to the L2 and L3 inductance of our circuit given in Fig. 8-10. Also, if the surge device is lacking in common-mode protection, placing it nearer the neutral-to-ground bonding point presents a relatively lower impedance path toward the nearest power source than what might be presented by a path through stray capacitance or a ground loop in the computer system.

Of course, most of us do not have the skill or bravery to go mucking about in the breaker panel. So the product that plugs into a wall outlet is the typical purchase. It is good to know that these other devices are available, both since their application in front of a panel will protect every branch circuit and for the reasons stated above.

But surge protectors have limitations no matter how fancy they are. Product life, ruggedness, noise bandwidths with the inability to attenuate transients at all points on the sine wave, and common-mode noise conversion are among those limitations. As we will see in the next chapter, there are products that overcome these limitations entirely. But the single most important difficulty that a buyer must face when selecting a product is to see through all the hype and fancy packaging so as to compare designs, power ratings in joules, and see the protection per dollar that is being delivered.

9 Power-Line Conditioners

In this chapter, we will introduce another device that is used to solve power problems—the *transformer*. But before we get deeply involved in a discussion of transformers, we must take yet another look at terms we are using.

The term, *power-line conditioner*, is a term that might be applied to most any product that is connected to the electrical line. Filters, surge suppressors, UPS, and voltage regulators are all power conditioners of one type or another. We can further define *conditioning* as "changing" or "modifying" something. To further narrow our terms, let's define conditioning as something that is always changing or modifying. This would eliminate filters and surge suppressors since they do not always change or modify something; they are inactive until the right set of circumstances take place.

On the other hand, there are products that do condition power all the time but perform other enhanced functions as well. Voltage regulators, for example, not only condition power, but they also adjust for variations in voltage, while UPS products provide power when the utility supply fails.

In this chapter, we will be talking about products that *only* condition power and that *always* condition power. This may seem a bit confusing. Why are we going to this extreme to explain this fairly simple point? Simply because the uncomplicated, bare-bones, no-frills power conditioner is the single wisest investment that the average user can make. It is a far better product than a surge suppressor, although it costs more. And it will solve the vast majority of all the power problems that we will ever encounter, far less expensively than many of the other products we will discuss.

And, yet, the simple power conditioner is probably the least popular of all power products on the market. Why? Because what they do is not simple to explain. They don't just suppress spikes. They don't regulate voltage. They don't provide backup power. So what do they do? They condition power, and that doesn't paint a dramatic mental picture for marketing executives to sell to the public. In fact, some executives have changed their terminology and now use the word "filter" to better describe the product's function. But "filter" implies something that can act only on an engineered band of noise frequencies. Power conditioners act to eliminate *all* noise frequencies, and that's the beauty of the product. Before we can explore these seemingly mystical qualities, we need to understand the heart of the technology involved.

Isolation Transformers

Transformer. Now there is a word we have heard a time or two. We know from Chapter 2 that transformers are amazingly efficient, around 96–97% efficient. We also know that "power in" equals "power out."

We made a fleeting comment in Chapter 6 about a transformer's propensity to pass normal-mode noise. But if a transformer will pass noise, why call it an *isolation transformer*? Remember that in Chapter 2, we discussed the construction of a transformer as being one coil of wire inside another, both wound jelly-roll style.

These two coils, the primary and the secondary transformer windings, are physically separated from one another by air and other insulating material. This type of construction inherently isolates the primary from the secondary. So, in that sense, all of these type transformers are isolation transformers. But we are talking about *noise isolation*. This type of isolation calls for some special design considerations.

Capacitive Coupling

Because of the proximity of the primary and secondary windings, a transformer will display a characteristic called *interwinding capacitance*. This is the effect of the facings of the windings displaying capacitive-like qualities at certain noise frequencies. This stray capacitance can be illustrated as one capacitor that bridges the distance between the primary and secondary windings (Fig. 9-1).

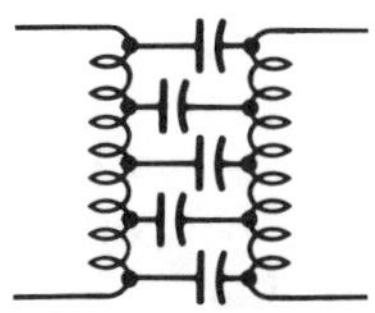

(A) Multiple stray capacitance.

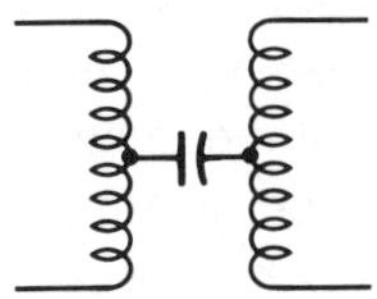

(B) Stray capacitance simplified to one value of capacitance.

Fig. 9-1. Stray, interwinding capacitance exists inside a transformer.

High-frequency noise can, therefore, use this path to travel from the primary to the secondary of the transformer. In order to prevent this, or at least attenuate it, we can significantly reduce the interwinding capacitance by installing a *Faraday electrostatic shield* between the primary and secondary windings (Fig. 9-2).

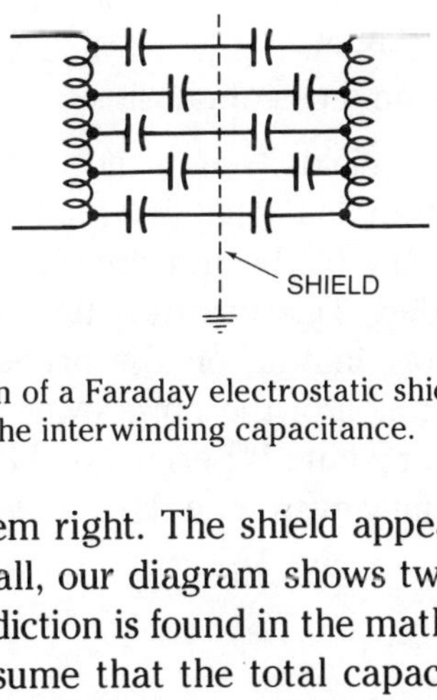

Fig. 9-2. The addition of a Faraday electrostatic shield greatly reduces the interwinding capacitance.

Wait! That doesn't seem right. The shield appears to produce twice as much capacitance. After all, our diagram shows twice as many capacitors. The answer to this contradiction is found in the mathematics of electricity. It would seem logical to assume that the total capacitance would equal the total of each individual capacitor being added to the next, or

$$C_T = C1 + C2 + \ldots$$

In fact, that is the formula for finding the total capacitance of capacitors in parallel. The formula for finding the total capacitance of capacitors in series is

$$C_T = \frac{1}{C1} + \frac{1}{C2} + \ldots$$

In other words, we are using the reciprocal of each individual value. Now it is apparent why we can state that the addition of a shield greatly reduces capacitive coupling.

Well, if one is good, might not two be better? In fact, this is usually the case. A second shield tied to the primary winding acts as a low-impedance path for common-mode noise to travel from one shield to the next. This path diverts common-mode noise away from the winding, thus eliminating common- to normal-mode conversion by the transformer. Double-shielded isolation transformers are a popular product in the three-phase power world. Large products can accommodate the additional material and associated costs much better than a product which is oriented toward PCs. In fact, some of the transformers for PCs have no shield at all. While this holds the top-end normal-mode attenuation to around −20 to −40 dB, they do have something that helps just as well, which we will discuss shortly. Certainly, a double-shielded isolation transformer would be a rare find in the PC world.

Let's take this one step further. What about triple shielding? Again, this is something a specifying engineer might call for in the plans for a large three-phase installation. It is never found in PC products. And there is considerable controversy as to whether three shields actually help reduce noise coupling much more than double shielding. Most manufacturers of large, computer-grade transformers do not offer a triple-shielded device, except on a custom basis.

The shield, itself, is most often a solid copper sheet—a little thicker than aluminum foil—that is wound, jelly-roll style, between the primary and secondary of the transformer. Notice in Fig. 9-2 that we show the shield grounded. This has the effect of completing a noise-current path for any noise originating on the primary side of the transformer (Fig. 9-3). This keeps much of the noise away from the secondary and the sensitive load. Not everything is perfect, and it is possible for some noise to transfer to the secondary even with the addition of a shield. We will deal with this problem later.

Common-Mode Noise

A glance at Fig. 9-3 shows that the noise the shield is designed to deal with is mainly in the common mode. Any time that ground is a path for noise, we

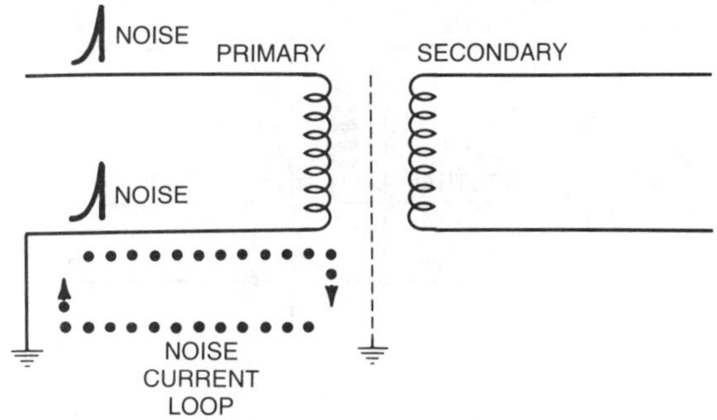

Fig. 9-3. The addition of a shield produces a loop for the flow of noise current, without its being transferred to the secondary.

are talking about common-mode noise. The addition of a shield will raise the noise attenuation characteristic of a transformer to about −60 dB. This means that a 1000-volt impulse will appear as 1 volt on the secondary. There are manufacturers who make claims of much higher noise attenuation. And, in fact, even a standard shielded transformer will display a wide range of attenuation, depending on the frequency of the signal applied. This device is better at lower frequencies than at higher. Overall, −60 dB is a good average and more than adequate for the PC environment. A company that is making wild claims about noise attenuation, over −100 dB, is making a dubious and almost unprovable claim.

There is another valuable feature of transformers that will totally eliminate common-mode noise as a concern. It is a *National Electric Code* safety requirement that one leg of an isolation transformer's secondary be grounded and identified as a neutral. Fig. 9-4 shows how this is accomplished. This is the neutral-to-ground bond we have been talking about all through this book. A power conditioner allows the ground to be reestablished close to the computer. Now, neutral is solidly referenced to ground through the impedance of the bonding strap and not through any stray capacitance that may exist in the load. Any common-mode voltage that might appear from either side of the transformer has its current short-circuited to ground through the bond. And, of course, any voltage developing across the bond will be extremely low.

Fig. 9-5 shows before and after photographs of common-mode noise. Obviously, there exists significant noise on the line, but the addition of the power conditioner has eliminated it. As we have stated, common-mode noise is the most serious problem that PCs must deal with. Tying the neutral and ground together near the computer is the answer.

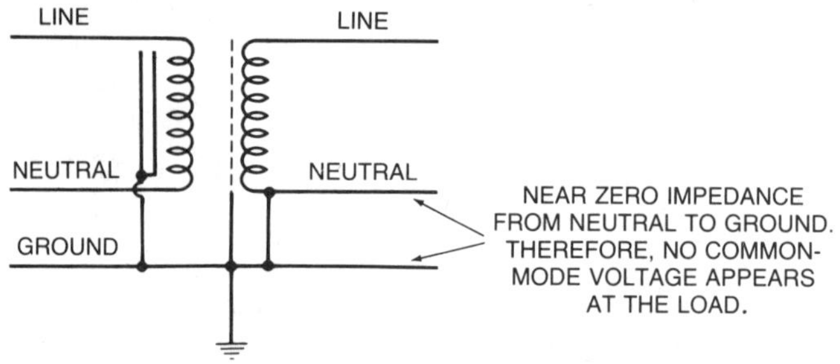

Fig. 9-4. The neutral-to-ground bonding point is established on the secondary winding, thus eliminating common-mode voltage drops.

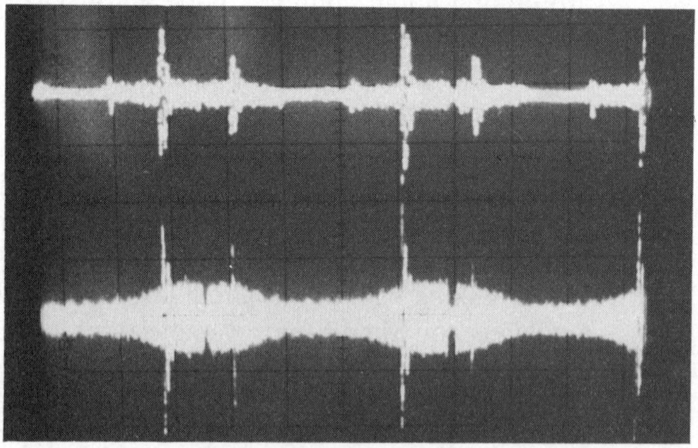

(A) Before conditioning.

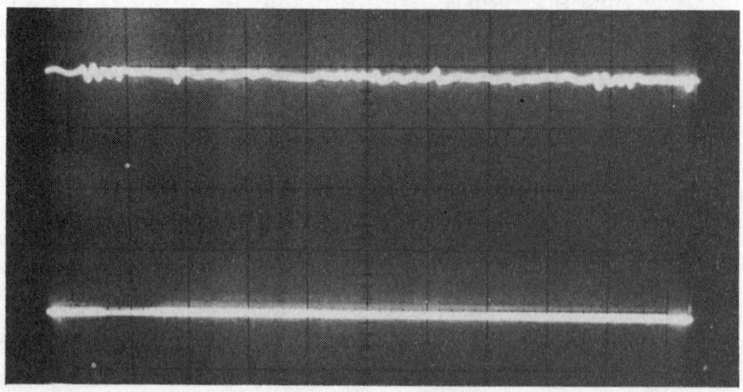

(B) After conditioning.

Fig. 9-5. The addition of a power conditioner with the neutral and ground bonded together virtually eliminates common-mode noise.

Before we leave this subject, let's take another look at Fig. 9-4. We see that the neutral and ground are tied together. We also see that the shield and core of the transformer are tied together. This is single-point grounding. Another ground element that we do not see in the diagram is the chassis of the power conditioner itself. It is clear that all chassis are tied to ground. But we bring this up to emphasize what the designer of such a device is trying to do. Every effort is being made to hold ground and anything referenced to it to the lowest possible impedance with respect to one another. This eliminates stray paths through the case of the unit, through the load, or differentials between the primary and secondary windings. We have established a clean, single point of ground reference for anything connected to this device.

There is another advantage to this design setup. Often, printers and other computer peripherals are a considerable source of common-mode noise or ground-loop voltages. This grounding of the neutral line is a direct path for those signals, thereby keeping them from propagating to other loads.

Normal-Mode Noise

Normal-mode noise is noise that appears from the line to neutral. The 120-volt supply voltage is a normal-mode signal. It is transferred from the primary windings to the secondary by currents induced by the changing magnetic field. It stands to reason that normal-mode noise would behave in much the same way.

An increase in any current flowing in the primary windings will result in an increased current flow in the secondary windings, regardless of the frequency of the applied voltage. The transformer principle applies to all frequencies, not just 60 Hz. We must realize that the ability of a transformer to pass normal-mode signals does vary as the frequency of the applied signal varies. After all, a supply transformer is engineered to pass 60-Hz power with efficiencies of about 97%.

The efficient transfer of energy at other frequencies will be different. And this frequency response will not be uniform as the frequency increases. Because of this, we can expect some distortion in the noise-impulse waveform as it passes through the transformer. But, the overall magnitude of a normal-mode noise impulse will be relatively unaffected by the insertion of a transformer in the circuit.

Before we talk about how to solve this problem—the problem of normal-mode noise passing through a transformer—let's talk about another source of normal-mode noise: *conversion*. By conversion, we mean common- to normal-mode conversion. Fig. 9-6 shows common-mode noise appearing on the primary windings of a transformer while it becomes normal-mode noise on the secondary windings. How can this be?

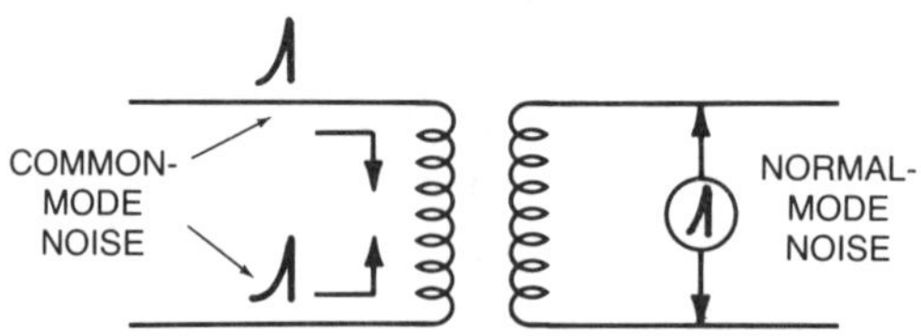

Fig. 9-6. A transformer converts common-mode noise into normal-mode noise.

In Chapter 6, we discussed how common-mode noise appears at the terminals of a transformer. Since the impulse is common to both the line and neutral, these two impulses appear across the transformer 180° out of phase. Ideally, this means that a cancellation will take place in the primary coil. Theory is one thing, reality is another.

Because of imperfections in the construction of transformers, reactive as well as capacitive discontinuities exist. This affects the speed of the noise travelling through the primary windings, as well as the distribution of current along the wires. These imperfections result in an imperfect "bucking" or "cancelling" of the common-mode signals. The resultant current from these variations produces a differential from the line to neutral in the secondary windings. This action causes common-mode voltages in the primary to produce normal-mode voltages in the secondary windings.

Lumped Capacitance

Whether the normal-mode noise on the secondary is coupled directly from the primary or converted by the transformer into normal-mode noise, there are two things that can be done to dramatically eliminate it. The application of *lumped capacitance*, connected from line to neutral on the secondary side, can provide a lower impedance path through the capacitive elements than through the load. Also, the application of an MOV from line to neutral will assist in handling high-energy impulses that might pass through the transformer (Fig. 9-7). We also see a second shield introduced specifically to eliminate

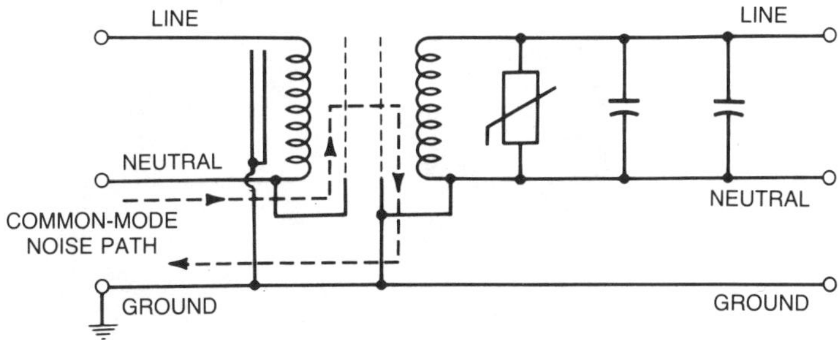

Fig. 9-7. The addition of an MOV, along with lumped capacitance, will dramatically attenuate normal-mode noise and high-energy normal-mode impulses.

common- to normal-mode conversion. This shield, however, is almost never to be found in products designed for the PC market.

Let's see how this combination of MOV and lumped capacitance works to attenuate normal-mode noise. Fig. 9-8 shows a photo of normal-mode noise. Wow, that's a lot of noise. Actually when the photo in Fig. 9-8 was taken, the gain on the oscilloscope was turned up as far as possible. Or, put another way, the sensitivity was turned to the highest setting. The noise at this setting literally fills the screen. Next, we put the power conditioner into the line, using the same settings. Nothing else was changed. Notice the dramatic difference (Fig. 9-9).

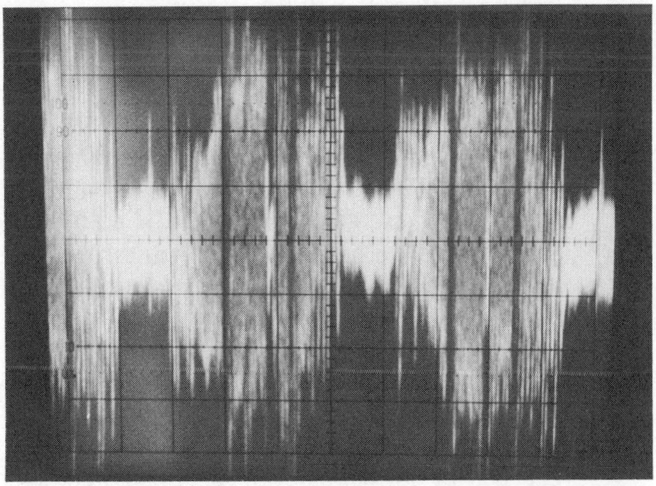

Fig. 9-8. Normal-mode noise fills the oscilloscope screen.

The power conditioner has obviously done several things to the noise. Most obvious is the magnitude of the noise, which has been reduced significantly.

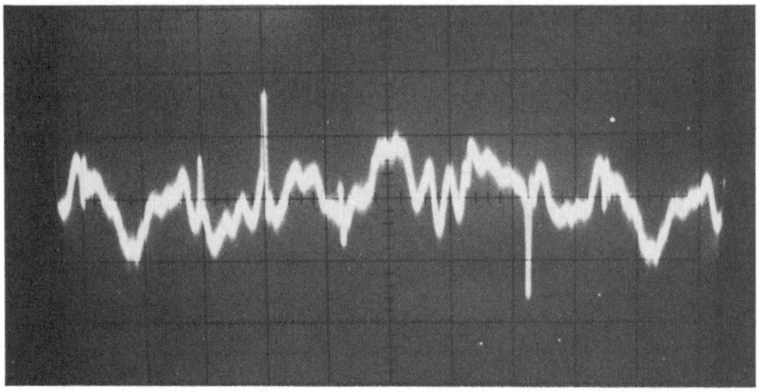

Fig. 9-9. The same noise shown in Fig. 9-8 after a power conditioner, using the circuit design shown in Fig. 9-7, is put in the line.

This is the most important effect of the power conditioner. Secondly, all the high-frequency components seem to have been stripped away. And lastly, the noise that is left has a much rounder look to it. Another way of describing this might be to say that the slope of the noise is less steep.

These last two effects are a result of the transformer working with the capacitors, much in the same way that a filter works. The inductance of the transformer windings has slowed down the rise time of the noise, while the capacitors have provided a return path. This action shunts the noise away from the load as we see it on the screen.

Clearly, care must be taken to select the proper values for the capacitors. It is not unheard of for these capacitors to form resonances with the load elements, causing disruptive problems, including the burnout of capacitors in the load devices. The capacitors work together with the inductance of the transformer. As frequency increases, capacitive reactance decreases. This means more and more noise sees the path through the capacitors as a much lower impedance path than the path through the load. Meanwhile, the inductive reactance associated with the windings in the transformer increases, opposing the flow of high-frequency current. This combination, if engineered properly, can be an effective normal-mode filter. This is why some companies call their product a filter instead of a power conditioner.

There are more benefits to this lumped capacitance than merely the reduction of normal-mode noise. Should common-mode noise appear on the live side of the transformer secondary, the lumped capacitance provides a low-impedance path to ground. This works both ways. The common-mode source may indeed be upstream from the conditioner. This is the main perceived mission of the conditioner, to block noise from moving downstream. There might also be significant common-mode noise generated on the load side. The capacitors complete a noise-current loop, in much the same way as the neutral-to-ground bond, again keeping the noise from propagating to other devices.

Other Benefits

We stated earlier in the chapter that power-line conditioners will solve most of the power problems that a PC will experience. As we will see more vividly in the next chapter, a simple transformer will not compensate for line-voltage drops or power outages. We will also see why we needn't be concerned about "sags" except in regard to certain types of equipment. "Outages" will be covered later.

It is the software disruption and hardware damage that most users are worried about. The power-line conditioner is a complete, portable, friendly, electrical environment for the personal computer. Because of its efficiency, the power-line conditioner gives off very little heat—certainly very little acoustical noise. Conditioners come suitably packaged for the home or office environment, and, for the most part, they are UL listed. More on that subject in a moment.

Another benefit of the power-line conditioner is that it is a low-impedance device. What this means is that, to the load, it appears as if the transformer is not even there. When the load's instantaneous current demands an increase, the transformer delivers the required current. An isolation transformer has an impedance of from 3%–6%, with 5% being about normal. How this percentage is derived is beyond the scope of this discussion. But there are devices on the market with ratings of around 15%. What this really means is that a low-impedance device does not impede the passage of current through it. An isolation transformer can pass currents that are 500% to 1000% of its rated load for very short periods of time. Devices with higher internal impedances cannot do so, and may even damage themselves or starve the load for current if they tried.

In Chapter 6, we discussed the current demands of a *switching power supply*. It draws all the current it needs at the peak of the sine wave. Earlier, we discussed *inrush currents*. Motors starting and stopping, devices being turned on and off, and a R/W head seeking across a disk—all these things combine to make a computer system an ever-changing, dynamic load. The power source servicing this system must be able to deliver current on demand. This task a low-impedance isolation transformer can do admirably.

UL Listed Devices

For years, Underwriter's Laboratories, Inc. (UL) has been testing equipment to certain performance standards. The UL listing and the associated label have long been a sign of safety for the user. We certainly do not want to argue UL's ability to certify product safety—safety cannot be sacrificed.

But, as of July 2, 1987, Underwriter's Laboratories took a giant step forward. It was then that a brand new standard was introduced—the *UL 1449 Standard for Transient and Surge Suppression*. UL's new standard starts where the IEEE 587 standard leaves off. It uses the IEEE standard as a starting point and then clarifies many of the areas left open previously.

The waveshape that is used is a 6000-volt impulse with a 1.2-μs rise time. This then decays over 50 μs. For plug-in-type devices, 500 amperes are used. After this initial hit, a series of smaller impulses are fed to the units.

The standard covers areas of ground continuity and safety as well as performance. UL 1449 is a welcome step forward and a criteria the cautious buyer should be aware of.

Power Distribution

Our discussion so far has assumed a particular kind of power conditioner. Most small power conditioners come in sizes like 200, 300, 500, 800, 1000, 1500, and 2000 VA (voltamperes). These units generally plug right into a standard wall receptacle. They often will have two or more receptacles for power distribution. Each unit has a particular rating, either in VA, as stated above, or in amperes. It is important that the rated load not be exceeded either by plugging too many devices into the conditioner or by using a lot of extension cords. Several units can be used where more power is desirable. Each unit should be tied together with the others, by using a heavy bonding strap to equalize any chassis voltage differentials.

Often, as the size of the unit goes up, the number of receptacles on the back panel go up. Because of the larger size of the cabinet, as well as the ampacity of the unit, more outlets can be accommodated. Also, with increased ampacity comes the capability of mounting 20-ampere receptacles on the unit. Most manufacturers have a variety of combinations that are standard. We mention this subject for the simple reason that proper power distribution is vital for the optimum use of a line conditioner. As stated in Chapter 5, it is desirable to avoid ground loops by using a common power strip. In the case of power conditioners, all peripherals should be plugged into the unit. This may not be possible, and when it is not, a grounding strap should tie all chassis to a single-point ground.

There is another type of power conditioner that has no power distribution. These devices follow the same design criteria that we have laid out in this chapter. However, they are meant to be "hard-wired" upstream from a power panel. This means that every branch circuit fed from the panel board will enjoy fully conditioned power. Typically, these devices are in commercial, as opposed to consumer, enclosures and are meant for installation in equipment rooms and electrical closets.

To take advantage of a commercial-grade power conditioner, it is necessary for each branch circuit to feed some type of computer or related equipment. It would not do, for instance, to condition the power for a panel that fed both office electronic equipment and some type of corrupting equipment, like copiers or air conditioners. If the panel feeds devices that are common power polluters, the computer equipment must be serviced from another panel, or the conditioning should take place downstream from the panel.

These types of conditioners are available in sizes from about 2 kVA to hundreds of kVA. In the office environment, their application could be used to support networks or large numbers of work stations. We will explore this concept where other products are concerned at a later time.

The concept of conditioned power is one that we will find throughout the rest of the book. We will see other ways of doing it using different technologies. Or, as will be found in the next chapter, we will see this basic concept expanded to include other more exotic features.

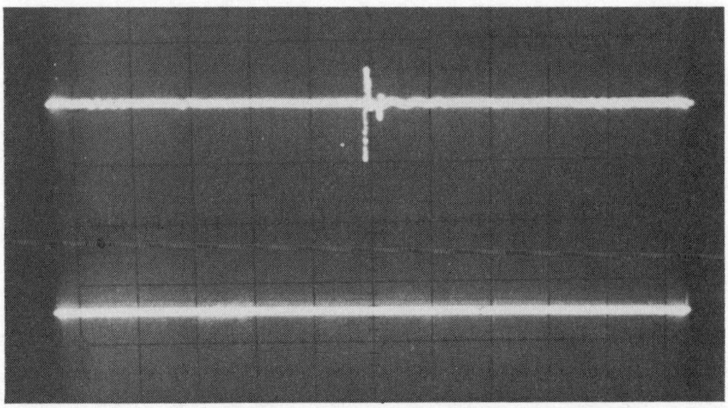

Fig. 9-10. A power-line conditioner has attenuated the 900-volt impulse to 7.5 volts, but has not converted the noise from normal to common mode.

But, before we leave this chapter, you may have wondered how a power-line conditioner handles our 900-volt impulse. Fig. 9-10 shows a photo of this. No normal- to common-mode conversion has taken place, and the device has attenuated the impulse to 7.5 volts.

10 Voltage Regulators

We will discuss two basic kinds of voltage regulators in this chapter. But, before we do, we must put the entire subject of voltage regulation in some kind of perspective where PCs are concerned. On the face of it, voltage regulation sounds like a very attractive proposition. If we look back to the subject of power quality, we will see that there are a significant number of power-line sags and surges throughout the year. Surely we want to properly protect our machines from these kinds of electrical variations.

However, a glimpse back at Chapter 6 will confound this notion to a large degree. In that chapter, we discussed the historical transition of computer power supplies from linear supplies to switching power supplies. Linear power supplies must have a constant flow of supply voltage within certain well-defined limits. Switching power supplies, on the other hand, must have a steady unimpeded source of current. Remember that we pegged the voltage range for a switching power supply at about 80 volts to 135 volts. This window varies from one manufacturer to another.

As we will see in this chapter, this is approximately the same range as that of a good voltage regulator. To put it more directly, a voltage regulator has a range roughly approximating the acceptable limits of a switching power supply. If that's true, who needs voltage regulation? Almost no one!

Like many things in life, there are no simple answers, and there are perfectly legitimate circumstances where voltage regulation is the correct application of technology. But strictly speaking, personal computers and their peripherals do not require voltage regulation.

Why Use Voltage Regulation?

Why use voltage regulation? If all of the preceding statements are true, why would a manufacturer build a voltage regulator in the first place? And, furthermore, what are the circumstances where voltage regulation is a requirement?

Let's look at the first question first. As we will see, voltage regulation is a side benefit of some power-conditioning technologies. But it is also a costly add-on to others, which may significantly reduce the reliability of an otherwise superior power conditioner. Why would a manufacturer do this? A lack of understanding of the PC marketplace and of technology is the only answer. The explanation for this leads us to the next question.

When is voltage regulation necessary? The obvious first answer to this question is in linear power supplies. There are a few applications where older or exotic equipment is used that contains linear power supplies. These pieces of equipment not only need power conditioning, but they need voltage regulation as well. Some of these applications might involve industrial, military, or medical environments. But even then, the power supply of choice is usually a switch that doesn't care much about the voltage it sees.

Another area where voltage regulation may be required is in the mini- and mainframe environment. For many years, it was standard practice for power-supply engineers to design shutdown features into the power supplies of the larger computers. For a wide variety of reasons, they did not want their machines running on power that had surged or sagged beyond acceptable limits. When the power supply sensed the voltage wandering, it would shut down the equipment. It was for this reason that voltage regulation became so popular. No DP manager wants to go down every time the power fluctuates.

This practice has continued until today. Even after the rationale for such circuits has gone away because of design advancements, like switching power supplies and smaller machines, minicomputer manufacturers may include this feature in their units. This can bedevil a site for no good reason. But voltage regulation is stuck in the psyche of many in the industry. And many manufacturers of computer power equipment started by designing products for this industry. Now they are manufacturing equipment for the PC market and this prejudice toward voltage regulation has followed. This explains why they might include it as a design criteria.

While the problems of minicomputers do not affect PCs directly, they may affect some environments where PCs are installed and this will cause a need for voltage regulation. But beyond these general areas, the need for voltage regulation for PCs is questionable.

Tap-Switching Regulators

In an earlier chapter, we talked about a concept called "turns ratio." We know that "power in" equals "power out." So if the turns of the primary winding equal the turns of the secondary, the voltage on the output will equal the voltage on the input.

Let's look back at Fig. 9-7. We know that this power-line conditioner will give us a clean noise-free environment. But since "power in" equals "power out," we will always see the same voltage at the output that appears on the input. The voltage may sag, and the voltage may surge—all slow-moving voltage changes will pass right through.

But what would happen if we could change the number of turns in the primary as the voltage fluctuated? Let's say we could take a few turns off of the primary. Now the voltage at the secondary would be slightly higher since the turns ratio would have changed. More turns on the secondary in relation to the primary would mean a higher voltage.

For years, engineers have been trying to figure out how to change the turns ratio to achieve a stable voltage at the output of a device as the input changed. A number of unique approaches have been used. Most of these methods used some sort of mechanical motion to make and break new connections on the windings of a transformer, and thus change the turns ratio. But mechanical action proved far too slow for typical voltage changes. Then, with the revolution in semiconductor devices, engineers found solid-state switches that could handle the job of changing taps electronically. Fig. 10-1 shows this basic concept at work.

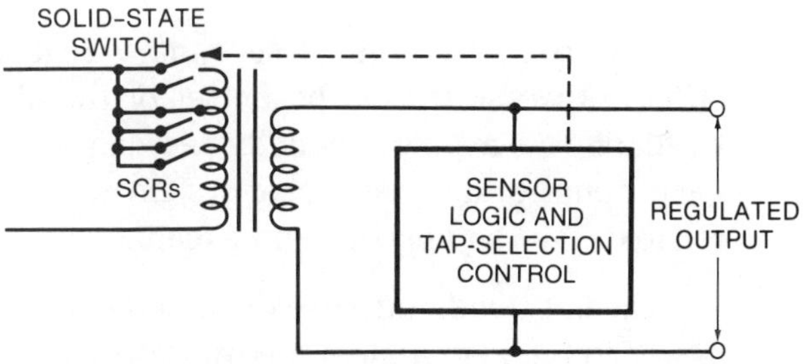

Fig. 10-1. A tap-switching regulator changes the output voltage by changing the turns ratio of a transformer.

Silicon-controlled rectifiers are usually used as solid-state switches to adjust the turns ratio for line-voltage fluctuations. A sensing circuit measures the voltage, and as it changes, the circuit sends the proper bias voltage to the correct SCR. The SCR begins conducting through the tap to which it is attached. Each tap is embedded in the windings of the primary or secondary, depending on the design. By properly placing these taps, the turns ratio can be adjusted in precise steps as the input voltage varies.

The design shown in Fig. 10-1 measures the voltage on the secondary side of the transformer and feeds this information back to the SCRs on the primary side so action can be taken. This primary-to-secondary separation is somewhat slower than the next two designs we will see. The ability to switch fast is essential if the unit is to respond to sags and surges.

In order to improve this, a design like the one shown in Fig. 10-2 can be used. Here we see the taps have been moved to the secondary side, where the association of the taps with the sensing circuit make for a few milliseconds faster response time. We might note that the advantage of having the taps on the secondary is a much finer voltage adjustment for the load. Dynamic changes in the load can affect voltage just as a sag might. Therefore, taps on the secondary can respond to both load changes and supply changes.

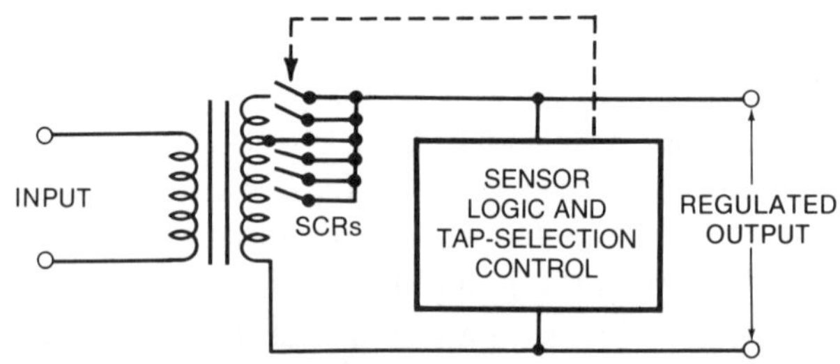

Fig. 10-2. Changing taps on the secondary provides finer voltage adjustments.

Another advantage of secondary regulation is the placement of the SCRs. As we stated at the outset of the chapter, the addition of voltage regulation to a power conditioner can sacrifice reliability. Increasing the parts count of any electronic system will inherently make the system less reliable. Tap switchers are no exception.

The line conditioner we discussed in the last chapter will always provide power to the load, unless the transformer burns up. That is extremely rare. Certainly, the capacitors and MOV may fail, but power will still flow to the computer. Forcing supply current to flow through a solid-state device, like an SCR, will make the unit less reliable. Putting the SCRs on the secondary side of the transformer will provide inductive cushioning that will protect them to a certain degree.

It is no secret that switching creates noise. And placing SCRs on the load side of a transformer will transmit any noise created by the switching action directly toward the PC. In order to get away from this problem, a design like the one shown in Fig. 10-3 is used. This combines the advantages of the noise-reduction capabilities of the transformer with a fast switching action. Obviously, it sacrifices SCR vulnerability and load-side regulation.

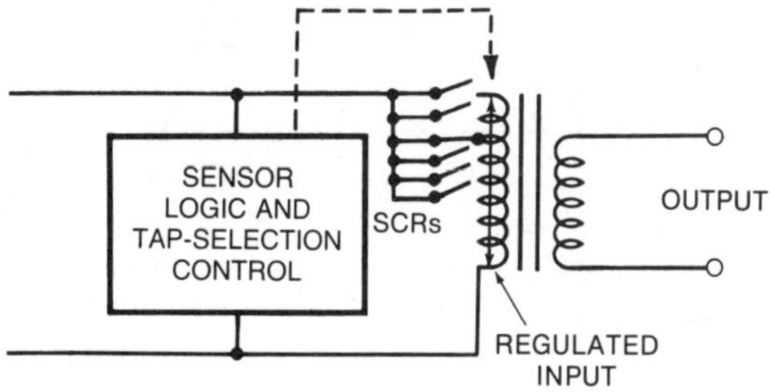

Fig. 10-3. Tap switching with a regulated input.

Let's look at one more design consideration. In the early days of tap-switching technology, voltage was used as the switching trigger. In other words, the sensing circuit would wait until the voltage dropped to zero before switching. But, as can be seen in Fig. 10-4, significant current is still flowing at the zero-voltage crossing point of the sine wave if the computer has a lagging power factor. This switching action created large impulses that often interfered with computer operations.

The answer to this was to sense for the zero-current crossing point and turn the SCRs on and off when no current was flowing through them. This change dramatically decreased the amount of switching noise generated. Superior tap switchers use the zero-current crossing design.

The typical range of regulation from tap switchers designed for the PC market is −15% to +10%. Or, to put it another way, from about 102 volts to 132 volts. There are some families of products that regulate −27% to +15%. Even this is still within the range of a switching power supply. Not only that, but as the voltage sags, the load draws more current to compensate. At some point, enough current should be drawn along a branch circuit that a circuit breaker should trip.

A note on SCR reliability. The reliability issue cannot be ignored. SCRs have a high initial mortality. Studies have shown it to be as high as 14% in some cases. We are not saying that products fail. We are saying the SCRs fail. That is why proper burn-in is absolutely essential in order to weed out those semiconductors that are likely to fail during the first few days of operation. If care is

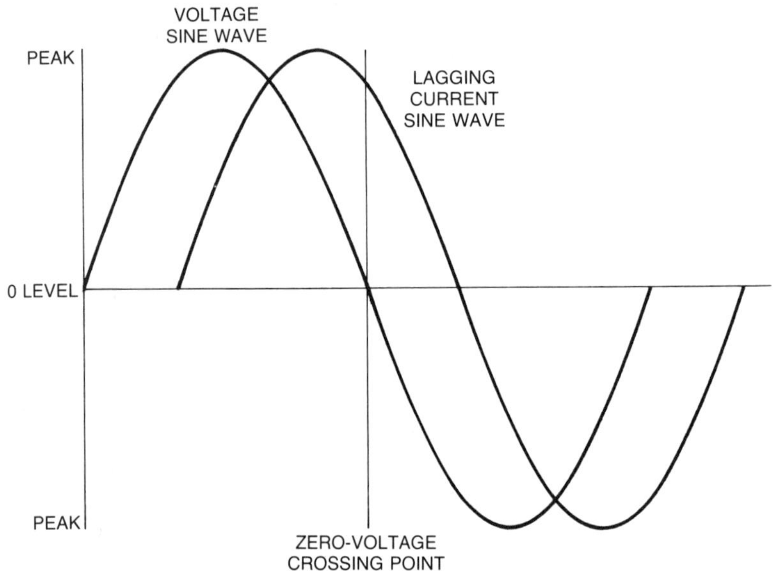

Fig. 10-4. When voltage is zero, significant current flows.

taken in selecting the right SCR with the proper current-handling margin of safety, and if proper testing is done before the unit leaves the factory, tap switchers can be manufactured that are very reliable.

We will move on now to the other kind of voltage regulator that we find on the market. But, before the chapter is over, we will come back to the subject of tap switchers—once we have put the entire subject in perspective with a discussion of ferroresonant regulators.

Ferroresonant Voltage Regulators

Ferroresonant voltage regulators, or *ferros*, depend on a technology that is radically different from either tap switchers or the kind of power-line conditioners which we have been discussing. These products are also known as *constant-voltage transformers*, or *CVTs*, but we will refer to them as *ferros*. There are companies that like to call them other things which are meant to throw the buyer off the track. But most reputable manufacturers will state in their literature that ferroresonant technology is being used.

We mentioned that ferros are referred to as constant-voltage transformers. This indicates that there must be something about the way they operate that delivers a constant output for a varying input. This is true since ferroresonant transformers operate in a way that is different from the simple isolation transformers we normally find in power-line conditioners and tap-switching regulators.

We know from earlier discussions that the current flowing in the primary winding of a transformer induces current in the secondary winding, because magnetic lines of flux cut through the windings of the secondary. As current in the primary increases, the total amount of flux increases. More lines of flux means that more current is induced in the secondary. There is a point at which additional current flow in the primary will not create more flux in the core of the transformer. This point is called *saturation*. The core of the transformer becomes saturated with flux, and a further increase in primary current cannot create more lines of flux, and, therefore, no additional current is induced in the secondary.

A *ferro* uses the principle of saturation to its advantage, in order to regulate voltage. If we could construct a transformer core so that it would easily achieve saturation, we would have a natural voltage regulator. We can't do this with an isolation transformer since current at saturation is close to short-circuit levels. Fig. 10-5 shows a simple diagram of a ferroresonant transformer.

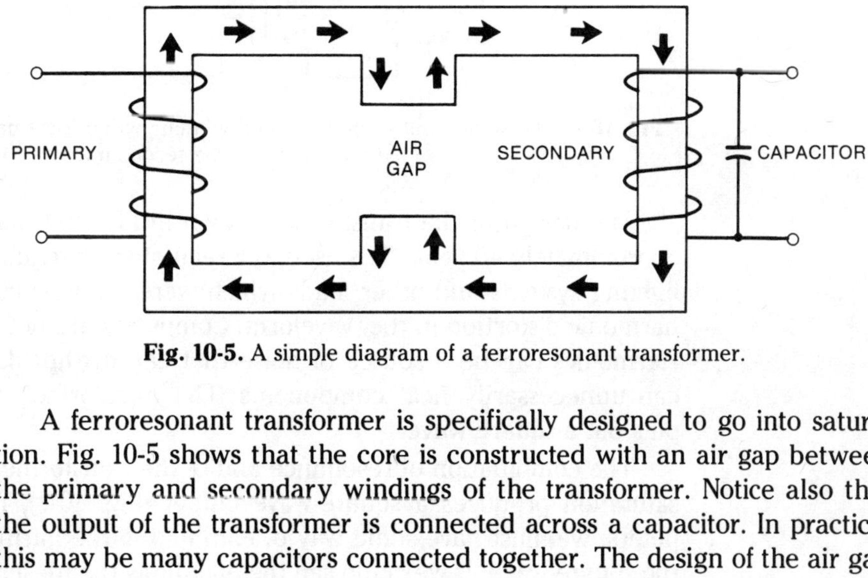

Fig. 10-5. A simple diagram of a ferroresonant transformer.

A ferroresonant transformer is specifically designed to go into saturation. Fig. 10-5 shows that the core is constructed with an air gap between the primary and secondary windings of the transformer. Notice also that the output of the transformer is connected across a capacitor. In practice, this may be many capacitors connected together. The design of the air gap and the value of the capacitance are the key design elements affecting the operational characteristics of the transformer.

The air gap gives the transformer a high reluctance as current flow starts at a low level. This means that the flux is primarily through the outer regions of the core. As the current flow increases, secondary voltage is determined by the turns ratio. As the flux lines increase, the current in the secondary also increases, causing the reactance of the secondary winding to increase. When the inductive reactance of the secondary winding becomes equal to the capacitive reactance, the capacitor and the winding become resonant. This causes the reluctance of the center core to drop and the transformer to go into saturation. Subsequent increases in primary current have a small influence on the secondary.

To compensate for these small voltage variations, another winding is added to the transformer. Strangely enough, this is called the *compensation winding* (Fig. 10-6). It is placed in the electrical circuit of the transformer, in series, opposing the secondary. This works to offset small voltage fluctuations that may come through the transformer even though it is in saturation.

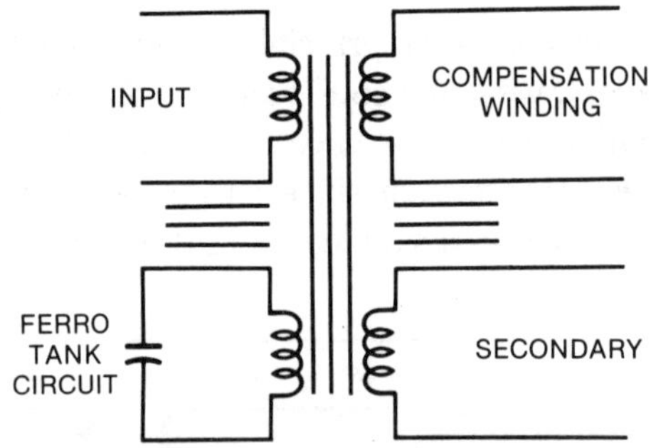

Fig. 10-6. The addition of a compensation winding will offset small voltage variations that appear on the secondary.

The design of the transformer shown in Fig. 10-6 has been around for approximately 40 years. It is used as a regulator for regulating the voltage to lighting systems and other loads which were not particularly disturbed by harmonic distortion in the waveform. Computers are not one of those loads. Harmonics can be a source of noise that can disrupt data processing and can unnecessarily heat components. The transformer shown in Fig. 10-6 puts out a square wave.

The combination of resonance and of the transformer being driven into saturation produces a square-wave output (Fig. 10-7). For use with computers, we must have some way of eliminating the harmonics contained in the square wave. If we could see the equations that describe a sine wave, as opposed to a square wave, we would see that a sine wave is derived in a very straightforward manner using the sine of a function, along with values of time and frequency. The equation for a square wave has all the same elements, along with the numbers 3, 7, 9, 11, 13, 17, . . ., etc. These numbers represent the derivation of odd harmonics that actually compose this type of waveshape. We will not reproduce these equations here since they are full of expressions that would take too long to explain and are not much fun to read—to most readers anyway.

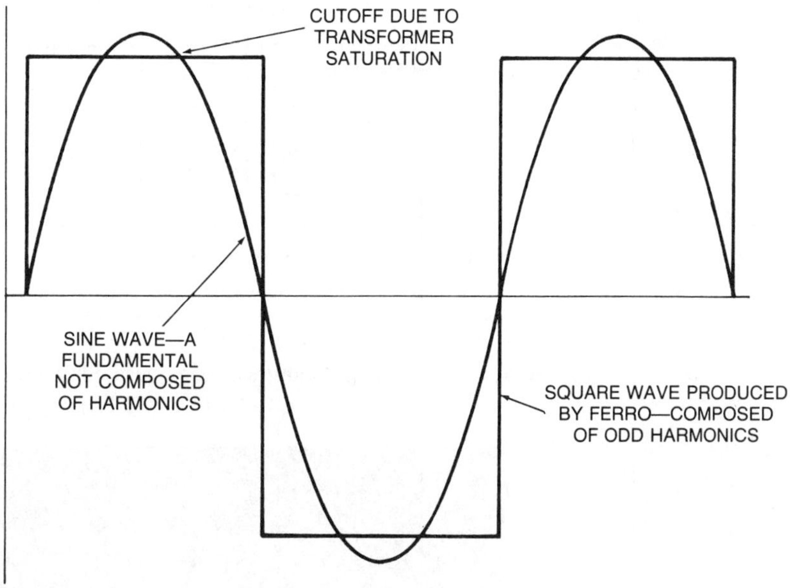

Fig. 10-7. A ferroresonant transformer produces a square-wave output.

To get around this problem, a neutralizing winding is added to the circuit. This winding is magnetically linked not only to the primary but to the secondary (Fig. 10-8). The purpose of this neutralizing winding is to allow the harmonic voltage to appear on this winding, having been coupled from the primary. This harmonic voltage is then fed to the secondary in series opposing, thus cancelling out those nasty odd harmonics. This, along with some filtering, produces a sine-wave waveform that is suitable for use with computers (Fig. 10-9). A note of caution: Not all manufacturers include a neutralizing winding.

A comment about Fig. 10-9 needs to be made. This picture looks like a fairly decent sine wave. What is even more impressive is that Fig. 10-10 shows the sine wave that was fed to the primary of the ferro. This is the same old, rumpled, flat-topped, distorted power waveform we saw in an earlier chapter. The ferro is literally putting out its own sine wave, with little regard for what is feeding it.

The transformer we have presented here is the ideal ferro, or CVT. The picture in Fig. 10-9 was taken at the output of an actual product that is sold

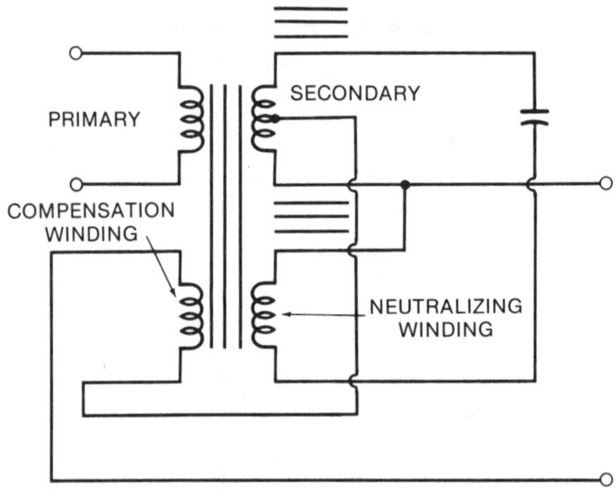

Fig. 10-8. Adding a neutralizing winding, plus additional filtering, will produce a sinusoidal output.

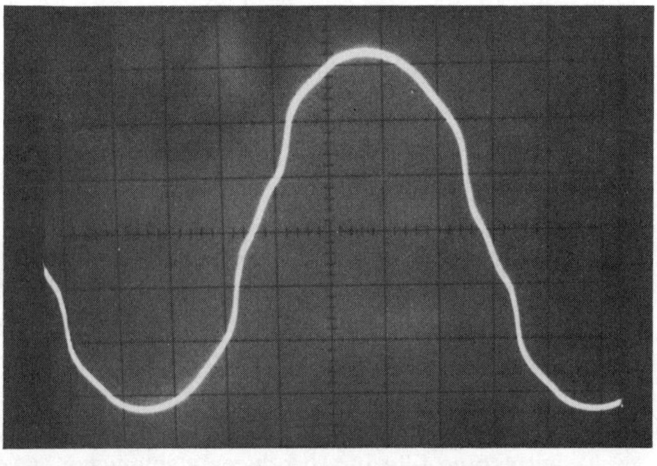

Fig. 10-9. This is the actual sine wave produced by a ferro.

for PC users. It may very well not have the exact same winding design we have discussed, and it probably has no additional filtering, but the principles we have illustrated are common to all of these devices.

Ferros have a wide regulation window—in some cases, from −40% to +20%. They are rugged. Other than the capacitors, which do fail with some regularity but which do not cause the load to loose power in most cases, there are no parts to fail—mechanical or electronic. They also have an inherent ability to suppress normal-mode noise. Because of the saturation of the transformer, impulses cannot penetrate to the secondary wind-

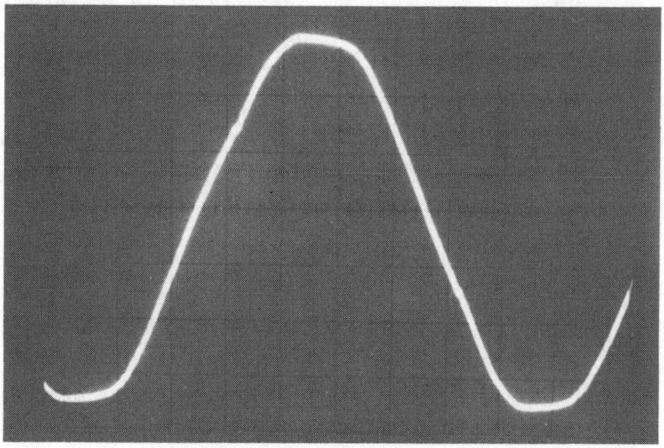

Fig. 10-10. A picture of the sine wave feeding the ferro that produced the output shown in Fig. 10-9.

ings. In other words, when an impulse appears across the primary windings, no additional flux lines will be created since the transformer is in saturation. This normal-mode immunity is in stark contrast to the isolation transformers we talked about earlier. They required additional filtering and surge suppression in the normal mode. On a ferro, neutral and ground are bonded together on the output for common-mode protection.

So far, the ferro, or CVT, sounds like the absolute answer to any power problems. But before we compare the products we have discussed, let's look into some of the drawbacks of ferros. Every technology has some inherent strengths and weaknesses. Usually the strengths are inextricably tied to those weaknesses. In the case of a ferro, this is once again true.

One of the ferro's major shortcomings is its ability to transfer energy. A ferroresonant transformer is a high-impedance device. This means that its resistance to the flow of current is high. Now high is a relative term, but we are talking about the internal impedance of a ferro as opposed to an isolation transformer. The net effect of this high impedance is that a ferro reacts more slowly to instantaneous current demands placed on it by the computer system connected to it.

On the other hand, an isolation transformer instantly reflects the demand of the load back up the line to its power source. This difference in internal impedance is the source of much controversy between rival manufacturers. The argument centers around the current demands of the switching power supply.

It may have already occurred to you that a ferro is the ideal product for linear power supplies. Their need for a constant source of stable voltage makes a ferro one of the best choices for an ideal electrical environment, although the same could be said of a tap switcher. Where switching power supplies are concerned, the matter is entirely different. Remember the switch wants to pull all of its current during a very short portion of the sine wave. This pumping of short bursts of current places an unusual demand for current on the power source.

In the case of a ferro, all the available current must be circulating in the resonant tank circuit, a circuit made up of the secondary windings and a capacitor. If this circuit were to suddenly become drained of its current, the transformer would loose resonance and would no longer be in saturation. The job of the transformer is to pull enough current from its source to hold the transformer in resonance and, therefore, saturation, plus providing for the changing current demands of the load. If the transformer is not sized properly for the load, it is possible for the switching power supply to gradually become starved for current, resulting in computer malfunctions.

This current starvation results from the fact that the time taken to transfer all the needed energy (from primary to secondary) can be too slow to react to the dramatic demands of the switching power supply. (Again, this is the subject of much argument between manufacturers.) This kind of thing would never happen with a low-impedance transformer. This high-impedance factor leads to another related liability—inrush currents.

Since the startup-current demands of most computer devices are on the order of six to ten times their ordinary running levels, it is possible that a ferro might not be able to meet these inrush demands. Most ferros cannot service current demands of more than 125% to 150% for more than a few milliseconds. The result of this is that the entire system might have to be brought on line, one device at a time. There have been instances where a properly sized ferro simply could not start up some system combinations at all, because of the inrush demands.

But let's be reasonable. This almost never happens. The reason is simple. Designers of ferroresonant products are well aware of the problems we have been discussing. In order to avoid these situations, they often build anywhere from 20% to 30% more capacity into their products to avoid current-demand problems. If the device is oversized to begin with, the likelihood that switching power supplies or inrush demands could cause problems becomes nearly insignificant.

Of course, nothing comes without a cost. A little more capacity means more steel in the core, more wire, more cost, and more weight. Watt for watt, a ferro has far more steel and copper in it than a low-impedance transformer. This is due to a core that is built to be driven into saturation, along with the addition of neutralizing windings and compensation windings. Also, adding hidden capacity to avoid field collapse and current starvation makes this difference even greater.

Efficiency is another concern. As we stated earlier, an isolation transformer of the type found in power-line conditioners and tap switchers is about 96% efficient. The efficiency of a ferro varies with the load placed on it. When a ferro is fully loaded, efficiencies approach 90%. But, as we have seen, running a ferro fully loaded runs the risk of overloading the capacity of the tank circuit, which will cause the field to collapse. As the load drops to 60% of rated capacity, efficiency can drop to as low as 65% to 70%. Remember that no matter how light the load, the transformer still must be driven into saturation. This uses energy even when nothing is plugged into the unit.

Inefficiency results in heat. This, coupled with the dynamics of the circulation of energy within the transformer, creates audible noise. Compared to isolation transformers, ferros are heavy, hot, noisy, and big. But let's not get too carried away. At 500 VA, for instance, the differences are minor. At 10 kVA, they are larger. And, as we stated in our other book, *Computer Electrical Power Requirements*, three-phase devices display enormous variances. The differences are relative, according to the size of the requirement.

Let's touch on two other areas of potential concern before we move on. Overload protection of the branch circuit supporting a ferro can be a problem. Since the current demands which a ferro places on its source of power are little different from no load to full load, even a short circuit across the output may not pull enough additional current to trip an "upstream" circuit breaker, in some cases.

The other problem is that in order to go into resonance, the ferro tank circuit must see a constant flow of 60-Hz power, plus or minus a fraction of a hertz. Since this is a tuned circuit at 60 Hz, minor variations in source power frequency may cause the transformer's magnetic field to collapse. This is almost never a problem except when on-site generation of power is used—for example, during prolonged outages. Diesel generators have long been notorious as a source of frequency drift.

Technologies Compared

So how is one to choose? Tap switchers are smaller, more efficient, more able to provide for large short-duration current demands. Ferros, on the other hand, have a greater regulation range, are probably more reliable, and have better normal-mode noise rejection. Let's be honest. In the size required by PCs, the differences between these technologies shrink to insignificance. Arguments rage between rivals in the industry, but the customer will make his or her determination more on price than on any other point.

This is where ferros have a big edge. To date, it is far cheaper to build a ferro than to build a tap switcher for personal computer systems. Often the difference in price between two equal-sized units can be significant. When all the facts are considered, it is hard to see how tap switchers can beat ferros as the regulator of choice for systems under 2 kVA. However, technology changes, and different manufacturers do creative things that may nullify this assumption, and after all, the choice is not all that clear-cut in every circumstance. For readers of my earlier book, *Computer Electrical Power Requirements*, this may seem to be an about-face, but, not at all. As power requirements increase, the disadvantages of ferros grow. This tilts the scales in favor of tap switchers for minicomputers and mainframes, especially as soon as we get into the three-phase power ranges.

But this is not the important conclusion to this discussion. The real decision for the PC user is not between tap switchers and ferros. The real decision is between power-line conditioners and ferros. This is clearly because of the lack of need for voltage regulation in small personal computers.

Let's twist our perspective away from voltage regulation for a moment. We can do this because we have already learned that switching power supplies do not need voltage regulation except under rare circumstances. With this in mind, we can evaluate a ferro in terms of its qualities as a power conditioner, with voltage regulation as a mere side benefit.

Having stripped away regulation as an issue, we are left with three key areas of interest: noise rejection, physical characteristics, and the device as a power source. We have already shown that a ferro is a better conditioner for normal-mode noise, although a low-impedance transformer with some filtering is good. Both units have their neutral and ground lines bonded together, so let's assume that they have comparable common-mode attenuation. We know that a simple power conditioner is smaller, lighter, more efficient, and less noisy. But these differences are tolerable in most cases, so let's give the power conditioner a slight edge here. Now, we are left with the concept of the device as a source of power. We know that a power-line conditioner is a low-impedance power source that can deliver ample current on demand. The ferro, however, is limited in this respect since it is a high-impedance device.

Being a good source of current for switching power supplies and short-term overloads is one aspect of power-source behavior. Another is, how does the device handle noise or harmonic distortion placed on the line from the load side? In order to test this, we fed our 900-volt spike generator power from both a ferro and a low-impedance transformer. Thus, we plugged the power conditioner into the wall and then connected the generator as the load into the power conditioner.

Figs. 10-11 and 10-12 show the results, which are fairly dramatic. Fig. 10-11 is a photo of the power waveform available at one of the unused outlets of a low-impedance line conditioner. Fig. 10-12 is the picture of the power sampled from a ferroresonant transformer. While the simple power conditioner shows clearly that the spike is gouging a hefty divot out of the peak of the sine wave, the ferro is showing us something radically different. Some sort of ringing oscillation has been set up by the windings and the resonant circuit caused by the pulsing of the generator. The generator is firing only once per cycle.

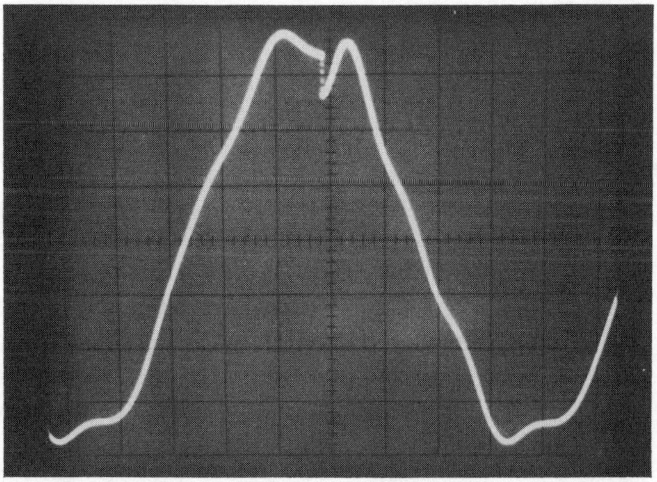

Fig. 10-11. The effect of a spike generator on a simple power conditioner, when used as a power source.

A more realistic example of this kind of problem would be found with devices like printers or outboard tape backups. Large starting or cycling currents could reflect back enough of a transient to cause the kind of pattern shown in Fig. 10-12. Let's be careful not to exaggerate this. The chance of peripherals back feeding 900-volt impulses is rare. But we will see a device in the next chapter that generates impulses in excess of 300 volts every half cycle, and it could easily be connected to a ferro.

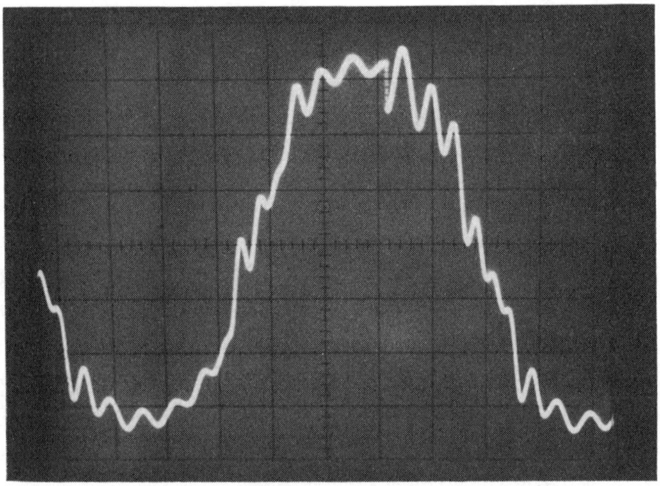

Fig. 10-12. The effect of a spike generator on a ferroresonant regulator when it is used as a power source.

Summary

What does this really mean? Is this some horrible secret defect in ferroresonant power conditioners? No. What it means is that the interrelationship of elements within the device makes it more susceptible to generating harmonic distortion in certain unusual circumstances. If it sounds like we are building an enormous case against ferros, we are not. There are many interesting things to be said on the subject that the thoughtful buyer should be aware of.

In the final analysis, the decision of which unit to buy can be evaluated by answering a few direct questions.

1. Do I need voltage regulation?

   If so, the choice between tap switchers and ferros is a matter of the needs of the specific site and the comfort of the buyer with the points we have discussed. Price will no doubt make the choice clearer.

2. Do I need power conditioning?

   If so, the choice is between a ferro and a simple power-line conditioner. The relative strengths and weaknesses of both product types have been described. The potential buyer of multiple units should obtain evaluation units and "try before you buy" to measure actual on-site performance against the technological differences presented here. Price differences between the two are slight.

3. Do I need backup power?

   Backup power will be the subject we will move to next. We include the question here only to lay the framework for further discussions of the subject of power conditioning. We will return to the subject of power conditioning and voltage regulation as we look at some new approaches to the issues. This includes the subject of providing power when the utility source fails.

11 Standby Power Systems

Too often, the first thought of standby power comes a few seconds after we have lost several thousand words of a word-processing project, or an enormous spreadsheet, due to a power failure. In my case, it took many disasters before I learned to save my work often and to back up my disks. What I needed was a power source that would keep me going when the utility power failed. What I needed was a *UPS*.

Right away, we are entering the controversy of words. UPS stands for *uninterruptible power system*. In this chapter, we will talk about standby power systems. We will see that they are not uninterruptible at all, but only turn on when the power fails. However, there is a rationale for calling them UPSs. We will see why later, and then in the next chapter, we will learn about true UPSs. Meanwhile, before we leave this chapter, we will see a product type that combines a standby power system with a ferroresonant transformer. But first, we must discover the basic building blocks of an *SPS*, or *standby power system*.

SPS Building Blocks

It comes as no shock to most readers that backup power must come from batteries. But batteries are only capable of putting out direct current, and computers run off of AC power. Right away, it can be seen that some method of converting DC into AC must be used if we wish to make battery power useful. And, if we drain the power from a battery, we must have some way of recharging that battery. The obvious answer is a battery charger.

Hold on now. Anyone who has ever charged a battery knows that you must have DC power to charge a battery. This means that some rectification must take place to change the AC input current into DC.

To summarize the path that current must flow in an SPS, let's look at Fig. 11-1. We see two current paths controlled by a switch. The normal path for current is directly through the unit. However, some current is diverted through the charger to keep the battery fully charged. We have shown the charger converting a portion of the AC power into DC in order to accomplish this. This might leave one with the impression that some straight-line value of DC is available at this point. Actually this charger is small, and fairly inexpensive in most units. The charger's output will have a large AC component in the form of ripple, and it will probably be pulsing instead of a steady current flow.

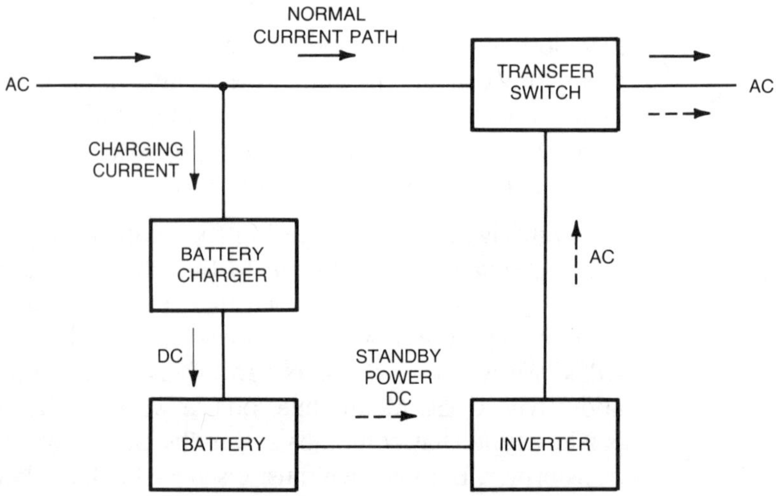

Fig. 11-1. The functional block diagram of a standby power system.

If the power goes out, or for some products, drops below a predetermined voltage level, the inverter is turned on and the switch activates the path from the battery through the inverter. We will spend some time looking at these components as the chapter progresses. By now, it is clear why this is a standby system. The inverter is basically cold until the utility power fails. The switch must be activated very fast so the load does not experience the power failure.

Transfer Time

One of the battles that rages between rival manufacturers of SPSs is who has the fastest *transfer time*. The more legitimate makers advertise and achieve transfer times in the 4- to 10-millisecond range. Others that advertise 4-millisecond transfer times are lucky to experience 15- to 20-millisecond times. Still, there is a class of manufacturers that claim transfer times of under 1 millisecond, or even in the nanoseconds.

Earlier in the book, we dealt with the length of time that a PC can stand to loose power. Anything beyond that time limit and the unit goes down. This is why the successful switching on of the inverter—before the internal ride-through of the PC's power supply is extinguished—is so important. All the batteries in the world won't help if they don't come up on line fast enough.

This is a particular concern in the minicomputer market. But, why should this be included in a book about personal computers? The simple fact is that many low-end computers made by the larger commercial vendors can be powered by 1000–2000-watt SPSs. Many of the readers of this book may have had occasion to apply these product lessons to machines of this variety, since computer power requirements fall with these physical sizes. Most of the major computer manufacturers have models that require only about 1500 watts, but must have an excellent electrical environment. Many of these computers, along with some of their fully loaded PC brethren, cannot tolerate any transfer time. In these cases, an SPS is not the correct product.

Let's examine first those products that claim to transfer in the nanosecond range. This would appear to be a highly desirable thing. After all, the faster a product switches, the less likely the computer will be affected. But the vast majority of PC installations don't need switching that fast. Earlier in the book, we discussed an envelope of time and magnitude, inside of which events that don't affect reliable computing could take place. Super-fast switching must respond to the events occurring in this envelope. This means that the SPS would be activated often, over and over again, while most SPSs would ignore the event. This cycling on and off would, on the face of it, lead to excessive battery wear, lowered inverter life, and other annoyances, such as warning buzzers constantly going off. Believers in this super-fast switching system have failed to show any reliable data to substantiate their claims, or answer any of the healthy skepticism that surrounds their claims.

We are then left with those products that claim a 4-millisecond transfer time. This is plenty fast enough if the claims of the manufacturer are actually true. Most products will switch inside 10 milliseconds, under worst-case conditions. And, 4 milliseconds is usually a best case. But how is one to know? It is not unusual to find specifications that cannot be verified under even the most optimal circumstances. In recent years, there have been a number of articles written in the major computer magazines that compare SPSs. Transfer time is one of the normal benchmarks of these tests. But not every manufacturer agrees to buy advertising in that particular issue so their product may not have been included in the testing.

Possibly, the reason many call their product a UPS is apparent. Since the PC can tolerate loss of power for as long as 30 milliseconds, any standby unit that is switched on in time to keep the system up and running might be considered uninterruptible. This point is technically debatable, but it makes marketing sense not to cloud the issue with the facts.

How switching times are measured is important too. Some manufacturers include *detection time*, or the time it takes to know when it's time to switch, in their transfer times. Others do not. The proper way to specify transfer time is to include detection time in the total.

Another gray area is the point along the sine wave that is used to sense that power is actually lost. Clearly this variable can make a difference of several milliseconds. What is important in all of this, then, is to choose a reputable manufacturer rather than the fastest transfer time. As we stated earlier, we don't want a unit so sensitive that it is constantly reacting to minor power fluctuations. A good design is a compromise between fast reaction and sensitivity.

Making Waves

When the power goes off and batteries become the power source, an inverter must convert the DC power from the batteries into AC power that is usable by the power supply. With this in mind, let's take a step back and consider the general market conditions. This is the PC market. It is highly competitive. Every dollar of cost put into a product risks sales volume. The consumer is not particularly well educated about the technological differences between products, and, ordinarily, won't pay for features they can't see or touch. It is into this type of environment that we probe into the heart of any UPS or SPS—the inverter. The inverter is the most complicated component of the device. It must take DC power and convert it into AC. If ever there was money to be saved, it is here.

Not every inverter puts out the same kind of waveform. For the concerned user, this is the vitally important factor, although it may come as somewhat of a shock. Most users may have assumed that AC is AC, and the

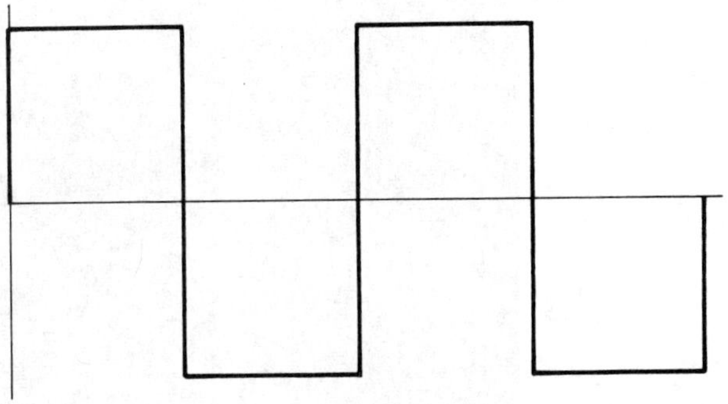

(A) Square wave.

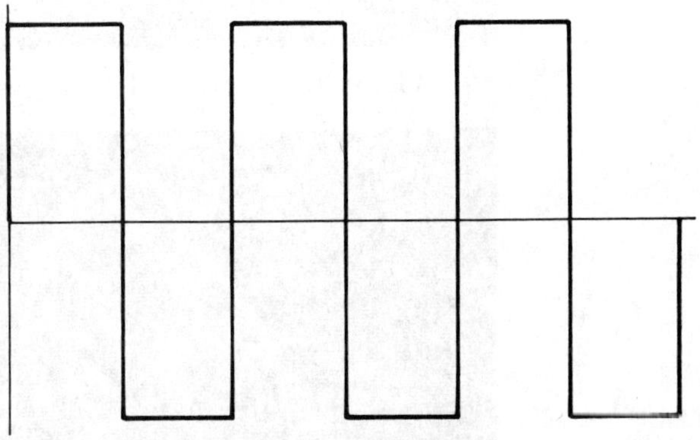

(B) Rectangular wave.

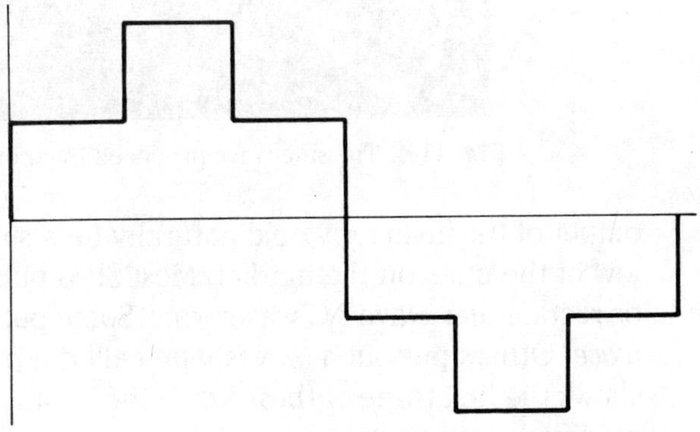

(C) Step wave.

Fig. 11-2. These are popular alternative waveshapes to a sine wave. The inverters that produced these waveshapes are considerably cheaper than one that produces a sine wave.

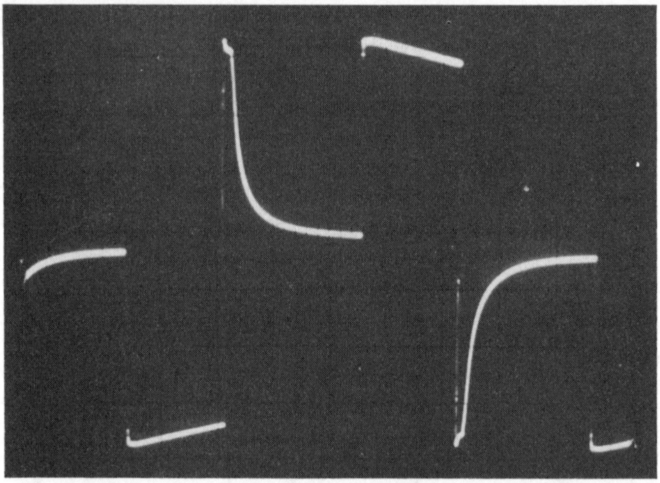

Fig. 11-3. The "modified" square wave from an SPS.

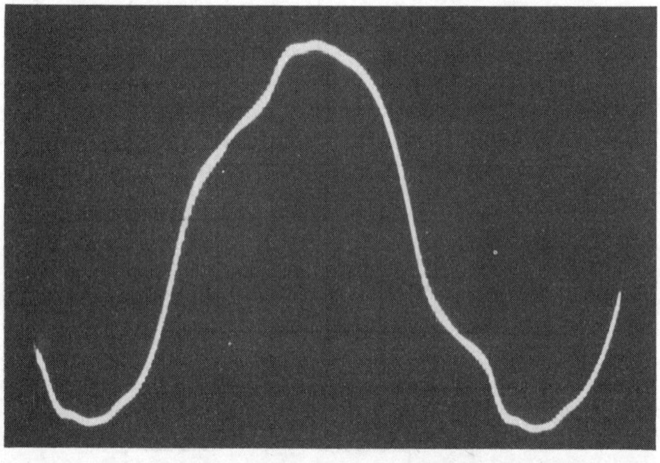

Fig. 11-4. The sine wave produced by another manufacturer's SPS.

output of the inverter would naturally be a sine wave. This is true for only a few of the units on the market. Most SPSs put out square-wave waveshapes, or rectangular-wave AC waveforms. Some put out a waveshape called a *step wave*. Others put out a waveshape called a *modified square wave*. Fig. 11-2 shows the first three of these while the photos in Figs. 11-3 and 11-4 show the modified square wave and a sine wave, respectively.

Obviously, these waveshapes deserve some comment. But before we do that, let's go back to something that came up in Chapter 6, when we discussed power supplies. We talked about the peak voltage and RMS voltage of a sine wave. For a square wave, these two values are one and the same (Fig. 11-5). The job for a design engineer is to decide what the most reasonable compromise voltage will be for a square wave when given the fact that the equipment is designed to accept a sine wave.

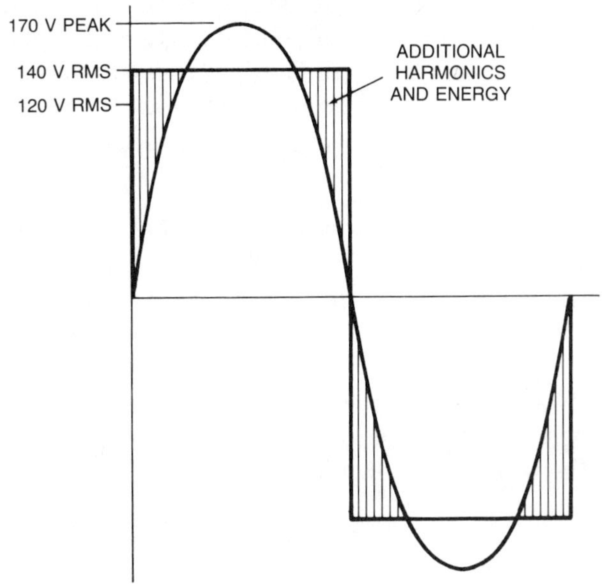

Fig. 11-5. A square wave as compared to a sine wave.

This is especially critical when considering the needs of a switching power supply. Some experts claim that a switching power supply requires 148-V AC peak voltage during the conduction period of the switch in order to maintain a regulated output. On the other hand, some loads are sensitive to rms voltages. This results in a compromise voltage that may be around 140-V AC.

As Fig. 11-5 shows, there are harmonics in a square wave and, at any point, a square wave contains more energy than a sine wave. These factors cause an additional heating of filter elements and some kinds of AC motors. This means that power supplies, printer motors, and some disk drives must digest this additional energy.

The rectangular wave is an answer to some of these problems. Less energy is contained at any point under the curve in a rectangular wave than there is in a square wave. The trade-off for this is maybe just a bit more noise output. We will address noise later in this chapter.

Another potential problem with square-wave inverters is that as the battery is drained, the output voltage tends to fall. In an attempt to reduce costs, many manufacturers do not regulate their output. This may cause problems in meeting the peak-voltage demands of switching power supplies and other equipment that is peak-voltage sensitive.

Let's not deceive ourselves, however. These low-cost alternatives do work. When the power fails, even the modified square wave will keep the computer running. For short outages, we might not care if our computer's power supply is stressed and overheated. These designs allow the manufacturer to offer a popular product at lower prices, in a market where that is all that matters. There are significant performance trade-offs that must be considered.

The sine wave is obviously the best way to go. It is exactly what the PC was designed to anticipate. It is a fundamental, with no harmonic content. It will cause no performance problems. Today's sine-wave outputs are generated with a pulse-width-modulated inverter. PWM inverters are not new to us. They are part of switching power supplies. When properly filtered, a PWM inverter puts out a sine wave like the one shown in Fig. 11-4. Even here we see some slight distortion, but this is negligible when compared to the waveform shown in Fig. 11-3.

Noise

An inverter is a very fast switch. And like switching power supplies and other electronic switches, it is the source of noise at the output of a UPS or an SPS. Fig. 11-6 shows the noise envelope of a PWM inverter. While this may look frightening, it is on the order of 10-volts peak-to-peak. This noise is too small to be of any concern.

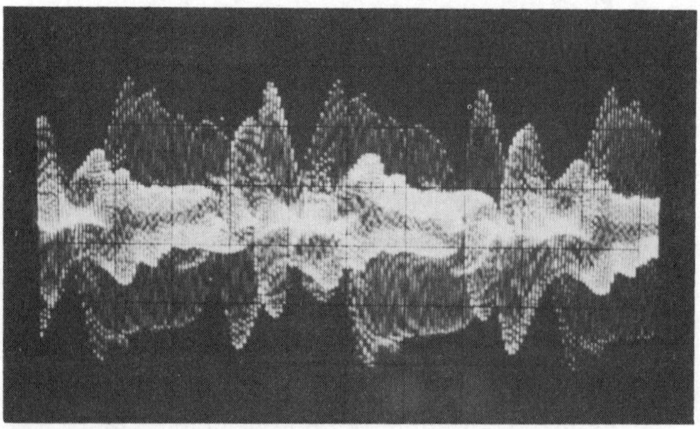

Fig. 11-6. The noise envelope of a PWM inverter.

As we stated earlier, the noise output of cheaper inverters can be significant. To illustrate this, look at Fig. 11-7. This is the noise output of the unit that produced the modified square wave in Fig. 11-3. This doesn't look as bad as the noise from the PWM we just saw. Just a few little spikes. Unfortunately, this unit has a noise envelope just like the PWM inverter does. It's just that we can't see it with the gain of the scope turned so far down. The little spikes that are shown in the photograph are impulses greater than 350 volts. That's right, 350 volts, being repeated every cycle. Is that what we want to feed our machine, even for the short durations when utility power has failed?

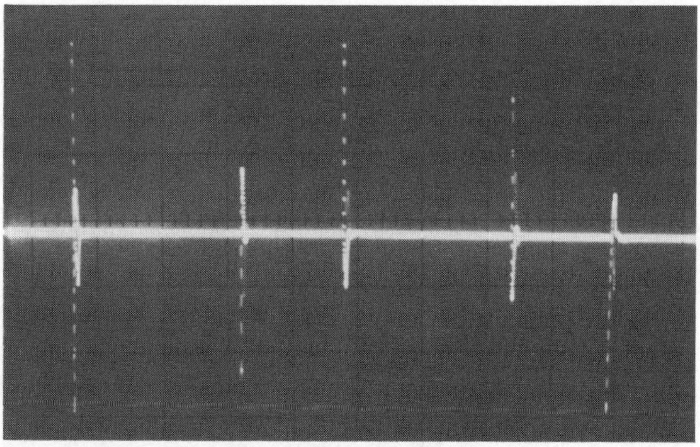

Fig. 11-7. This modified square-wave inverter puts out noise impulses that are greater than 350 volts.

Obviously, every inverter puts out some noise. But the cheaper units are cheaper because of the kinds of technological sacrifices that are made. Will the PC run while being bombarded with noise, harmonic distortion, and energy it can't use? The simple fact is that it will in many cases. But wait until you hook up that modem or connect your computer to a network. It's hard to relate that unexpected investment in a power supply to some vague problem with the battery back-up unit.

The point, here, is that these products may be purchased for legitimate reasons. Let's analyze those reasons for a moment. We need back-up power because our data is valuable, and our time is valuable. Isn't our investment in equipment valuable? Why not spend a few dollars more, or look a little deeper before following bad power with worse? A sine-wave output, with little noise output, should be the goal every user should try to accommodate, given their own personal financial constraints. Furthermore, it remains to be seen that worse is always less expensive. In many cases, a fine product is available at very competitive prices.

Synchronicity

The problems with low-end SPSs don't just end with switching times and waveforms. There is a sticky little problem called *synchronization*. To illustrate this, let's look at Fig. 11-8. This photo will take some explanation. Since this is a time exposure of about one second, we see three distinct waveforms in this picture. From a time standpoint, the first waveform traced across the screen of the scope is the "modified" square wave of the same SPS output we saw in Fig. 11-3. The second trace is the faint "S"-shaped trace. The third looks a little like a bright "S."

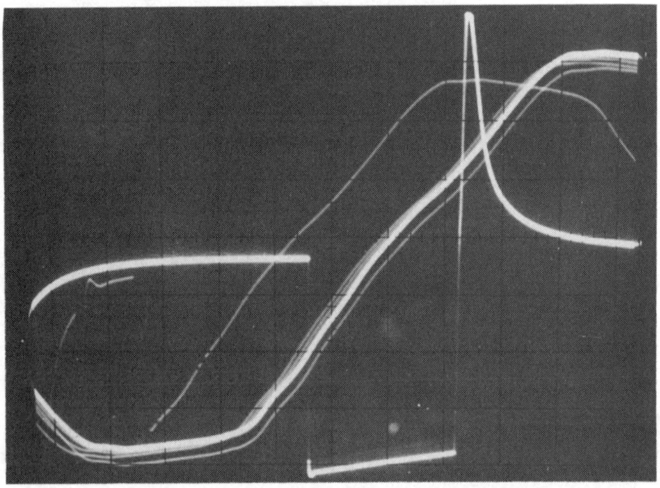

Fig. 11-8. This photo shows the switching of an SPS that does not sync to the line.

The faint "S"-shaped trace and the bright "S"-shaped trace are the waveforms of the utility power after the SPS has switched from batteries back to the line. Here we assume that power has gone off for some period of time, and the batteries and inverter have powered the load. Then, the utility power is restored, and the unit switches from the inverter back to the utility line. The faint "S" trace is the actual first cycle that swept the screen after the switch was activated. During this cycle, the oscilloscope synchronized itself with the line and thus we have the bright "S" trace which is shifted away from the first "S" trace. So let's ignore the bright trace and deal with only those events which occurred just before and just after the switching action.

Notice that in the lower left-hand side of the picture (Fig. 11-8), bordered by all the traces, are some faint markings. This is the actual switching, captured in process. It is at that moment that the retransfer takes place. We can see directly below this the faint tracing of the first cycle of utility power. We can see that the direction of this waveform is up. As it climbs, we see the previous "modified" square-wave waveform move down. Despite the crude shapes, we can see that these two waveshapes are virtually 180° out of phase.

It is this phenomenon that the photo is supposed to illustrate. If the waveform prior to switching and that one which occurs after switching are not synchronized, the computer may be ready for more power moving in one direction, and will get it for a long period (say one and one half cycles) in entirely the wrong direction. This could have the same effect as an outage and could cause the system to crash.

Other possible consequences of nonsynchronized switching are changes in the operational frequency of those devices that need a relatively stable frequency source as a reference. (The reference is for clocks and motors, as well as other sensitive timing circuits.) The photo shows that the power which was delivered to the PC was moving in exactly the opposite direction during the same cyclical slice of time.

The best engineered units on the market have circuitry that sense the phase relationship of the new utility power. It then shifts the inverter output to match the phase angle of the incoming power, prior to retransferring. This not only eliminates the problems we have discussed but it protects against an important event.

When power is restored after an outage, devices are waiting for it and greedily gobble up current as soon as it is available. This enormous demand of inrush current forms a virtual short circuit across the power source. This situation results in a transient pulse of immense proportions. Power engineers have long known that it is this impulse, which propagates downs the line, that causes most of the actual hardware damage, rather than the outage itself. Obviously, this transient pulse will not impact the PC that is connected to an SPS with synchronized switching, since it will be busy phase-matching, leaving the PC still on inverter power while this destructive event is taking place.

Brownouts

This section takes us back to our original discussion of transfer to batteries. There is a point at which every SPS must decide when to go to batteries. This is an extremely important design-and-buying consideration. Does the device wait until there is a total power outage, or does it transfer at some predetermined low-voltage state, regardless of whether the power is really going off?

A product that advertises a 4- to 10-millisecond transfer time may actually wait until the voltage has dropped to an extraordinarily low level before sensing an outage. This additional time adds up to an unacceptably long overall transfer time. What happens during a brownout when the supply voltage sags for more than a few cycles? Don't we need some sort of backup then?

The more sophisticated units are designed with this problem in mind. They have a preset voltage level, say 103 volts, that causes the switch to battery power. This makes the unit a voltage regulator in effect. However, a word of caution is in order. There are many commercial sites where the voltage may sag for extended periods at regular intervals every day. The danger is that the SPS will transfer, and the voltage would not reach a high enough level to trigger retransfer before the batteries are drained. It is also important to remind ourselves that the switching power supply will run fine under most brownout conditions, unless they become severe. With this in mind, a compromise must be reached between switching time and switching level to satisfy all conditions. The most reasonable approach is to design the SPS with the capability of being switched to higher or lower transfer points according to the dictates of the site itself.

Batteries

Standby power systems come with an infinite variety of battery times. But before we consider why this is so, let's understand what an SPS is really for. Since the invention of the UPS, they have been used for two basic purposes. The first is to ride through short-term outages. The second is to have time to do an orderly shutdown during long-term outages.

These are precisely the considerations that a buyer must have in mind before making a decision on one SPS or another. A unit that advertises 10 to 20 minutes of battery time will be heavy and large. But, depending on the needs of the site, it may be the best possible choice. However, longer battery times are desirable in those locations where brownouts are common. Battery time is critical if a particular processing job, say an accounting function, must be completed before shutdown can occur. In another chapter, we will talk about networks. If an SPS is supporting a file server, sufficient battery time must be available for every user to finish their job, close files, and log off the system.

Short battery time, on the order of five minutes or less, is available in the smaller sleeker units. Often these machines are designed to fit under a monitor and on top of the CPU. These short-battery-time units have advantages. They allow for better cosmetics in the design of the package, as the SPSs are not big, bulky boxes. They are attractive low-profile units. But their basic function is to give you enough time to save files and shut down the equipment. In most cases, this is adequate.

The vast majority of power outages are of the under-a-few-seconds-in-duration variety. The ability to ride through those events is the primary utility of an SPS. But when it comes to longer outages, there is yet another battery consideration—end voltage. *End voltage* is that voltage which the cell of the battery reaches, where any further discharge will result in damage to the cell. Most SPSs have no provision to shut down the inverter when the end voltage is reached. As a result, it is common to find batteries that have given their life and must be replaced.

In other words, during a long outage, the SPS manufacturer must assume that the alarm on the unit has warned you of the loss of power and that you have taken appropriate steps. As the outage is prolonged to near the rated backup length, the batteries become drained of their charge. At the point where the end voltage of the cell is reached, the manufacturer must provide a circuit that senses this and shuts off the inverter before the cells are damaged. Again, you get what you pay for. Reputable manufacturers are aware of this need and build this safety feature into their units. The cost differential is nowhere near the cost of a new set of batteries to replace those that have been damaged due to a total discharge beyond the cells' end voltage.

Battery Times Again

Before we move on, there is another important point a buyer must keep in mind. This market, the PC market, is extremely price competitive. This forces a cutting of corners and outright deception. Batteries are no exception.

Batteries don't fit well into the PC market anyway. They are big, bulky, heavy, and they don't have the high-tech image of a turbo board or a laser printer. It is for this reason that manufacturers build smaller and smaller boxes. The look of the package is important in making the sale. It is for these reasons that some vendors stretch the truth about battery times.

Often a manufacturer will reason that most people will not fully load their SPSs. They reason that the typical user will only load an SPS to about

60% to 70% of the unit's rated load. So a 1000-watt SPS will probably only be loaded to 600 or 700 watts. This is why 500-VA units are so popular. Most users only need 360 VA, but by the time they add in a margin of safety, they are shopping for a 500-VA product.

Some unscrupulous manufacturers have guessed this to be the case. They advertise a 10-minute battery, but then size their battery for about 65% load. By doing this, they can get away with a smaller, lighter cabinet that is a sleeker marketing package, and at a lower cost. There is no way it will deliver 10 minutes at full-rated load, but who is going to know?

The Ideal SPS

The ideal SPS for personal computers will vary somewhat from one application or site to another. However, what we have laid out in this chapter suggests some basic guidelines. We can say the ideal SPS will have the following qualities:

1. Transfer time that always switches fast enough so that the PC never experiences an outage.
2. Retransfer is done in-phase with the new utility power so the PC is not affected by inrush transients or by sudden changes in frequency.
3. An inverter waveform that is a sine wave with little distortion.
4. A battery time that will carry the full load for the rated time.
5. Battery protection, to keep the batteries from reaching excessive discharge levels, thereby damaging the batteries.

Power Conditioning

Many ads for SPSs claim that their product conditions power. This "power conditioning" is usually in the form of some sort of surge suppressor built into the unit. Fig. 11-9 shows a photo of the input and output of an SPS. Notice that the white wire from the power cable enters the unit and immediately is routed to the output receptacles. Nothing touches the neutral. No surge suppressor can be seen. The only surge suppression in this unit is an MOV and a couple of capacitors connected between the line and ground. What's even more ridiculous is that these components are mounted on the circuit board that contains the inverter section and all the other circuitry.

Fig. 11-9. This SPS boasts surge suppression. Notice that the white wire (neutral) enters and leaves the unit, and is never touched by any form of surge suppression.

This is the height of folly. First of all, this arrangement is difficult to classify as surge suppression, and surely not "conditioned" power. Secondly, diverting energy on the same circuit board that contains sensitive circuitry jeopardizes every component mounted on the board. Marketing hype is one thing. Being competitive is another. There is no way that adequate power conditioning can be built into an SPS and stay competitive in the market. As buyers, we should know this and not deceive ourselves. It is for this reason that we highly recommend the setup shown in Fig. 11-10.

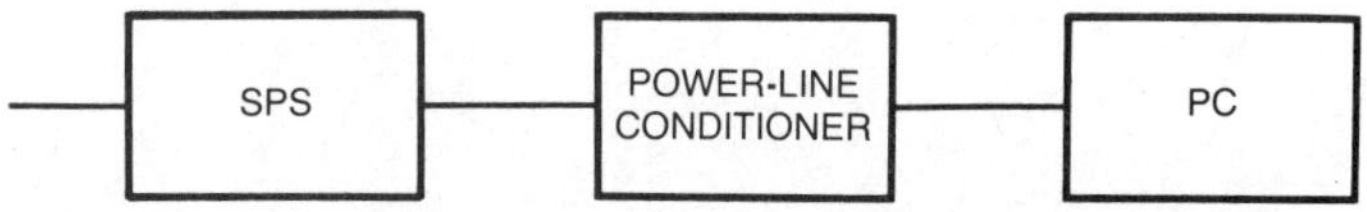

Fig. 11-10. The ideal electrical arrangement for a PC.

This setup combines the benefit of standby power with the low-impedance isolation-transformer line conditioner we described in an earlier chapter. The line conditioner will fully condition the power from the utility, as well as eliminate the noise output from the SPS when it provides power. Care must be taken when selecting the SPS. If the unit puts out great quantities of noise and harmonics, like the "modified" square wave we saw earlier, it will cause the capacitors across the secondary of the line conditioner to burn up. With the proper SPS and a power conditioner, we have an ideal electrical environment for a PC.

But, Fig. 11-10 suggests something to us that applies throughout this book and to the largest computer installation. Putting a transformer between a UPS or SPS and the computer is never a bad idea. The normal-mode rejection, along with common-mode elimination through neutral-to-ground bonding, gives the advantages of clean power along with continuous power.

Recently, one company introduced a novel design. The SPS is placed between the secondary of a low-impedance transformer and the neutral-to-ground bonding point. This also gives the advantages shown in Fig. 11-10—all in one cabinet.

There are other ways of accomplishing this same thing, as we will see in the next chapter.

12 UPS Designs

We named this chapter *UPS Designs* for a reason. We will be discussing not only what many people call "true on-line UPS," but we will touch on several other designs that are arguably not on-line but are still not standby types. These designs are line-interactive (tri-ports or load sharing) and ferroresonant standby power systems.

We will start with on line UPS designs since they are the products which really fit the definition of being uninterruptible. Fig. 12-1 shows the block diagram of an on-line UPS. We can see that the incoming AC power is converted to DC by the rectifier/charger. This DC provides charging current to the batteries, which float on the DC bus. Meanwhile, the inverter converts this DC back into AC to power the load.

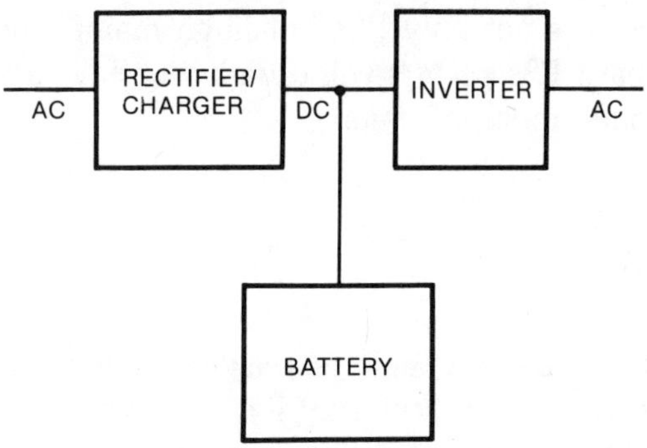

Fig. 12-1. The block diagram of a true UPS.

When utility power fails or drops below a certain point, power is automatically pulled from the batteries. The physics of the way that the batteries float on the DC bus is such that no switching ever takes place. If the batteries need charging, they pull current from the bus. If the batteries are charged and the bus voltage is low, the batteries will deliver the needed current to the bus.

This AC-to-DC conversion process not only eliminates the need for any switching, it also has the facility of conditioning power at the same time. Fig. 12-2 shows a photo of the output waveform of a UPS designed for PCs. We are feeding our 900-volt impulse into it. Notice the output shows practically no effect of the impulse and is a perfect sine wave.

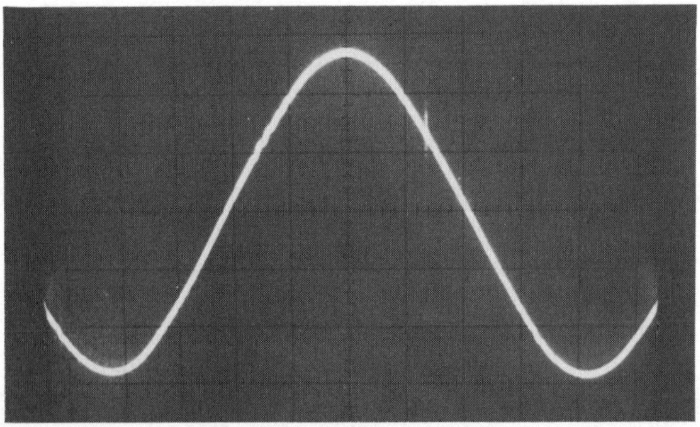

Fig. 12-2. The output waveform of a UPS, with a 900-volt impulse across the UPS's input.

Since the inverter is on all of the time and is always providing power to the load, we call it an "on-line" UPS. This on-line design is the basic unit that powers not only PCs but huge mainframe computers. We should mention that UPSs for PCs will usually not have a bypass switch such as is normally found in larger units.

Why a UPS?

There are a couple of reasons why someone would want a UPS in a PC environment. Primarily, it is the uninterruptible nature of the power that the UPS delivers. There are a number of larger systems which cannot tolerate switching that fall into the PC power range, but, they are not really PCs.

And, there are a number of PCs used in exotic systems which integrate special hard drives or other peripherals which are sensitive to any disruption of power.

The other reason, as we mentioned before, is the power-conditioning aspect of the AC–DC–AC conversion that takes place. This virtually eliminates any impulse coming down the line. To illustrate this, we have included the pictures shown in Figs. 12-3 and 12-4. Fig. 12-3 shows the noise that was on the line before the insertion of the UPS. Both the common-mode and normal-mode signatures were virtually identical. Fig. 12-4 shows the normal-mode and common-mode tracings of the output of the UPS.

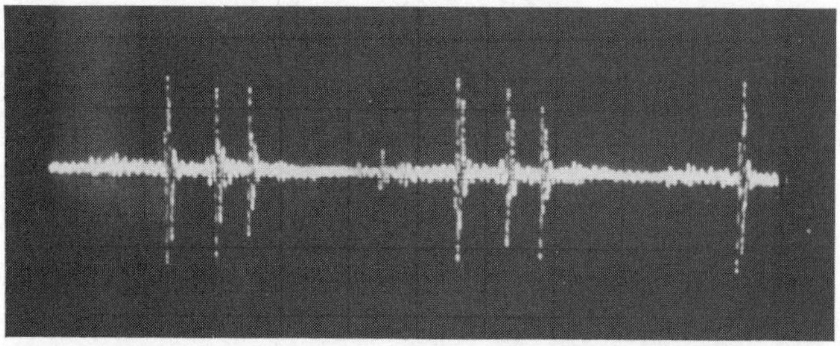

Fig. 12-3. Illustration of the noise on the line before the insertion of a UPS.

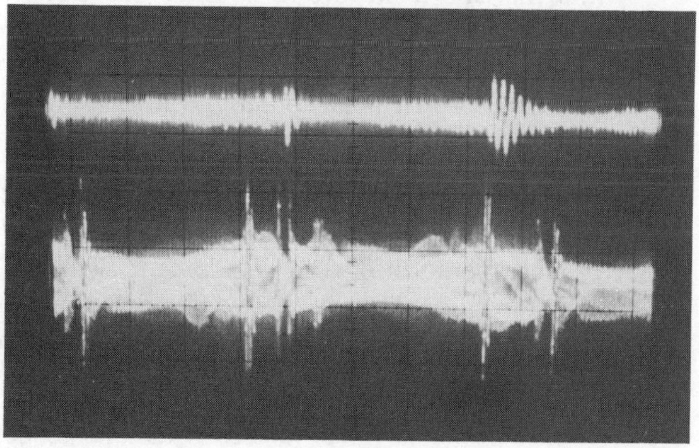

Fig. 12-4. The normal-mode (top) and common-mode (bottom) output of a UPS.

Fig. 12-4 shows something interesting about on-line UPSs. Notice how normal-mode noise has been eliminated. All that remains is some high-frequency component of the PWM inverter. The common-mode output is an entirely different story. We see a noise envelope that has developed between neutral and ground, along with the noise that was on the line before. In some cases, we might observe an increase in common-mode noise due to a UPS. To make this point even more dramatic, let's go back to

Fig. 12-2. What does the high-frequency noise output of the UPS look like with our 900-volt impulse being fed into it? Fig. 12-5 shows us the answer.

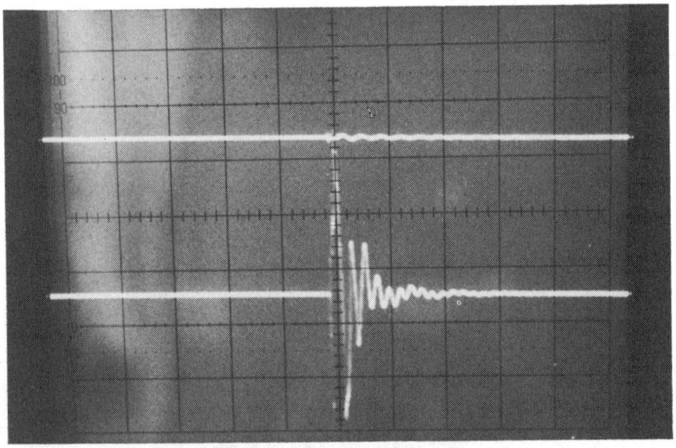

Fig. 12-5. The output of a UPS with a 900-volt impulse fed to the input. Normal-mode to common-mode conversion has taken place.

Clearly, the impulse has been stopped in its tracks as far as the normal-mode noise is concerned. This is significant since the impulse was being fed into the UPS from line to neutral. But inside the UPS, some coupling has taken place, and the impulse has been converted from normal-mode noise to common-mode noise. This new impulse is not as large as the one that created it, but it is large enough to cause significant problems for the PC downstream.

This raises an interesting issue with regard to UPSs. It is not uncommon for the harmonic distortion and noise output of a UPS to interfere with the proper operation of some equipment. This will usually manifest itself with symptoms like displays that wiggle and dance, or other kinds of interaction with the frequency output of the PWM inverter. Does this mean we shouldn't buy a UPS? Not in the least.

All products have various trade-offs to consider when balancing one technology against another. We will see this dramatically as this chapter progresses. On-line UPSs have a distinct place in the market where uninterruptible power cannot be sacrificed for anything else. But they do have shortcomings other than common-mode attenuation and a noise output. They tend to be less efficient than other products because the inverter is on all the time. They also put out heat and are noisy in comparison to other products. These problems, like the negative points we listed for ferros, may or may not be significant, depending on the site-specific needs and tastes of the user.

Ferroresonant UPSs

A popular product design that has really come into its own, in the 1000-VA to 10-kVA area, uses a ferroresonant transformer in a unique way. We have not yet talked about a "quality" of ferros that makes them useful in many applications with UPSs. This quality is *ride-through*.

Because of the large amount of wire and steel in a ferro and the energy circulating in its tank circuit, a ferroresonant transformer has the curious property of being able to deliver stored energy to the load for many milliseconds after utility power has failed. We must point out that this stored energy is proportional to the size of the load. If the load and the capacity of the transformer are closely matched, very little ride-through exists. However, under normal circumstances, there will be sufficient ride-through to switch on an inverter without disturbing the flow of current to the load.

Fig. 12-6 shows us the block diagram of this type of UPS. Under normal operation, power is delivered through the ferro to the load. This affords all the advantages we discussed in Chapter 10. The load receives regulated and conditioned power at all times. The ferro eliminates normal-mode noise, and since the neutral-to-ground lines are bonded on the secondary, no common-mode noise appears across its output.

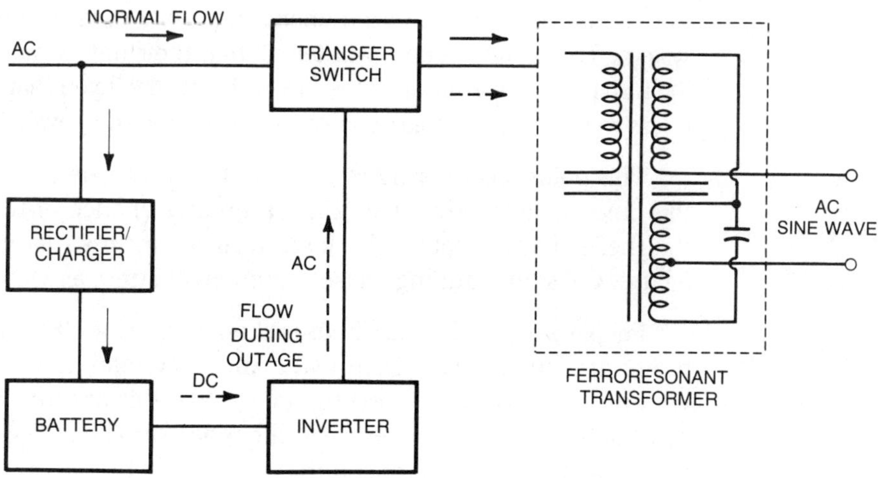

Fig. 12-6. The block diagram of a ferroresonant UPS.

When the utility power fails, the inverter is turned on and the ride-through of the transformer provides continuous power to the load. No inverter noise or switching transients are passed on to the load, as we have seen with UPSs and SPSs. Since the output of a ferro, without additional windings, is a square wave, and since the inverter is only on during an outage, the manufacturer of these devices can get away with an inverter that is significantly less costly, lighter in weight, and less critical in terms of its waveshape output.

This design has a lot going for it. It also meets my personal prejudice in favor of transformers. Even though it uses a ferro, a transformer on the output of a UPS is a design criteria that is optimal. But let's look a little deeper. Everything has its price in terms of trade-offs, both economically and technologically.

In comparing this design over an on-line UPS, several things must be pointed out. First of all, we are not going to get away from the problems of ferroresonant transformers. But there are problems with on-line UPSs too. Let's assume these concerns balance out. More often than not, this unit will be too large in terms of its available sizes, as well as its physical size, for most PC installations. However, where there are multiple PCs, this unit can be a central power source. Even the 500-VA units that are available weigh about 90 pounds. This may hold back some purchasers.

The real controversy between manufacturers of on-line UPSs and the producers of the ferro product is a dispute over another issue which we have not touched on so far—reliability. From a load standpoint, this ferro design is truly an on-line unit. But, from an inverter point of view, it is a standby power system. The on-line people will tell us that their unit is more reliable because their inverter is operating all the time. They will tell you that a standby inverter is less reliable since it must cold-start every time the power fails.

This point has the ring of truth to it. But, on-line units are operating all the time, meaning they may have a greater chance of failing. It is not just the thermal stress caused by large inrush currents that causes component failure. Constant running causes component stress as well.

People who live in glass houses shouldn't throw UPSs. The UPS manufacturers have problems of their own. And, new solid-state components, along with proper burn in and testing, may make this argument mute. All equipment fails. Who knows where it will happen or when? The plain truth is that batteries are the single most unreliable element of a UPS.

The standby people would not survive long in a market that placed the burden of reliability on them so competitively. Knowing this, they must go to extraordinary lengths to turn out a reliable product. However, this does not mean that an on-line manufacturer will or will not go to great lengths to turn out a reliable product. At 10 kVA, when powering a minicomputer system with 75 terminals attached, this discussion is of vital importance, and many DP professionals may feel more comfortable with one technology or the other. Although this comfortable feeling may be deceiving, there are strong pros and cons. But at 1000 VA, the whole discussion is somewhat misplaced. The economics of the marketplace force everything to take a back seat to cost considerations. Here an argument over reliability has a hollow echo.

Against the Ideal

In the last chapter, we held up Fig. 11-10 as the ideal electrical environment for the PC. How does this ferroresonant UPS affect that ideal? Obviously, it was the addition of a transformer downstream from the SPS that was so attractive. But in the case of the ferro UPS, we have those same advantages. The question becomes one that is related to the site and the needs of the user. The ferro has advantages like voltage regulation and ride-through, but normal PCs don't need either. However, if either becomes a concern, the ferro must become an option.

If we bring the on-line UPS into this framework, we loose all the benefits of a transformer. Possibly the mind is not built to balance all these variables. Add to this the fact that the ideal unit, as pictured in Fig. 11-10, is contained in two boxes.

How does one decide? The site, the computer, the peripherals, and the needs of the users are all factored together, and this will suggest the proper product choice. All things being equal, there is the matter of money. Typically, the SPS, coupled with a line conditioner, is the least expensive. Ferroresonant UPSs are substantially more expensive, but still somewhat under the cost of most on-line UPSs.

Tri-ports

The *tri-port* design is relatively new to the UPS field. Currently, this design is not to be found in the PC market. However, it is beginning to make an impact on medium-size systems. Nevertheless, we feel that it warrants discussion here since its entry into the PC field in one form or another is inevitable.

Fig. 12-7 shows a diagram of the tri-port design. This product is a combination of a UPS and a tap-switching regulator. The incoming utility power is fed through a low-impedance isolation transformer via a set of SCR switches that can be adjusted for surges and sags. The output of the transformer is noise free, just like the line conditioners we talked about earlier. It also has the neutral and ground bonded together.

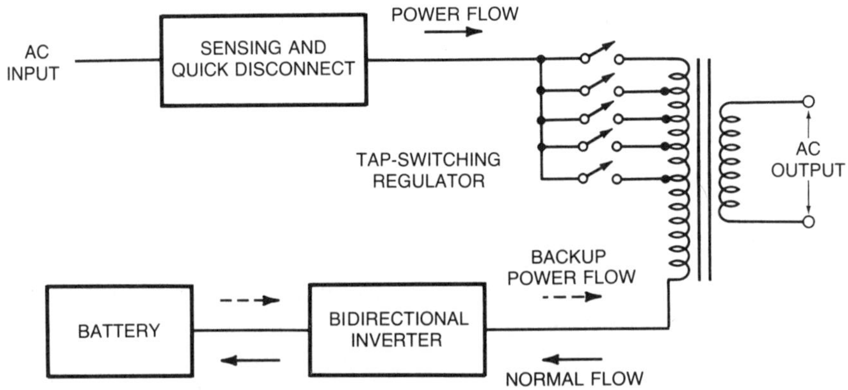

Fig. 12-7. Diagram of a tri-port UPS.

During normal operation, the inverter draws enough power to keep the batteries charged. Some additional circuitry has been added to allow the inverter to act like a battery charger. While it charges the batteries, power flows from the primary of the transformer through the inverter and then into the batteries. When utility power fails, the inverter changes the direction of current flow and pulls power from the batteries, thereby becoming the source of power for the load. The sensing circuit must do two important things. First, it must acknowledge the outage and turn on the inverter. Secondly, it must disconnect the input feeder so that the inverter does not try to operate and back feed the unit's own power source.

The tri-port design has several advantages. First, the inverter is on all the time. Some think this makes the unit more reliable than an SPS, although still somewhat less reliable than an on-line unit since it is not carrying the entire load all the time. However, engineers will argue that being on-line all the time is less reliable. Again, for small systems, this point is not particularly important. It has the advantage of being a low-impedance power source that provides a good electrical environment, and, of course, all the noise-attenuation characteristics of a power conditioner.

The problem with the design in the form presented here is likely to be "cost." This unit has all the advantages of the ferro UPS except ride-through, without the disadvantages of a ferro. Its inverter could be more reliable while its regulator may be less reliable. But to produce this device at a price that would compete favorably with a ferro would probably not be possible in sizes for PCs.

If this product design ever makes it to market, it will probably have to eliminate some features, like the tap-switching section, in order to be a price competitor. Even at that, it would still be attractive since it provides both conditioned and standby power. We have included it here since the design has important distinctions which fit well into our overall UPS discussion.

Line-Interactive UPSs

As the name implies, *line interactive* is a UPS designed to be on-line only to interact. Tri-ports are a variety of line-interactive units since they interact with the lines changing state. While tri-ports have yet to make an appearance as products for PCs, there is a line-interactive type of UPS that is making an appearance. It is called a *load-sharing* UPS. Fig. 12-8 shows us this basic idea.

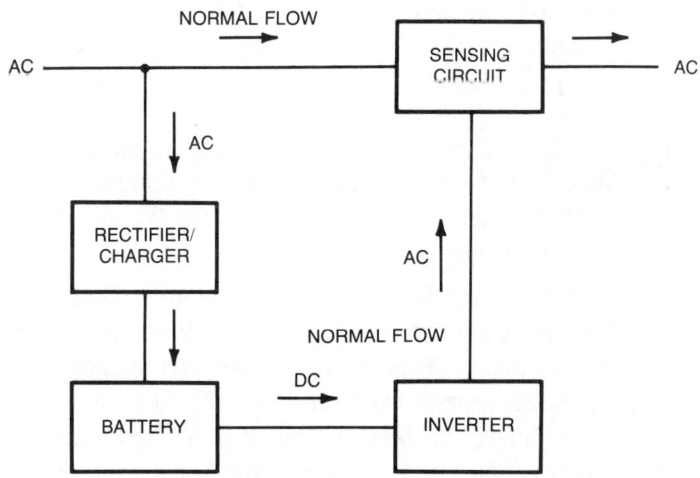

Fig. 12-8. The block diagram of a load-sharing, line-interactive UPS.

This design looks strangely like an SPS. But there is an important difference. This is an on-line UPS. In other words, the UPS circuit from the rectifier charger to the battery, and through the inverter, is on all the time. The sensing circuit, which is very simple in this case, governs the amount of current that the load actually needs to draw from the inverter section.

During normal operation, the inverter might provide a small fraction of the current needs of the load. The bulk of current would be drawn from the line. Let's say that the line voltage begins to sag. As this occurs, the inverter would be called on to provide more and more power to the load. Finally, if the power went out completely, the inverter would supply 100% of the power required by the load.

This design accomplished some marketable concepts. It is on line all the time, so any concern about cold starting an inverter is gone. There is no switching time since it is on line. Devices sensitive to the 4- to 10-milliseconds delay typical from an SPS would have nothing to fear from a load-sharing design.

On the other hand, there is no ongoing power conditioning with this approach. Of course, the inevitable answer to this is to throw a few MOVs into the unit and call it a surge suppressor as well. This design is beginning to crop up in those under-the-monitor-type control-center packages.

The RUPS

We can't leave a chapter about UPS without touching on *rotary technology*. A more complete discussion of this topic is contained in my earlier book, *Computer Electrical Power Requirements*. Fig. 12-9 shows the basic block diagram of this type of device. Notice that the incoming utility power is used to drive a spinning motor which is mechanically linked to an AC generator. When utility power fails, there is enough inertial mass in the motor/generator set (MG Set) to ride through until the inverter section is able to provide power to the unit.

This seems like a strange technology to find in a book about PCs. However, this unit is being built in sizes clear down to 1000 VA. This is almost unbelievable to many DP professionals who remember RUPS as being found only in large data centers. Presently, the military is the only real customer for this kind of technology in sizes that might fit in the PC environment. We include it here on the off chance that its use might become more widespread, although this is a remote possibility. Even so, the thoughtful reader may find it valuable to know such a technological approach does exist.

UPS Wrap-up

We have seen quite a plethora of power products in the last two chapters. To be sure, the most popular UPS for PCs is the SPS, especially in the sizes

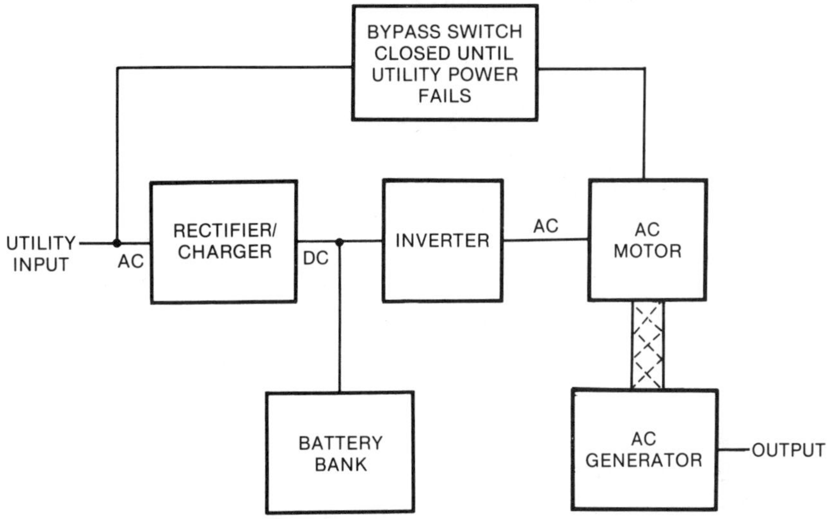

Fig. 12-9. A block diagram of one type of rotary UPS (RUPS).

under 1000 VA. Above 1000 VA, applications often call for the advantages of on-line UPSs. At two to three times the price, this can be a difficult decision.

The load-sharing design is an attempt to get at this price differential, while other technologies, like the ferro design, really compete head on with the on-line varieties.

In the next chapter, we will see two growing applications for power products—networks and desktop publishing. It is in considering these kinds of installations where we must put our knowledge to the test. Which will be the best, most cost-effective application of technology? This book now serves us as a handbook for determining what makes the most sense in each situation.

13 LANs, Desktop Publishing, and Other Final Thoughts

Throughout this book, we have talked about virtually every technological approach to solving, perhaps, virtually every power problem that might be encountered. We have looked at the electrical environment and the quality of utility power and the problems with it. Yet there are still tens of thousands of personal computers that are plugged right into the wall outlets, which never have had and probably never will have a problem.

For those of us who make a living solving computer power problems, and advising various companies on how best to install computers, both big and small, this comes as no particular surprise. I'm not even tempted at this point to say that these are disasters waiting to happen. After all, the interesting thing about PCs is that, in some cases, the thing could blow up and it would be no big deal. In other cases, it would be a disaster of biblical proportions. *Local area networks (LANS)* fall neatly into the latter category.

Local Area Networks

Not too long ago, a friend of mine, a well-paid executive in a very large bank, complained that the LAN which serves her department is so unreliable that no one uses it to do any important work. What a shame! Sounds like just another power horror story to justify the expense of a UPS or something.

Let's put this into better perspective. This local area network is a part of an $8,000,000 computer upgrade that was made by the bank; the upgrade included every one of the bank's departments throughout the country. As anyone knows, who has ever had to install new equipment, like phone systems, computers, or other high-tech stuff, the first impression of the end users in the organization is absolutely critical. If everyone is afraid of the equipment, or turned off during their first few experiences with the system, it will never see its full potential utilized or its cost justified.

My executive friend was leary of using the LAN because the power kept going off. She and none of her subordinates wanted to loose valuable data if the system were to suddenly go down. So they didn't use it, period. They still don't. This is a shame, but not unexpected. LANs are without a doubt the single most vulnerable systems when it comes to power disturbances. There are four major areas of concern we want to highlight. They are:

- Corruption of data from outside interference.
- Ground loops.
- Protection of equipment.
- Losing power without losing data.

Data Cabling

Often, in large data centers, every effort is made to distribute the data-cable wiring in an orderly fashion. Often it is not. And, most certainly, in local area networks is when it usually is not. Cable is stretched here or there, around this and over that. Data-cable wiring is a common source of data corruption by outside influences.

There are several ways of distributing data using various kinds of cable. Typically, *coaxial cable*, commonly call *coax*, is used and few problems result. But, it is usually a mistake to run coax any great distance without adhering to special grounding practices, as described earlier in this book. Of course, using coax throughout an extensive network is an expensive alternative.

Most larger installations have discovered the unexpected advantages offered by *twisted-pair wiring*. That's right. More often than not, there are unused pairs of telephone cable in existing trunks which can be used economically to transfer data. There are some advantages to using existing telephone cables. First of all, it is significantly less expensive than coax. Second, it can be interfaced with *baluns*, matched to *coax interfaces*, and mated with *patch panels* for a versatile installation. Granted, twisted pair is more vulnerable to noise than coax. However, if existing cable is used, the lines are probably clear of noise influences since the voice system is already working properly. This is no guarantee, but it is a hopeful first step. Rearranging twisted pair away from noise influences is easier than with coax. Finally, it can be purchased with a shield sheathing, if necessary.

If at all possible, stay away from ribbon cable. There may be some systems that use RS-232 connections to link certain types of terminals, peripherals, or remote devices, but ribbon cable is a notorious source of noise interference. For example, a recent client of mine had a keyboard which wouldn't operate properly. Whenever the welding equipment in the next room was operating, the keyboard locked up. The problem was resolved when it was discovered that a ribbon cable had been substituted for the normal shielded cable between the terminal and the keyboard, and the cable was replaced. Normally, we would expect nothing to work in such a hostile environment. The use of ribbon cable guaranteed it.

Ground Loops

A LAN is a *ground loop*. There is no way to get around it. It's all well and good to talk about single-point grounding, but when Sally is in accounting, and Betty is in clerical, and Joe is in shipping, this might be a little unrealistic. Fig. 13-1 shows the problems typical of a LAN and how ground currents can flow.

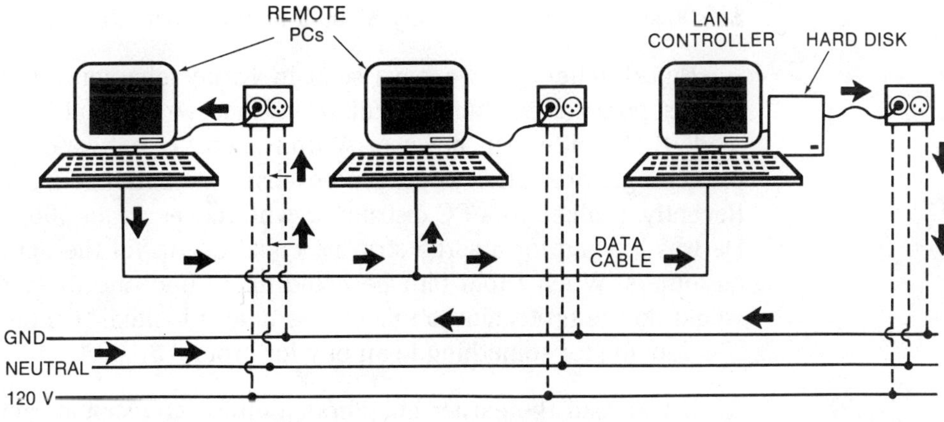

Fig. 13-1. A simple LAN may form many ground loops. The arrows show the paths that noise might take.

Ground loops can foul communications, create hard disk errors, and/or render one or more terminals useless. The answer to LAN-generated ground loops is not always simple and straightforward. Chokes, baluns, optical isolators, and modems—any or all of these may be the answer. But the simplest form of cure is proper *bonding*. Practices would include connecting power grounds and data-cable shields where the cables penetrate walls. In some cases, heavy copper strapping can be used to bond the ground buses of two separate panel boards. Bonding to steel building columns can be a cure in some cases. What we are trying to do is give the ground noise a lower impedance path other than the one through the data cable.

Liberal use of three techniques will stop most ground-loop problems. These are bonding, shielding, and isolation. We have talked about bonding. *Shielding* involves the use of shielded cable, but the term also refers to the practice of using grounded metal barriers between equipment and any potential noise sources. *Isolation* brings us back to the use of power-line conditioners as a barrier to the entry of noise into a system. The neutral-to-ground bonding on the secondary of a transformer effectively shunts ground noise away from LAN data circuits. The situation may require just the use of one device, or the use of one device on *each* LAN terminal. Careful application of bonding, shielding, and isolation is the answer to the LAN ground-loop situation.

Protection

Corporate America is buying surge strips by the boxcar. This usually happens with the assistance of a corporate buyer who has figured out how to buy a $40.00 surge protector for only $9.99 if he buys them in case lots.

Unfortunately, as we have seen in earlier chapters, finding the right surge suppressor can be a difficult task. Underwriter's Laboratories, Inc. has made that a bit easier, however. With the cost of networks in the five-digit price range, protection and economy have become like bazaar antonyms. Recently, I talked to a PC distributor who moves about 500 units a month. He was looking for a surge strip he could use to fill the demand from his customers. When I told him he could likely find one for about $100 that would do the protection job nicely, he nearly fainted. "Oh no," he told me, "I'm looking for something I can buy for around $6.00."

If you read the earlier chapters carefully, you should remember that I showed a strong bias toward an isolation transformer that has the neutral and ground bonded together. Since a LAN is almost always subject to ground loops, and since the data tied up in the network is so valuable, it seems logical to at least give the file server this kind of high-quality protection. The cost associated with losing a 40-Meg hard drive and the data it contains ought to justify the expense of a $200 or $300 power conditioner.

Each PC connected to the LAN should have the same kind of protection. While it is hard to keep two widely spaced safety grounds from moving electrically apart, it is surely desirable to keep these noise potentials from appearing across the LAN cable and power ground. A power conditioner with the neutral and ground lines bonded does just that. A surge suppressor will not accomplish this in every desirable instance, even if it has been well engineered to handle common-mode transients.

If the ground-offset potentials are only a few dozen volts, data lines can be corrupted and chips may be damaged by the current flow that results. The voltage levels may be far below the functional threshold of an MOV, so a surge device will not help in this situation. The only threat that remains, if proper power conditioning is used, is that the ground offset caused by the physical distance of the devices, themselves, may cause loop currents to flow. Then bonding becomes another line of defense. We can recognize that these ground currents may exist and can give them a lower impedance path to follow.

This relates to our earlier comments. Running supplemental grounding straps between the breaker panels, or even along cable runs, can accomplish this. Often times, significant potentials can exist between two building columns. Bonding can equalize these voltages. Shorter, thicker wires will divert ground current away from cabling. Another approach, as we stated in an earlier chapter, would be to bond the actual shield of the data cable to building steel at short distances, in order to equalize loop currents traveling in the cable itself.

Application of a UPS

It's time to make one of those sweeping statements that will no doubt haunt me as I travel around the country giving seminars and workshops. It is one of those unqualified, broad generalizations that at first may seem a bit harsh, but here goes.

If you have a LAN without a UPS, you didn't need the LAN in the first place. The whole concept of networking is to share data between intelligent machines. Sometimes the data resides in a file server, and users share its large hard drive and, possibly, a printer. Less often, systems make use of a number of PCs, each with its own individual hard drive.

A hard disk is a delicate instrument that communicates with its magnetic media through a Read/Write head that literally flies in the air. Like an airplane, a sudden loss of power makes the head crash. A head crash is usually a disaster. It can destroy information, make a disk unreadable, and/or can cause actual hardware damage. Head crashes caused by power outages are common events.

Fortunately, not all power outages cause head crashes. What does happen when the power goes out is that the head stops writing to the disk. The volatile memories all fade, and the screens go blank. Depending on the software, intermediate work—meaning work generated but not yet saved in a closed file—may be lost.

At a minimum, the hard disk must have a backup power source. It is essential that the mass of data be protected, files not left open, and hardware not be jeopardized. Each workstation should be evaluated for the possible need for standby power. In expensive systems, SPSs can be added that will give each user just enough time to close files and log off the system.

Orderly Shutdowns

Let's take this entire concept one step further. Many networks are set up for 24-hour continuous operation. It is highly desirable that the system have some way of coping with an unplanned termination on its own. For this system to be effective, three elements are needed. First, the file server must be on a UPS capable of sending a signal to the file server that the power has failed and the system is now operating on batteries. Secondly, there must be some software resident in the system which will take appropriate action when this signal is received. Finally, the PCs on the network must be on some form of UPS in order to take advantage of Elements One and Two, above.

In fact, there are systems on the market that do all this and more. Let's step through an outage and see what happens. The moment the power goes out, the UPS sends an "on battery" signal to the file server. This activates a program already resident in memory. Immediately, a message appears on every screen of each PC logged onto the network, saying, "Power Outage, Approximately 5 Minutes Battery Time Remaining." With each succeeding moment, the minutes are counted down as the battery time expires.

At somewhere near the 1-minute mark, a keyboard alarm sounds at each workstation. The power software begins closing files. But it does two very important things in the meantime. First, it retrieves each active workstation's log on sequence into a macro file. Also, it begins developing a macro of keystrokes that will preserve work done after the files are closed.

When the power returns, the power software automatically reboots the system and activates the macro files. Each user is logged back onto the system without their touching their terminal. They are placed into the program exactly where they were before, and their last few dozen keystrokes appear on the screen. If all works properly, no data is lost, no time is lost, and more importantly, no confidence in the system is lost.

The scenario that we have outlined is actually in use and readily available from network vendors and distributors. Depending on the application, even the keyboard macro options may be a necessity. What does all this cost? Probably somewhere in the range of from 7% to 15% of the cost of the network.

Wow! You mean I pay all this money for the network, and then I have to buy all this power stuff?

Take my advice. Look at your network needs, including the power requirements, up front in the budget. The power products are a part of what the network is all about. It should be included in the original proposal. Vendors that don't include it don't have your best interests in mind.

Now, possibly, our statement about the absolute necessity of a UPS with a LAN seems more grounded. Of course, when we talk about LANs, we are talking about a system where real computing is going on, in a commercial setting. Clearly, very small networks that only swap files from the disk is not what we mean. LANs that include a proper power environment will be used more and will be relied on more by their users. The productivity of data sharing will soon justify not only the expense of adding power conditioning and UPS, but the LAN itself.

Desktop Publishing

We are devoting special consideration to LANs and Desktop Publishing not only because they are popular and growing, but because they represent a significant investment for the organization. Desktop publishing presents a very different set of problems than does a local area network. But what are the individual elements of a desktop system, and how do they add up in terms of power protection needs?

Most basic, yet powerful, publishing systems consist of the following elements: a high-speed PC, a large-capacity hard drive, a laser printer, possibly a scanner, and possibly an outboard tape-backup system. Each one of these elements performs a distinctive role at separate times during the process of inputting, manipulating, and printing.

We will assume that all of these elements are involved in a system that we must protect. It seems simple enough on the face of it. Why should protecting this system be any different than any other system? Let's just add up the power requirements of each element and then buy the device of our choice in the proper size. Well, will that approach work? Let's try it and see.

The high-speed PC with an internal hard drive of 20-Megabytes needs about 360 VA of power, including the monitor. The external tape-backup system might only need 250 VA. The scanner—about 250 VA also. Gee, we're only at 860 VA and we have only one item left. The problem is that one item. Many laser printers have ratings of around 1000 VA. Now, quite suddenly, our power requirement has jumped to almost 2 kVA. A 2-kVA power conditioner will cost in the neighborhood of $1000 to $1400. An SPS at the same size will cost in the range of $2500 to $3000. And, hold on to your hat, a true UPS may be in the $4000 to $5000 range.

Before you rush out to buy any of these items, can we find other alternatives that might afford the kind of electrical environment we are after without breaking the bank? The answer is, "Yes." Unlike a LAN, where continuous processing is a must, a publishing system requires a one-step-at-a-time process.

The real concern is the PC itself. This is where all the work is done, and the arguments here for good power are just as compelling as if it were an important stand-alone PC on some executive's desk. The fact that so much in-process work will be resident in memory at any one time should indicate that an SPS would be desirable. Depending on how often the actual composition is saved to disk will determine the operator's exposure to rebuilding lost work after a power outage. This is a judgment that must be made. The SPS to back up this part of the system will cost around $600.

It almost goes without saying that the high-speed PC needs a line conditioner. This is the finest electrical environment available for this equipment, and at a cost of around $300, it is well worth the protection to the hardware and all the data contained on the hard drive. What about the tape backup system and the scanner? These items might, for a couple hundred dollars more, be included on the same line conditioner that feeds the PC. If not, a high-quality surge suppressor will protect this equipment.

And, this is also the answer to protecting the laser printer. Since the laser, scanner, and tape backup are not part of on-going processing, the damage done by corrupting influences is easier to deal with. If, for example, a bothersome electrical event fouls the data stream from the PC to the laser printer, the corrective action is to print the page over again. This one-step-at-a-time job processing allows us to look at these outboard devices more in the light of protecting them from actual hardware damage than from worrying about the actual processing itself. If the result of their function is not satisfactory, we simply repeat the process. On a LAN, however, the process is interactive and the stream of data requires a higher level of power purity.

It is for this reason that the peripherals, including the laser printer, can be protected with less expensive items. Please take note. We are not suggesting a cheap surge strip or anything of the kind. If we are going to substitute a surge device for a power conditioner, let's be clear that it must be a high-quality design which is fully capable of handling common-mode as well as normal-mode events in such a way that the connected device is completely protected.

What if the publishing system is part of a network? The same thing holds true in that case. The network needs full-time power, as well as power conditioning, to ensure the integrity of data stored and in process. The peripherals that don't interact with the network, but job process, can be protected from damage at a lesser overall cost.

One point is vital. If a variety of power peripherals are used for economy sake, as we are suggesting, it is imperative that they all be referenced to the same ground, as close to the computer as possible. This can be done by bonding the power units together, or by simply plugging them into the same receptacle on the wall. We must not create a ground loop while trying to solve potential power problems. Also, under normal circumstances, we would never recommend using more than one different type of protective device. After all, buying a power conditioner large enough to accommodate the PC, printer, and any other peripheral will cost only a few more dollars than one sized only for the PC. The exception is a laser printer. Its high-power usage makes it a candidate for exploring the alternatives.

Final Thoughts

One of the important issues that the discussion on LANs and Desktop Publishing exposes is the importance of the application of the PC. The application makes all the difference in terms of evaluating the type of appropriate product technology to be applied. And it is hard to generalize. All home computers are not equal. Some commercial settings have site-specific considerations. Different software applications, hardware configurations, and consumer expectations have everything to do with the kind and level of protection needed.

Now that all the technological options have been laid out, the reader can evaluate the specific needs of his or her application and choose wisely. There is a magic scale that exists, with the need for protection on one side and dollars on the other. Finding the proper balance is not always easy. This book has covered enough of every area of power protection so that the thoughtful decision maker, who is concerned with the wise use of personal or company money, can make purchases that fit the application and will perform appropriately.

We have tried to develop this book logically by first arming the reader with the basic knowledge required to understand the subject of computer power. We talked about environmental issues like power quality, grounding, and the PC's own power supply. When we got to those chapters that dealt with the actual products, we started with the simplest, cheapest, and smallest first, and then built up from there. Finally, we applied the technology to two of the fastest growing areas of computing—LANs and Desktop Publishing.

What's left? *The future.*

What will the future of computing bring? One thing we know that may be coming is *nonvolatile memory*. This is memory that is not lost when the power goes out. Certainly, faster clock speeds are on their way. And storage media that is more densely packed, with faster scanning rates, is a phenomenon we don't have to wait for. It's happening on an ongoing basis.

The real question is, "Will the pace of rapid advancement of computing technology make power protection obsolete?" The answer is, "No." The trend has been that advancements have created a greater need for power products. Even some of the enhancements made to make computers less vulnerable to certain kinds of power disturbances have generated a need for other kinds of protection.

Another inevitable question I get at my workshops is, "Will computer manufacturers ever build power conditioning into their products?" I can only say, "Not in my lifetime." The way that the price wars have been going, the public is lucky to find a power supply in their PC. Nothing that adds a dime's worth of cost, and which doesn't return a dollar's worth of profit, will ever be put in a PC. There have been one or two attempts at including a UPS in PCs, but they have not sold well.

Strangely enough, another industry has done this with great success. The telecommunications industry has been including battery backup as part of their systems for many years. Their power requirements are somewhat different, however. This has not and probably won't happen in the computer industry.

One thing that is rumored to change, however, is the power supply. New designs are coming out every day. A recent introduction to the field claims to draw current in a sinusoidal waveshape. Whether this will appear in PCs is not clear. But the window is still wide open for new power-supply designs to enter the market. When they do, it will no doubt be necessary to take a new look at the kind of protection that may be appropriate.

There are a number of new chips that are making their way into the market which we should mention. The first is a member of a family of rectifiers that is impervious to EMI. Obviously, the military is the biggest market for these chips. As of yet, these chips have not made their way into the PC market. Another advancement is chip technology that monitors the power, and takes action on a nanosecond basis to thwart power fluctuations. How this interfaces with the machine's intelligence is not clear. One possibility is that it will halt processing temporarily, in order to ensure the integrity of the data. In a location where power is particularly bad, this might bring processing to its knees—requiring the installation of a UPS or power-conditioning equipment. History has shown that what designers have thought was an advancement, in the way computers deal with utility power, usually requires a new computer power strategy.

Of course, this is the purpose behind this book. Every computer user needs a computer-power strategy. The information contained here should assist the reader in matching the proper technological solution to their particular needs, without wasting money. To illustrate what this book was written to avoid, consider the following true story.

A hospital was having power problems with a computerized phone system. The facilities manager called his electrical contractor and both agreed that they probably needed a UPS. The contractor called his electrical supply house and ordered a 1500-watt SPS to solve the problem that the hospital was experiencing. The cost of the item was about $2000. After installing the UPS, problems with the phone system still persisted. An "expert" was called in to analyze the situation. He connected a BMI, which is an expensive power-line analyzer, to the input and the output of the SPS in order to test and see if the unit was performing properly. The tape of the BMI showed that the telephone system was experiencing impulses of up to 173 volts. They simulated an outage by pulling the plug on the SPS and the output low voltage of the SPS was recorded at 103 volts.

The "expert" concluded that there was no way the telephone system could survive in an electrical environment like that. At this point, everyone descended on the electrical wholesaler. Why had they sold a product that didn't work? What were they, a bunch of thieves? In a panic, the wholesaler called in their own expert (me).

After a thorough and professional analysis of the BMI tape, and studying the specifications of the SPS, the real expert knew exactly what the problem was. The SPS had a surge protector, but, beyond that, was not designed to condition power in any way. In fact, the peak of the voltage sine wave is 170 volts. No surge to protect here.

Next, the real expert checked the transfer point of the SPS. Surprise! It was 103 volts, which is the typical transfer point of most SPSs. The real expert concluded that the SPS was performing exactly as it was supposed to perform. The problem all along was the facilities manager, the contractor, and the "expert"—none of them understood the technology of the product they needed to purchase. They had heard that UPSs would cure problems so they bought something without really knowing what it was. The result—hard feelings, finger pointing, and $2000 wasted.

Now that you have read this book, this should not happen. We must look at our problem or our potential problem. We should evaluate our financial resources. And, we should balance the knowledge contained here against the claims of the manufacturers. The result will be the kind of trade-off that we are willing to live with. We can now go back to computing, knowing that we have the foundation laid for PC power protection.

Bibliography

Bent, Rodney; Lewis, Warren; Clark, O. Melville; Martzloff, Francois D.; Richman, Peter; Tetreault, Maurice; Kalbach, J. Fred. *Surge Protection of Computers and Other Electronic Systems*. Madison, WI: University of Wisconsin, n.d.

Bowyer, Richard N. "Rotary and Static UPS Both Convert DC to AC but Total Costs Vary," *Computer Technology Review* (Winter 1985).

Brill, Kenneth G. *Computer Power Protection Equipment: An Introductory Guide*. California: Atlas Energy Systems, 1977.

Brown, John F. "Trends in kw-size rack-mounted power supplies," *Powertechnics Magazine*, n.d.

Cannon, Don L. and Luecke, Gerald. *Understanding Communications Systems*. Dallas, TX: Texas Instruments Incorporated, 1984.

Carr, Joseph J. *Digital Electronics Troubleshooting*. Blue Ridge Summit, PA: Tab Books Inc., 1981

Clark, O. Melville. *EMP Transient Suppression Using the Transzorb®*. Tempe, AZ: General Semiconductor Industries (December 1979).

Clark, O. Melville. *Long-Term Pulse Life and Design Criteria for Transzorb® Transient Voltage Suppressors*. Tempe, AZ: General Semiconductor Industries (April 1979).

"Computer Power Systems." *Guide Specification: EDP Site Grounding*. Carson, CA: CPS, n.d.

Con Edison. *Electric Power and the Computer*. New York: Con Edison, 1984.

Conwill, Norman B. "The Computer Power System," *A New Concept in Power Distribution*. Carson, CA: Computer Power Systems, n.d.

Cronin, Daniel J. *Microcomputer Data Security*. New York, NY: Prentice Hall, 1986.

Crosby, Ben G. "Power Conditioning," *Journal of Healthcare Material Management* (January 1987).

Crosby, Ben G. "Total System Reliability," *Microservice Management* (October 1987).

Daughtry, Vicki C. and Keller, David. "New Ferro Power Conditioners Deliver Computer Grade Power," *Computer Technology Review* (Summer 1986).

Devore, Tim. "Nonlinear Loads and UPS Systems," *EC&M* (July, 1985).

Douglas, John. "Quality of Power in the Electronics Age," *EPRI Journal* (November 1985).

Dranetz. *How to Correct Power Line Disturbances*. Edison, NJ: Dranetz Technologies, Inc., 1985.

Dranetz. *How to Identify Power Line Disturbances*. Edison, NJ: Dranetz Technologies, Inc., 1985.

Dranetz. *Understanding Power Line Disturbances*. Edison, NJ: Dranetz Technologies, Inc., 1985.

DWP. *Power Supply for Los Angeles*. Los Angeles, CA: Los Angeles Department of Water and Power, 1982.

EPE. *Power: Problems and Solutions*. Costa Mesa, CA: Emergency Power Engineering, Inc., n.d.

Goldstein, M. and Speranza, P.D. *The Quality of U.S. Commercial AC Power*. Whippany, NJ: Bell Telephone Laboratories, 1982 (IEEE).

Gottlieb, Irving M. *Regulated Power Supplies. 3rd. ed.* Indianapolis, IN: Howard W. Sams & Company, 1986.

Gould Deltec. *AC Power Handbook of Problems and Solutions. 3rd. ed.* San Diego, CA: Gould, Inc., Power Conversion Division, 1975.

GSI® *Product Data Book—10th Edition.* Tempe, AZ: General Semiconductor Industries, n.d.

IEEE. *The Gold Book: Recommended Practice for the Design of Reliable Industrial and Commercial Power Systems*. ANSI/IEEE Standard 493-1980.

IEEE. *The Gray Book: Recommended Practice for Electrical Power Systems in Commercial Buildings*. IEEE Standard 241-1983.

IEEE. *The Green Book: Recommended Practice for Grounding Industrial and Commercial Power Systems*. ANSI/IEEE Standard 142-1982.

IEEE. *The Orange Book: Recommended Practice for Emergency and Standby Power for Industrial and Commercial Applications*. ANSI/IEEE Standard 446-1980.

IEEE. *The Red Book: Recommended Practice for Electric Power Distribution for Industrial Plants*. IEEE Standard 141-1976.

IEEE. *IEEE Standard Dictionary of Electrical and Electronic Terms*. New York: IEEE, 1977.

Kalbach, John Fredrick. *Interaction Between Computer Systems and Their Power Sources*. Boston, MA: Kalbach Engineering, 1984.

Key, Eugene George. *Principles of Electricity*. New York, NY: Harper & Row (1967).

KW Control Systems, Inc. *Introduction to the Uniblock UPS System*. Middletown, NY, n.d.

KW Control Systems, Inc. *Uniblock Analysis: Reliability and System Availability*. Middletown, NY, n.d.

Lewis, Warren H. "A Dozen Electrical Mistakes," *Datamation* (May 1984).

Lewis, Warren H. *Electrical Power, Grounding, and Life Safety Systems for EDP Sites*. California: Computer Power Systems, 1981.

Lewis, Warren H. *Safe and Effective Grounding*. 1983.

Lonie, Bruce B. and Frost, Holly. "How to make sure electrical interference won't short-circuit your career as a telecom manager," *Communication Age* (July 1986).

MacDonald, Ian. *Solutions to Computer Power Problems: Uninterruptible Power Systems*. Santa Ana, CA: Emerson Electric, n.d.

MacGorman, D.R. et al. *Lightning Strike Density for the Contiguous United States from Thunderstorm Duration Records*. Washington D.C.: National Oceanic and Atmospheric Administration, 1984.

McEachern, Alex. *Changing Strategies for Using Power Line Monitors.* Foster City, CA: Basic Measuring Instruments, n.d.

McLoughlin, Robert C. and Redding, Randall J. "Protection of Electronics from Lightning and Other Larger AC Power Pulses," *EMC Technology* (September-October 1987).

McWhorter, Gene. *Understanding Digital Electronics.* Dallas, TX: Texas Instruments Incorporated, 1984.

Meyer, Charles. *SCR-controlled Loads, Waveform Distortion and Standby Power Systems.* Onan Corp., n.d.

Mutascio, Vince. "Selecting Power Supplies for Burn-In Systems," *Evaluation Engineering* (October 1986).

Nakagawa, Akio et al. "1,800 V Bipolar-Mode MOSFETs (IGBT)," *Toshiba Review No. 161* (Autumn 1987).

National Bureau of Standards. *Federal Information Processing Standards Publication 94.* Washington, D.C.: U.S. Department of Commerce, 1983.

National Electrical Code, NFPA-70-1981/84, National Fire Protection Association, Boston, MA.

Nielsen, Gwen and Brletich, Frank. "Changing Technology Leads to Changes in Power Requirements," *Computer Technology Review* (Winter 1983).

Nystrom, Peter. "Analyze System Needs before You Decide to Add Voltage Regulation," *Computer Technology Review* (Winter 1984).

Nystom, Peter and Cosgrove, Steven. "Power Conditioning Provides Documented Productivity Gains in Semiconductor Fabrication and ATE," *IEEE Proceedings of International Test Conference,* November 1985.

O'Connor, James. "Power's Electrical Reference File," *Power* (October 1953).

The Office of Business Research and Analysis. *The Effects of Electrical Power Variations Upon Computers: an Overview.* Washington, D.C.: U.S. Dept. of Commerce, n.d.

ONEAC Corp. *Case Studies on Reliability in Telecommunications.* Libertyville, IL (1986).

Paulin, William and Drabkin, Mark. "Series-Hybrid Circuits Protect Sensitive Loads from Power Anomalies," *Computer Technology Review* (Spring 1986).

Raiger, John R. "Power Line Conditioning," *BTT* (May/June 1987).

Rechsteiner, Emil B. "Comprehensive Power Protection Requires a Static or Rotary UPS," *Computer Technology Review* (Spring 1986).

Rechsteiner, Emil B. *Power to Computers; Keep It Clean and Stable!*. Littleton, MA: Frequency Technology, Inc., n.d.

Robins, Marc. "Our Power Needs Cleaning," *Teleconnect* (November 1986).

Roehr, William D. and Clark, O. Melville. *AC Power Line Protection for an IEEE 587 Class B Environment*. Tempe, AZ: General Semiconductor Industries, Inc. (1984).

RTE Deltec. *AC Power Handbook of Problems and Solutions, 5th ed.* San Diego, CA: RTE Deltec Corporation, 1975.

Salzer Technology Enterprises, Inc. *UPS: Uninterruptible Power Systems and Other Power Protection Equipment*. Santa Monica, CA: Salzer Technology Enterprises, Inc., 1986.

Seki, Nagataka. *Gate Circuit on Gate Turn-off Thyristor*. Tokyo, Japan: Toshiba Corp. (September 1981).

Seki, N. and Ichikawa, K. "Gating Circuit Developed for High Power Thyristors," *IEEE Power Electronics Specialists Conference—1981*. Boulder, CO (1981).

Shambrook, Bill. "Burn-In Update," *Evaluation Engineering* (February 1985).

Shambrook, Bill. "How to 'Clean Up' AC Power Lines to Minimize Semiconductor Fabrication and Test Equipment Malfunctions," *Microelectronic Manufacturing and Testing* (August, 1985).

Sorgel Transformers. *Sorgel Dry-Type Transformer Study Course*. Milwaukee, WI: Sorgel Transformers, n.d.

Transient Voltage Devices—Fifth Edition. General Electric Company (1986).

Trcmaglio, Don. *Power Line Disturbances and How to Eliminate Them*. Bristol, CN: Superior Electric, 1985.

Westinghouse Architect's and Engineer's Electrical Data Book. Westinghouse Electric Corporation, 1957.

Wiswell, Phil. "Surge Suppressors," *PC Magazine* (May 1986).

Glossary

Actual Power—A term referring to the number of watts of power consumed by a load.

Alternating Current—Electrical current which reverses direction periodically, expressed in hertz or cycles per second. Abbreviated AC.

Ampere—The quantitative unit measurement of electrical current. Abbreviated Amp or A.

Ampacity—A term used to describe the current-handling capacity of an electrical device.

Amperage—A term synonymous with current; used in describing electrical current.

Antimony—An element found in lead-acid batteries; used to harden the plate material.

Apparent Power—The load power as expressed in VA or kVA. This value is usually greater than real power or watts, due to circuit reactance. This reactance causes the timing between the voltage and current to vary. Device sizing must be in accordance with Volts times Amps rather than in Watts, since Voltamperes is the apparent load seen by the power-handling device.

Arc—Sparking generated when current flows between two points of different potential, due to leakage through the intervening insulator.

Arrester—A device placed from phase to ground whose nonlinear impedance characteristics provide a path for high-amplitude transients.

Autotransformer—A transformer that uses common turns for both the primary and secondary windings, thus providing no isolation for the input from thc output.

Balance—A term used to describe the even distribution of loads on the legs of a three-phase system.

Battery—A group of cells connected in such a way that more current and/or voltage is delivered than from one single cell.

Battery, Sealed—A battery containing a gelled or liquid electrolyte that has no opening for water replenishment.

Blackout—The total loss of commercial electrical power. Sometimes refers to the length of time that the power must be off to bring the computer down. Used synonymously with *Outage*.

Branch Circuit—A discrete division of a load that is protected by one fuse or breaker.

Breaker—Short for *circuit breaker*.

Brownout—A long-duration undervoltage condition, usually hours or days in length. Brownouts can be caused by heavy usage during peak hours, or they may be planned as an energy conservation strategy.

Building Service Entry—That point where commercial power enters the building.

Bus—A heavy, rigid conductor. Often equipped with screws or some other means by which a number of smaller conductors can be connected to it. Also called a *bus bar*.

Bypass Line—An alternate electrical path around a device, usually a UPS, that allows the flow of power to the load. This bypass may "make" before breaking power to the load or may drop power to the load in the switching process. Bypass lines are used for three purposes: to allow the performance of maintenance on equipment, to bypass damaged equipment, or to pass fault current to a circuit breaker upstream. Also called a *bypass circuit*.

Calcium—An element used in lead-acid batteries to harden the plate material.

Capacitance—A term referring to the electrical properties of a capacitor or to a circuit that displays capacitor-like behavior.

Capacitive Reactance—The behavior of alternating current as it interacts with capacitance encountered in a circuit.

Capacitor—A discrete electrical device which has two electrodes and an intervening insulator, which is called the dielectric.

Cell—A combination of two metal plates suspended in an electrolyte which, when connected to an external circuit, causes a current to flow.

Charge Voltage—The voltage that must be applied to storage batteries to maintain their maximum charge.

Choke—A form of inductor which is constructed to allow desirable frequency signals to pass while acting with high impedance to other signals at some undesirable frequency.

Circuit Breaker—A resettable device that responds to a preset level of excess current flow by opening the circuit, thereby preventing damage to circuit elements.

Coax—A cable constructed by using two concentric conductors separated by an insulator.

Common-Mode Noise—Abnormal signals that appear between a current-carrying line and its associated ground.

Compensating Winding—A winding on the primary of a ferroresonant transformer that is connected opposite to the output winding in order to improve regulation.

Converter—A device that changes alternating current to direct current, or a device that changes direct current to alternating current, can be called by the general term of "converter." In this sense, a rectifier/charger and an inverter might both be termed converters. The term converter is also applied to any of a family of devices that convert the frequency of the alternating current.

Core—The iron structure of a transformer around which the windings are wound. A choke also has a core but does not act as a transformer.

Core Saturation—That point at which the iron material, the core, of an inductor or transformer will no longer produce more lines of flux when current flow through the windings is increased.

CPU—An acronym used for the central processing unit of a computer.

Critical Load—That portion of electrical/electronic equipment for which power quality is a vital consideration. The term "load" applies to all current-carrying devices on a given circuit or feeder. The term "critical load" refines the language to include only those current-using devices whose operation is considered essential.

CSA—An abbreviation for the Canadian Standards Association. This is a Canadian safety assurance agency similar to the Underwriter's Laboratories.

Current—The flow of electricity in a circuit as expressed in amperes. Current refers to the quantity or intensity of electrical flow. Voltage, on the other hand, refers to the pressure or force causing the electrical flow.

Current Balance—A term that describes the nearly equal flow of current on each leg of a three-phase power system. With this flow balanced, the theoretical flow of current in the neutral line, with respect to ground, will be zero.

Cycles Per Second—This term describes the frequency of alternating current. Frequency is more properly described using the term "hertz," which is synonymous with cycles per second.

Delta—A term describing a kind of connection in a three-phase circuit; often the primary side of a transformer. A delta connection may or may not have a neutral conductor.

Delta/Wye Transformer—A three-phase transformer with a delta connection on one side and a wye connection on the other. Most often the delta connection is on the primary side.

Dip—Another term for Sag.

Direct Current—Electrical current which flows consistently in one direction. Abbreviated DC.

Disk—A memory device which uses a magnetic media for the storage of information. Disk, as a term, has expanded into other areas often used to describe the shape of the storage media, that is: floppy disk, compact disk, laser disk, or hard disk. It sometimes refers to the way in which the storage media mimics a disk media; that is, RAM disk or bubble memory.

Distortion—The waveshape of a signal that is not normal is distorted. Distortion is a term that describes abnormal waveshapes.

Distribution—The way in which power is routed to various current-using sites or devices. Outside the building, distribution refers to the process of routing power from the power plant to the users. Inside the building, distribution is the process of using feeders and circuits to provide power to devices.

Dropout—A total loss of voltage for a short period of time.

Electrolyte—The acid or alkaline solution in which the plates of a battery cell are immersed.

Electromagnetic Interference—A term that describes electrically induced noise or transients. Abbreviated EMI.

Engine Generator—A combination of an internal combustion engine and a generator; often referred to as a diesel generator.

Feedback—Energy that is fed from the output of a circuit back to its input.

Ferroresonance—When an iron-core inductor is part of an LC circuit and it is driven into saturation, causing its inductive reactance to increase to equal the capacitive reactance of the circuit, this action is called ferroresonance.

Ferroresonant Transformer—A transformer that uses the principle of ferroresonance to regulate the output voltage.

Filter—An electronic device which opposes the passage of a certain frequency band while allowing other frequencies to pass. Filters are designed to produce four different results. A high-pass filter allows all signals above a given frequency to pass. A low-pass filter allows only frequencies below a given frequency to pass. A bandpass filter allows a given band of frequencies to pass while attenuating all others. A trap filter allows all frequencies to pass but acts as a high-impedance device to the tuned frequency of the filter.

Flashover—Arcing that is caused by the breakdown of insulation between two conductors where a high current flow exists, with a high potential difference between the conductors.

Flywheel—A heavy, wheel-like piece of metal or steel which acts as a governor to provide an inertial force generally found in motor generators.

Fuse—A device that automatically self-destructs when the current passing through it exceeds the rated value of the fuse.

Gassing—The process by which hydrogen gas is produced from the breakdown of the water in an electrolyte solution during battery charging.

Ground—A general term that refers to the point at which other portions of a circuit are referenced when making measurements. Power-systems grounding is that point to which the neutral conductor, safety ground, and building ground are connected. This grounding electrode may be a water pipe, driven ground rod, or the steel frame of the building.

Ground Fault—An undesired path that allows current to flow from a line to ground.

Ground Loop—The condition of having two or more ground references in a common system. When two or more grounds have a potential difference between them, current can flow. This flow of current is a new circuit or loop which can interfere with the normal operation of the system.

Harmonic—A frequency that is a multiple of the fundamental frequency. For example, 120 Hz is the second harmonic of 60 Hz, 180 Hz is the third harmonic, and so forth.

Harmonic Distortion—Excessive harmonic content that distorts the normal sinusoidal waveform is harmonic distortion. This can cause overheating of circuit elements and might appear to a device as data-corrupting noise.

Hertz—A term describing the frequency of alternating current. The term, hertz, is synonymous with cycles per second. Abbreviated Hz.

Impedance—Measured in ohms, impedance is the total opposition to current flow in a circuit where alternating current is flowing. This includes inductive reactance, capacitive reactance, and resistance. Symbol is Z.

Impulse—A disturbance of the voltage waveform that is less than about one millisecond. Voltages can rise to hundreds or even thousands of volts in a very short period of time. An impulse may be additive or subtractive. (Sometimes called a notch.)

Inductance—This term describes the electrical properties of a coil of wire and its resultant magnetic field when an alternating current is passed through it. This interaction offers an impedance to current flow, thereby causing the current waveform to lag behind the voltage waveform. This results in what's known as a lagging power factor.

Inductive Reactance—A term used to describe the impedance to alternating current offered by an inductive circuit. Reactance is expressed in a unit called the "henry."

Inductor—A discrete circuit element which has the property of inductance. It should be noted that at very high radio frequencies, a straight wire or a path on a printed-circuit board can act as an inductor.

Inrush—A term used to describe the high-current demand of a device when it is initially turned on, due to a low load impedance before the device has reached its normal operating value.

Inverter—The subassembly of a UPS that converts DC power into AC power.

Isolation—The degree to which a device can separate the electrical environment of its input from its output, while allowing the desired transmission to pass across the separation.

Junction Box—A metal box inside which electrical connections are made. Also called a *J-Box*.

Kilohertz—A term meaning 1000 cycles per second. Abbreviated kHz.

Kilovoltamperes—Abbreviated kVA. Voltage times amperage is expressed in kVA. Kilovoltamperes is the "Apparent Power," and can be found by dividing kilowatts by the power factor.

Kilowatts—Term for "Real Power," or the power actually used by the load.

LC—An abbreviation for the inductance and capacitance that is used in the same circuit.

Light-Emitting Diode—A semiconductor that emits light when a current is applied to it. Abbreviated LED.

Lightning Arrester—A device used to pass large impulses to ground. It is vital that this device be placed upstream from the computer ground.

Line—A term used generally to describe a current-carrying conductor.

Line to Line—A term used to describe a given condition between conductors of a multiphase feeder.

Line to Neutral—A term used to describe a given condition between a phase conductor and a neutral conductor.

Load—Any electrical device connected to a power source may be called by the general term of "load."

Magnetic Field—The lines of force that exist around an energized electrical conductor, magnet, or inductor.

Magnetic Synthesizer—A marketing term for a certain variety of ferroresonant regulator.

Maintenance Bypass—A line that allows power to be routed around a power device so maintenance or repair can be performed on the unit.

Mean Time Between Failure—A statistical estimate of the time a component, subassembly, or operating unit will operate before failure will occur. Abbreviated MTBF.

Mean Time to Repair—A statistical estimate of the repair time for a failed item. Abbreviated MTTR.

Megahertz—A term for one million hertz (cycles per second). Abbreviated MHz.

Motor Alternator—A device that consists of an AC generator mechanically linked to an electric motor, which is driven by utility power or by batteries. An alternator is an AC generator.

Motor Generator—A term used synonymously for "motor alternator."

National Electrical Code—A set of rules and regulations, plus recommended electrical practices, that are put out by the National Fire Protection Association. Abbreviated N.E.C.

Neutral—One of the conductors of a three-phase wye system is the neutral conductor. Sometimes called the return conductor, it carries the entire current of a single-phase circuit and the resultant current in a three-phase system that is unbalanced. The neutral is bonded to ground on the output of a three-phase delta-wye transformer.

Noise—An undesirable signal, which is irregular yet oscillatory, that is superimposed on the desired signal. *See* Common-Mode Noise and Normal-Mode Noise.

Normal-Mode Noise—A noise signal which appears between a set of phase conductors, irrespective of their associated ground conductor.

Notch—Slang for a negative or subtractive impulse.

Ohm—The unit of measurement for resistance (symbol R), impedance (symbol Z), and reactance (symbol X).

Ohm's Law—The mathematical relationship between Volts, Amperes, and Ohms: Volts = Amperes times Ohms.

Orderly Shutdown—The turning off of power to computer devices in such a way that data is not lost or corrupted.

Oscillation—Generally used to mean an electrical phenomenon that produces a number of occurrences above or below a given instantaneous voltage level.

Outage—A long-term loss of voltage resulting from a localized utility failure.

Overvoltage—Similar to a surge but for a longer period of time, over 2.5 seconds.

Peak—The maximum instantaneous measurement of an electrical event.

Phase—A term used to describe the timing between two or more events tied to the same frequency.

Phase Balancing—The practice of placing equal electrical loads on each leg of a three-phase system. *See also* Neutral, Balance.

Phase Rotation—The sequence in which a comparable voltage appears in all three phases (A, B, and C) of a three-phase system.

Planté Plate—A kind of lead-antimony grid used in the construction of battery plates.

Power—A general term which means the capacity for doing work. In the electrical environment, this is usually measured in watts.

Power Distribution Unit—A portable electrical distribution device that provides an easily expandable and flexible electrical environment for a computer and its associated peripherals. Abbreviated PDU.

Power Factor—Watts divided by volt-amperes, or the ratio of actual power to apparent power.

Power-Line Monitor—A measuring device which reports information on the changing conditions of electrical power.

Primary—The input winding of a transformer.

Pulsating DC—A voltage that periodically rises and falls but does not change polarity.

Pulse-Width Modulation—Process for varying the width of a train of pulses by tying it to the characteristics of another signal. Abbreviated PWM.

Radio-Frequency Interference—Electromagnetic signals of a frequency associated with electromagnetic radiation, which are coupled to a conductor either directly or as with an antenna. Abbreviated RFI.

Reactance—The opposition to the flow of alternating current in a circuit, usually described as either capacitive or inductive reactance.

Rectifier/Charger—A subassembly of a UPS that performs the function of converting the incoming AC into DC for driving the inverter and charging the batteries.

Redundancy—The practice of providing backup modules to support a function, in case other modules should fail.

Reflection—The wave that is generated when a traveling wave reaches the point at which line impedance changes.

Regulation—A term used to describe the action of holding a constant electrical value in the face of fluctuations.

Remote Emergency Power Off—A device that permits the total shutdown of electrical power devices from an exit, in the event of an emergency. Abbreviated REPO.

Resistance—A term describing the opposition of elements of a circuit to alternating or direct current. Symbol is R.

Resistor—A discrete electronic component designed to produce a DC voltage drop when current passes through it.

Root Mean Square—The square root of the arithmetic mean of the squares of a set of electrical amplitudes. Abbreviated RMS.

Rotary—A term used in describing certain electrical power equipment which functions through rotational mechanics.

Safety Ground—A conductive path that bonds all cabinets and conductor shields to the power-source ground.

Sag—A short-term RMS voltage decrease which exceeds an established upper limit for less than 2.5 seconds.

Secondary—The output winding of a transformer.

Shield—A conductive enclosure or barrier that prevents electrical interference from external sources.

Shunt Trip—A type of circuit breaker that can also be activated by a circuit other than the one it is protecting.

Sine Wave—A fundamental waveform produced by periodic oscillation that expresses the sine or cosine of a linear function of time or space, or both.

Single Phase—That portion of a power source which represents only a single phase of the three phases that are available.

Single-Point Ground—The practice of tying the power neutral ground and safety ground together at the same point, thus avoiding a differential ground potential between points in a system.

Surge—A short-term voltage increase that exceeds established upper limits for less than 2.5 seconds.

Synchronization—In the context used here, the term relates to maintaining a constant phase relationship between AC signals.

Tap—A terminal on a transformer winding.

Tap Switching—The action of changing from one terminal on a transformer winding to another, thereby changing the turns ratio of the device to maintain a desire voltage relationship.

Three Phase—An electrical system with three different voltage lines or legs, which carry sine-wave waveforms that are 120° out of phase from one another.

Total Harmonic Distortion—A term that refers to the alteration of a waveshape by the presence of multiples of the fundamental frequency of the signal. Abbreviated THD.

Transfer Switch—A device used to transfer the load of a power unit from itself to a bypass line.

Transformer—A device used for changing the voltage of an AC circuit and/or isolating a circuit from its power source.

Transient—An electrical event of a nonrepetitive nature. The term is used interchangeably with the term "impulse"; however, the term relates more to the intermittent occurrence of "surges" and "sags."

Transverse-Mode Noise—Often used as a synonym for normal-mode noise, it more clearly relates to noise that is the result of the conversion of common-mode noise to normal-mode noise after it passes through a transformer.

UL—The abbreviation for Underwriter's Laboratories, Inc., an independent United States product-safety assurance agency.

Undervoltage—Like a sag, but for a longer period of time; over 2.5 seconds.

Uninterruptible Power System—A power-conditioning and supply system that provides power during outages. Abbreviated UPS.

Volt—The quantitative measurement of electrical force or potential; also called *electromotive force.*

Voltage Regulator—A circuit that has a constant output voltage when input voltage fluctuates.

Voltampere—The unit of measurement of apparent power.

Watt—The unit of measurement of actual power.

Waveform—The graphic form of an electrical parameter.

Wye—A three-phase connection with a single common neutral conductor and three phase conductors.

Zero Signal Reference—The result of a properly installed ground structure is a constant potential over a broad band of frequencies between the devices that are part of the structure. This highly desirable state is called the *zero signal reference*, meaning the potential between points on the ground reference is equal to zero over a broad range of frequencies.

Index

H

I

K

L

R

S

T

U

V

W

Y

Z

Computer Electrical Power Requirements

Mark Waller

This in-depth examination of power regulation problems offers solutions that will help control electrical power input for mini, mainframe, and microcomputers. As a result, permanent and expensive damage to computers can be avoided.

Field engineers, technicians, and computer repair and maintenance professionals involved in problems with computer electrical power will benefit from this book. Its discussion of power regulators and how they can best be implemented to provide "clean power" for computers is especially valuable.

Topics covered include:

- Utility Power
- A Closer Look at Utility Power
- Inside the Building
- Lightning, Static, and Noise
- Grounding
- Personal Computers and Office Electronic Equipment
- Transient Suppression
- Isolation and Distribution
- Voltage Regulation
- M-G Sets, RUPS, and UPS
- Batteries for UPS Systems
- PC Power
- Appendices: The Future, Glossary, Bibliography

250 Pages, 7½ x 9¾, Softbound
ISBN: 0-672-22561-1
No. 22561, $19.95

IBM® PC Advanced Troubleshooting & Repair

Robert C. Brenner

Here is in-depth, advanced data for troubleshooting and repair of the IBM PC. This technical book compliments the circuit-tested COMPUTERFACTS™ service data with its descriptive text and expanded circuit explanations.

This book provides more sophisticated data than the author's earlier text, *IBM® PC Troubleshooting & Repair Guide.* It details PC operation and gives a full description of how to use test equipment with PC repair. Troubleshooting programs help locate failures while numerous oscilloscope screen photos and drawings help to identify problems.

Topics covered include:

- System Overview
- Detailed System Operation
- Troubleshooting Techniques
- Preliminary Service Checks
- Detailed Circuit Troubleshooting/Analysis: Power Supply, System Board, Monochrome Monitor/Printer Adapter, Color Graphic Monitor Adapter, Keyboard, Disk Drive Adapter, and Disk Drives (A & B) Type 1
- Appendices: Disassembly Instructions, Reassembly Instructions, Adjustments to System Board and Power Board, Schematic Notes, Switches & Jumpers, and Safety Precautions & Warnings.

304 Pages, 8½ x 11, Softbound
ISBN: 0-672-22590-5
No. 22590, $24.95

Troubleshooting with the Oscilloscope, Fifth Edition

Robert G. Middleton,
Revised by Joseph J. Carr

This 225-page book will help technicians and hobbyists obtain the maximum benefits from the wide selection of scopes now available for servicing and repair.

The new edition emphasizes digital troubleshooting and applications as well as the time- and data-domain analyzers and the logic state analyzer, with up-to-date information about television receiver troubleshooting.

Topics covered include:

- Introduction to the Oscilloscope
- How to Operate an Oscilloscope
- Using Oscilloscope Probes
- TV Signal Tracing in RF, IF, and Video Amplifiers
- Signal Tracing in the TV Sync Section
- Troubleshooting in the TV AFC and Horizontal Oscillator Section
- Waveform Tests in the Horizontal Sweep Section
- Troubleshooting in the TV Vertical Sweep Section
- Signal Tracing in the TV Sound-IF and Audio Sections
- Special Oscilloscopes and Their Applications
- Digital Logic Troubleshooting with the Oscilloscope

225 Pages, 5½ x 8½, Softbound
ISBN: 0-672-22473-9
No. 22473, $16.95

Advanced Digital Troubleshooting

Alvis J. Evans

Advanced Digital Troubleshooting provides comprehensive coverage of digital test equipment for intermediate-level electronics technicians, maintenance technicians, technical students, and hobbyists. The book emphasizes practical troubleshooting techniques, going into specifics at the board and even component level where necessary.

Beginning with a brief review of digital circuits, it presents successful approaches to troubleshooting and includes digital test instruments such as digital logic probes, oscilloscopes, logic analyzers, and an in-circuit emulator. Detailed coverage of microprocessor troubleshooting, digital system maintenance, and several helpful tips round out this well-illustrated tutorial.

Topics covered include:

- Electrical Characteristics of Digital Systems
- Digital Troubleshooting Methodology and Approaches
- Microcomputer Fundamentals
- Meet the Main Chips
- Software and the Diagnostic Program
- Using Basic Digital Troubleshooting Instruments
- The Logic Analyzer
- An In-Circuit Emulator
- Signature Analysis
- Preventive Maintenance, Repair, and Checkout

208 Pages, 8½ x 11, Softbound
ISBN: 0-672-22571-9
No. 22571, $19.95

Visit your local book retailer or call 800-428-SAMS.

Understanding Digital Troubleshooting, Second Edition

Don L. Cannon

Digital electronic systems are more reliable than the systems they replace, yet, at some point, they will need repair and maintenance. This book provides an insight into this highly technical world in a language that both technicians and nonengineers can understand. It presents the basic concepts and fundamental techniques needed to locate faults in digital systems and how to repair them.

- Digital Systems Fundamentals
- Digital Systems Functions
- Troubleshooting Fundamentals
- Combinational Logic Problems
- Sequential Logic Problems
- Memory Problems
- Input/Output Problems
- Basic Timing Problems
- Advanced Techniques

272 Pages, 7 x 9, Softbound
ISBN: 0-672-27015-3
No. 27015, $17.95

Understanding Communications Systems, Second Edition

Cannon and Luecke

In an easy-to-understand, self-paced learning format, this book presents a fascinating look at the world of electronic communications and its impact on our everyday lives. The book explores many of the systems that are used every day—AM/FM radio, telephone, TV, data communications by computer, facsimile, and satellite. It explains how information is converted into electrical signals, transmitted to distant locations, and converted back to the original information.

Topics covered include:

- The World of Communications
- Using Electrical Signals for Communications
- Basic System Functions and Conversions
- The Communications Spectrum
- Telegraph and Telephone Systems
- Radio and Television Systems
- Computer Networks and Systems
- Facsimile
- Satellite Communications Systems

288 Pages, 7 x 9, Softbound
ISBN: 0-672-27016-1
No. 27016, $17.95

Understanding CAD/CAM

Bowman and Bowman

For the newcomer to CAD/CAM, here's an in-depth look at this marriage between engineering design and manufacturing. From multi-color graphs and charts to 3-D depictions of machine parts, you will get the basic concepts and fundamentals underlying applications and future considerations.

Each description of this state-of-the-art communications tool is in everyday language that makes the book ideally suited for self-paced, individualized learning. Chapter quizzes and marginal notes allow for fast learning and increased retention.

The book discusses points to consider when buying a CAD/CAM system, including initial cost justification, purchase, and implementation. Training, system maintenance, and security are also discussed.

Topics covered include:

- CAD/CAM Overview
- Anatomy of a Graphics Workstation
- Input/Output
- Data Highways
- Artificial Intelligence
- The Engineer's Dialogue with the CRT
- CAD and the Personal Computer
- Applications: New Directions for Engineering
- The Third Wave in Engineering (Cost Justification)

304 Pages, 7 x 9, Softbound
ISBN: 0-672-27068-4
No. 27068, $17.95

Understanding Digital Electronics, Second Edition

Gene W. McWhorter

Learn why digital circuits are used. Discover how AND, OR, and NOT digital circuits make decisions, store information, and convert information into electronic language. Find out how digital integrated circuits are made and how they are used in microwave ovens, gasoline pumps, video games, cash registers, and other high-technology products.

Topics covered include:

- Let's Look at a System
- How Digital Circuits Make Decisions
- Building Blocks that Make Decisions
- Building Blocks with Memory
- Why Digital?
- Digital Integrated Circuits
- Mass Storage and Digital Systems
- How Digital Systems Function
- Programmed Digital Systems
- Digital Electronics Today and in the Future

264 Pages, 7 x 9, Softbound
ISBN: 0-672-27013-7
No. 27013, $17.95

Visit your local book retailer or call 800-428-SAMS.

Need More Information?

Just fill out the form and mail it to:

POWER MANAGEMENT ASSOCIATES
1545 N. Verdugo Road, Suite 203
Glendale, CA 91208

or call us at (818) 243-7256.

☐ I want to know about products that solve power problems and protect PCs. Do you have any recommendations?

☐ I want to learn more about the subject of PC power protection or large system power protection. Are there any workshops or seminars in my area?

☐ I am having strange problems I think might be related to power or grounding problems. Can you help me solve them?

☐ We are installing some new equipment or plan to build a new data center. Can you help us ensure we get a quality installation?

☐ Other needs: ______________________________

____

____

____

Name ______________________ Title ______________________

Company ______________________________

Address ______________________________

City ______________________ State __________ Zip Code ______________

Phone (   ) ______________________ Date ______________________

Type of computer ______________________________

22637